Elizabeth Parsons Ware Packard

Modern Persecution, or, Insane Asylums Unveiled

As demonstrated by the report of the investigating committee of the legislature of

Illinois. Vol. 2

Elizabeth Parsons Ware Packard

Modern Persecution, or, Insane Asylums Unveiled
As demonstrated by the report of the investigating committee of the legislature of Illinois.
Vol. 2

ISBN/EAN: 9783337370015

Printed in Europe, USA, Canada, Australia, Japan

Cover: Foto ©Suzi / pixelio.de

More available books at **www.hansebooks.com**

MODERN PERSECUTION,

OR

Married Woman's Liabilities,

AS DEMONSTRATED BY THE

Action of the Illinois Legislature.

By Mrs. E. P. W. PACKARD.

" Ye Shall Know the Truth."

Published by the Authoress.

Vol. II.

HARTFORD:
CASE, LOCKWOOD & BRAINARD, PRINTERS AND BINDERS.
1874.

INTRODUCTION.

"A wounded spirit who can bear." Spirit wrongs are the keenest wounds that can be inflicted upon woman. Her nature is so sensitively organized that an injury to her feelings is felt more keenly than an injury to her person.

The fortitude of her nature enables her to endure physical suffering heroically; but the wound which her spirit feels under a wanton physical abuse is far more deeply felt, and is harder to be borne than the physical abuse itself.

Her very benevolent, confiding, forgiving nature, renders it a greater crime to abuse her spirit, than to abuse her person. To most men, and some women, this position may appear absurd, yet it is true; neither do we feel disposed to blame this class for not appreciating it, for their coarser organization incapacitates them to understand us.

When woman is brought before our man courts, and our man juries, and has no bruises, or wounds, or marks of violence upon her person to show as a ground of her complaint, it is hard for them to realize that she has any cause for appeal to them for protection; while at the same time her whole physical system may be writhing in agony from spirit wrongs, such as can only be understood by her peers.

Spiritual, sensitive women, knowing this fact, suffers on in silent anguish without appeal, until death kindly liberates her from her prison-house of unappreciated suffering.

It is to delineate these spiritual wrongs of women, that I have given my narrative to the public, hoping that my more tangible experiences may draw the attention of the philanthropic public to a more just consideration of married woman's legal disabilities; for since the emancipation of the negro, there is no class of American citizens who so much need legal protection, and who receive so little, as this class.

As their representative, I do not make complaint of physical abuses, but it is the usurpation of our natural rights of which we complain; and it is our legal position of *nonentity*, which renders us so liable and exposed to suffering and persecution from this source.

In the following narrative of my experiences, the reader will therefore find the interior of a woman's life delineated through the exterior surroundings of her bitter experiences. I state facts through which the reader may look into woman's soul, as through a mirror, that her realm of suffering may be thus portrayed.

Mrs. E. P. W. Packard.

Chicago, Ills., *January*, 1873.

(1496 Prairie Avenue.)

Illustrations.

———◆———

CONTENTS.

MODERN PERSECUTION.

CHAPTER I.

Imprisoned at Home by My Husband.

The Trustees ordered Mr. Packard to take me out of the Asylum, as no other person could legally remove me. I protested against being again put into his hands without some protection, knowing as I did, that he intended to incarcerate me for life in Northampton Asylum, Mass., if he was ever compelled to remove me from this.

But like as I entered the Asylum against my will, and in spite of my protest, so I was put out of it, *into the absolute power of my persecutor* against my will, and in spite of my protest to the contrary.

Mr. Packard removed me to Granville, Putnam County, Illinois, and placed me in the family of Mr. David Field, who married my adopted sister, where my son paid my board for about four months. Mr. Packard instructed this family to prevent my ever returning home to my children, adding:

"If she ever does come to see them I shall put her into another Asylum!"

During this time Granville community became acquainted with me and the facts in the case. And finding how intensely I desired to see my children, and be re-instated again into the duties of the maternal relation, and seeing no reason why this natural yearning of my nature should not be gratified, they called a meeting of the citizens where this subject was fully discussed, and Sheriff Leaper was appointed to communicate to me the result.

Their decision was that I go home to my children, taking their voluntary pledge as my protection, that should Mr. Packard again attempt to imprison me without a trial, they would use their influence to get him imprisoned in a Penitentiary, where they thought the laws of this Commonwealth would place him.

They also presented me thirty dollars to defray the expenses of my journey home to Manteno, and offered me the protection of a Sheriff as my travelling companion, if I desired it.

I declined this kind offer, fearing its effect upon Mr. Packard's feelings. I preferred to come to him alone and unprotected, hoping thus to arouse his manliness into exercise towards me, as one wholly dependent *upon him* for protection and shelter. And coming alone under these circumstances, might possibly lead him to reconsider his plan for perpetuating my imprisonment. For since this entire community, after becoming personally acquainted with me, had combined in defense of my sanity, he might be led to fear that the popular current might interpose a barrier to his treating me as an insane person in future.

My Granville friends appreciated the force of my argument, and therefore allowed me to return home unattended.

It was about ten o'clock, on a cold morning in November, that I arrived at the depot in Manteno. A few inches of snow had fallen the previous night, and now this snow was melting so as to render it very wet and sloppy under foot.

Without speaking to any one, I left my trunk at the depot and started to walk to my home, about one hundred yards distant. But before I had stepped from the platform I thought that my trunk, containing my valuable papers, must be carefully looked after, lest Mr. Packard get access to it and rob it of its valuables. I therefore concluded to return and request Mr. Harding, the depot master, to retain the trunk until called for by myself or my written order.

But as I turned round, I saw for the first time a boy following me, and seeing how very sloppy the platform was, I asked this boy if he would please go back and tell Mr. Harding that:

" Mrs. Packard requests him to please retain her trunk until she calls for it—or, simply say, Mrs. Packard wishes Mr. Harding to not let Mr. Packard take her trunk."

The boy hesitated.

Said I, " an't you willing to do this favor for me ?   It is so wet I don't like to go back."

" I don't want to say anything against my Pa ! "

Raising his cap, I looked him full in the face, exclaiming:

" Who are you ?   Is this my little George ! Didn't I know my darling boy ! "

As I embraced my precious child, and bestowed upon him kisses of the tenderest affection, I said :

" My darling George shall have his mother again. We shall never be separated now. Kind people are going to protect me and your Pa can't take your mother from you again."

At this point he drew back from my embrace, saying :

" My Pa has done right. He has not done wrong."

" Yes, George, your Pa has done wrong to take your mother from you and imprison her, as he has, without cause. An't you glad to see your mother ? "

" Yes, mother ! Yes ! But—but"—and he burst into tears.

Seeing the conflict between filial love and filial obedience that was going on in his little breast, I remarked :

" We wont talk any more about your father," and taking his hand, I said :

" Go with me, George."

" No, mother, I can't, Pa said I must get the mail and come directly home."

" I will go with you then to the Post-office."

And as we walked on together, I said :

" Did you know me, George ? "

" Yes, mother, I knew you when you got off the train ; Pa said you were coming to-day, and he told me to go to the depot and see if you came."

" How did he know I was coming ? "

" He had a despatch from Chicago last night, saying you were on the way home."

While at the Post-office, I informed Mr. La Brie, the postmaster, of the offer of protection the Granville community had extended to me, and asked him to see to it that my mail was not interfered with, so as not to intercept communication with them.

He promised me it should not be disturbed.

Noticing George in tears, I said :

" What is the matter, my son ! "

" Pa said I must come directly home with the mail."

" You may go, then, my child, and I will come by-and-by."

And he left for his home.

My arrival had now become known throughout the village, and friends met in consultation as to what course to advise me to pursue. Mr. Blessing insisted that I should dine at his hotel, and then his team would transport me and my trunk to my house.

They also offered me a body-guard, not only to the house, but to remain with me in it if I chose. I declined both for the same reason I had refused my Granville guard.

Mr. Blessing accordingly landed my trunk upon the portico of our house, and left me to enter in alone. Before removing my trunk from the depot, I took from it my papers and delivered them into the hands of my friend, Mrs. Haslett.

I entered the front door and passed through the reception room and opened the door into the kitchen before seeing any one. Mr. Packard sat about opposite the door near the stove, in his stuffed easy chair, holding Arthur, my babe, in his arms. He simply bowed, without rising, and said :

" Good morning, Mrs. Packard."

I went up to my babe, and taking him from his father's arms commenced caressing him, when George and Elizabeth came in from the back yard. After embracing and kissing each other, I sat down with Arthur upon my lap and told them they were now going to have a mother again—that I had come to take care of them, and hoped we should be very happy, and never be separated again, adding:

" It is my desire to do you all the good I can, and promote your welfare in every possible way. My daughter, won't it be pleasant to have some one to relieve you of your cares and responsibilities ? "

Mr. Packard replied :

" No, you an't wanted here ! We get along better without you than with you ! "

Addressing my daughter, I said :

" I am thankful the law protects me in my *right* to my own home."

Said he : " You have no ' right' here ! The law does *not* protect you here ! *I* am your only protector ! "

I exchanged no words with Mr. Packard upon this or any other subject—I knew argument was useless, and every attempt at self-vindication would only add fuel to the flame of hatred and distrust which evidently still rankled within him. I had returned with the settled determination to *do* my whole duty in the family, as mother and housekeeper, so far as possible, without interfering in the least with his own duties or privileges.

With a sad, and yet joyful heart, I commenced to reconstruct my now desolate-looking home, by first cleaning it of its extra amount of defilement—the accumulations of three years.

Before going home after my arrival, I engaged a hired girl to come the next day and assist me in cleaning my house. She came, and although Mr. Packard knew I had engaged to pay her from the money Granville people had donated for my use, he ordered her out of the house, even before I had had time to welcome her in, and told her never to come to his house to assist his wife without his permission. Of course she left, as the married woman has no *rights* which her husband is bound to respect!

I then commenced alone with my own sleeping room by removing the carpet, and being unable to lift it alone I asked one of my children to assist me. Mr. Packard forbid their helping me at all, saying:

"It is of no use to clean—it don't need it—and you must not assist your mother at all in doing it."

I put some water upon the kitchen cook-stove to heat for the purpose of cleaning the paint. He took it off, saying:

"You shall heat no water upon *my* stove for cleaning."

I accordingly cleaned my room with cold water.

In passing through the kitchen I saw my little daughter rolling out some pie-crust. I stepped up to the table and said:

"Let me show you how to make your crust, my daughter, I see you don't understand how to do it right."

Mr. Packard came up to the table, and in a loud and most authoritative tone, with his hand upraised, said:

"I forbid your interference! I will attend to this business myself! Elizabeth shall make her pies as she pleases."

I thought the "interference" was on the other side—that it was he who was interfering with my duties instead of I with his. Nevertheless, I maintained my determination, never to *speak* in self-defense.

I sought for clean sheets for our beds, but found them locked up and the key in Mr. Packard's hands, and I could only get a change when in *his* judgment it was needed, not when I thought it even indispensable to health and cleanliness.

I sought for my wardrobe, but this too I found was under Mr. Packard's lock and key, and not even a decent pair of winter hose would he allow me from it, because in his judgment a useless worn out pair was all I needed.

One morning as I was doing the chamber work up stairs, I saw a bunch of keys left by the thoughtlessness of some of the children, who used them when they wished, in the closet door where our family stores and bedding and wardrobe were deposited to keep them from me ; and I took them into my custody, assuring myself that I, as my husband's partner, had some right to carry the keys part of the time at least, and I concluded now was the time to test this principle. As locks and keys were an article introduced into my family during my banishment, I ventured to leave the door so much used, unlocked, so that the keys would not be necessary to *their* comfort or convenience.

But when, behold ! the keys were missing, suspicion at once fell upon me, and Packard ordered my person and my room to be searched ; which was done most thoroughly.

Now I saw the wisdom of not having my papers in my trunk, for he took an inventory of every article, and would doubtless have taken my papers had they been there, and he might have done as Dr. McFarland advised, " Burn them ! "

But the search for the keys was all in vain—they were nowhere to be found !

This search was not confined to my person and my room merely, but the entire house and premises were most carefully and diligently searched in every corner, nook, and crevice— even the embers of my stove were examined. Both the front. and back yard were also included in Packard's " searchwarrant "—every stone, leaf, and shrub were upturned to find the missing keys—but all to no purpose ! He could not find them, for the simple reason he did not look in the *right place !*

He then locked me up in my nursery so I could have no opportunity for using them.

Thus was my imprisonment in my home secured, whereby

a writ of *habeas corpus* could be legally obtained. Thus, this my painful imprisonment of six weeks was the stepping-stone to my freedom.

I never was allowed to eat at the table with my family afterwards. My food was sent to my room in as good order as such cooks could prepare it. My health suffered much from confined air, as my windows were nailed down so my room could not be properly ventilated.

Mr. Packard cut me off from all communication with the community, and my other friends, by intercepting my mail—refused me interviews with friends who called to see me, so that he might meet with no interference in carrying out the plan he had devised to have me incarcerated again for life.

During the day he allowed my four children, Samuel, Elizabeth, George, and Arthur, to occupy the room with me, as my scholars, and great was the proficiency they acquired during this their short school term of six weeks, in the knowledge of arithmetic, grammar, algebra, reading, spelling, writing, composition, and elocution—Samuel especially being enthusiastic over his attainments during this school term—said he: "Mother, I have learned more here this winter under your teaching, than I learned during one whole term of twelve weeks at the Academy at Kankakee."

While in my room I demanded and received from all my children the respect and obedience due me, as their teacher. But when I attempted to dictate in reference to their personal habits in relation to their bathing, toilet duties, hours of rising and retiring, and their wardrobe, Mr. Packard required them to disregard my directions, whenever they conflicted with his own plans or wishes in these matters.

The door of my room was not kept locked during the day, when the front outside door was securely fastened and the back door sufficiently guarded to prevent my escape; but at night it was always locked by himself.

One evening I proposed to my children that we clean and polish our cook-stove in the kitchen which Mr. Packard now used as his study, to which they readily consented. And to avoid disturbance during the time, Mr. Packard removed his stationery and papers to my room to study by himself by my warm stove.

When our merry polishing party had completed their task to their entire satisfaction, insisting upon it that "Black Prince" looked now just as bright as he used to shine when mother was housekeeper, we cleaned ourselves and all retired to my room to warm before retiring for the night. Our entrance was the signal for Mr. Packard's leaving, of course, and in his haste or carelessness in gathering up his papers he overlooked a package of letters, which he left behind upon my table. These I did not notice until all had dispersed and Mr. Packard had locked me up for the night.

My first thought was not to examine them, as they were undoubtedly left by mistake. But upon second thought I concluded it not only right to see my husband's papers, but also to avail myself of every lawful means of self-defense which lay within my reach. Accordingly I spent several hours of this night in carefully reading these letters, received during my incarceration and since my discharge. From these replies to his own letters, his platform of action, both past, present, and future, was distinctly portrayed, bearing most fearful and unmistakable evidence that *I was to be entered in a few days into Northampton Insane Asylum for life!*

One of these letters from Doctor Prince, Superintendent of that Asylum, assured me of this fact, in these words:

"I will receive Mrs. Packard as a case of hopeless insanity, upon the certificate of Dr. McFarland that she is 'hopelessly' insane."

Another from Dr. McFarland, saying:

With this certificate he could get me entered *without any*

sort of trial, and thus I could be disposed of without jeopardizing their own interests, for he added:

" The dignity of silence is the only safe course for us both to pursue! "

Another from his sister, Mrs. Marian Severance, of Massachusetts, revealed the mode in which she advised her brother to transfer me from my home prison to my Asylum prison. She advised him to let me go to New York, under the pretence of getting my book published, and have him follow in a train behind, assuring the conductors that I must be treated as an insane person, although I should deny the charge, as all insane persons did, and thus make sure of their aid as accomplices in this conspiracy against my personal liberty. The conductor must be directed to switch me off at Northampton, Mass., instead of taking me to New York, and as my through ticket would indicate to me that all was right, she thought this could be done without arousing my suspicions ; then engage a carriage to transport me to the Asylum under the pretext of a hotel, and lock me up for life as a state's pauper! Then, said she :

" You will have her out of the way, and can do as you please with her property, her children, and even her wardrobe ; don't be even responsible this time for her clothing."

Mr. Packard was responsible for my wardrobe in Jacksonville prison, but for nothing else. I was supported there three years as a state pauper. This fact, Mr. Packard most adroitly concealed from my rich father and family relatives, so that he could persuade my deluded father to place more of my patrimony in his hands, under the false pretence that he needed it to make his daughter more comfortable in the Asylum. My father sent him money for this purpose, supposing Mr. Packard was paying my board at the Asylum ; but instead of that he appropriated it all to his own exclusive use.

Another letter was from Dr. McFarland, wherein I saw that

Mr. Packard had made application for my re-admission there; and Dr. McFarland had consented to receive me again as an insane patient!

But the Trustees put their veto upon it, and would not consent to his plea that I be admitted there again. Here is his own statement, which I copied from his own letter:

" Jacksonville, December 18, 1863. Rev. Mr. Packard, Dear Sir: The Secretary of the Trustees has probably before this communicated to you the result of their action in the case of Mrs. Packard. It is proper enough to state that I favored her re-admission!"

Then follows his injunction to Mr. Packard to be sure not to publish anything respecting the matter.

Why is this? Does an upright course seek concealment?

Nay, verily: It is conscious *guilt* alone that seeks concealment, and dreads agitation lest his crimes be exposed. Mine is only one of a large class of cases, where he has consented to re-admit a sane person, particularly the wives of men whose influence he was desirous of securing for the support of himself in his present lucrative position.

Yes, many intelligent wives and mothers did I leave in that awful prison, whose only hope of liberty lies in the death of their lawful husbands, or in a change of the laws, or in a thorough ventilation of that Institution. Such a ventilation was needed, in order that justice be done to that class of miserable inmates who were then unjustly confined there.

When I had read these letters over three or four times, to make it sure I had not mistaken their import, and even had taken copies of some of them, I determined upon the following expedient as my last and only resort, as a self-defensive act.

There was a stranger who passed my window daily to get water from our pump. One day as he passed I beckoned to him to take a note which I had pushed down through where the windows came together, adding:

" Stranger, please hand this note to Mrs. Haslet."

My windows were firmly nailed down and screwed together, so that I could not open them.

This note was directed to Mrs. A. C. Haslet, the most efficient friend I knew of in Manteno, wherein I informed her of my imminent danger, and begged of her if possible in any way to rescue me, to do so forthwith, for in a few days I should be beyond the reach of all human help.

She communicated these facts to the citizens, when mob law was suggested as the only available means of rescue which lay in their power to use, as no law existed which defended a wife from a husband's power, and no man dared to take the responsibility of protecting me against my husband.

And one hint was communicated to me clandestinely that if I would only break through my window, a company was formed who would defend me when once outside our house. This rather unlady-like mode of self-defense I did not like to resort to, knowing as I did, if I should not finally succeed in this attempt, my persecutors would gain advantage over me, in that I had once injured property, as a reason why I should be locked up.

As yet, none of my persecutors had the shadow of capital to make out the charge of insanity upon outside of my opinions ; for my conduct and deportment had uniformly been kind, lady-like, and Christian ; and even to this date, 1873, I challenge any individual to prove me guilty of one unreasonable, or insane act.

The lady-like Mrs. Haslet sympathized with me in these views ; therefore she sought counsel of Judge Starr of Kankakee City, to know if any law could reach my case so as to give me a trial of any kind, before another incarceration.

The Judge told her that if I was a prisoner in my own house, and any were willing to take oath upon it, a writ of *habeas corpus* might reach my case and thus secure me a trial.

Witnesses were easily found who could take oath to this fact, as many had called at our house and had seen that my windows were screwed together on the outside, and our front outside door firmly fastened on the outside, and our back outside door most vigilantly guarded by day and locked at night.

In a few days this writ was accordingly executed by the Sheriff of the county, and just two days before Mr. Packard was intending to start with me for Massachusetts to imprison me for life in Northampton Lunatic Asylum, he was required by this writ to bring me before the court and give his reasons to the court why he kept his wife a prisoner.

The reason he gave for so doing was, that I was insane.

The Judge replied, " Prove it ! "

The Judge then empanelled a jury of twelve men, and the following trial ensued as the result. This trial continued five days.

Thus my being made a prisoner at my own home was the only hinge on which my personal liberty for life hung, independent of mob law, as there was then no law in the State that would allow a married woman the right of a trial against the charge of insanity brought against her by her husband ; and God only knows how many innocent wives and mothers my case represents, who have thus lost their liberty for life, by this arbitrary power, unchecked as it then was by no law on the Statute Book of Illinois.

CHAPTER II.

My Release on a Writ of "Habeas Corpus," and my Sanity Tried by a Jury—My Sanity Fully Established.

BY STEPHEN R. MOORE, ATTORNEY AT LAW.

In preparing a report of this Trial, the writer has had but one object in view, namely, to present a faithful history of the case as narrated by the witnesses upon the stand, who gave their testimony under the solemnity of an oath. The exact language employed by the witnesses has been used, and the written testimony given in full, with the exception of a letter, written by Dr. McFarland, to Rev. Theophilus Packard, which letter was retained by Mr. Packard, and the writer was unable to obtain a copy. The substance of the letter is found in the body of the report, and has been submitted to the examination of Mr. Packard's counsel, who agree that it is correctly stated.

This case was on trial before the Hon. Charles R. Starr, at Kankakee City, Illinois, from Monday, January 11th, 1864, to Tuesday the 19th, and came up on an application made by Mrs. Packard, under the *Habeas Corpus Act*, to be discharged from imprisonment by her husband in their own house.

The case has disclosed a state of facts most wonderful and startling. Reverend Theophilus Packard came to Manteno, in Kankakee county, Illinois, seven years since, and has remained in charge of the Presbyterian Church of that place until the past two years.

In the winter of 1859 and 1860, there were differences of opinion between Mr. Packard and Mrs. Packard, upon matters of religion, which resulted in prolonged and vigorous debate in the home circle. The heresies maintained by Mrs. Packard were carried by the husband from the fireside to the pulpit, and made a matter of inquiry by the church, and which soon resulted in open warfare ; and her views and propositions were misrepresented and animadverted upon, from the pulpit, and herself made the subject of unjust criticism. In the Bible-Class and in the Sabbath School, she maintained her religious tenets, and among her kindred and friends, defended herself from the obloquy of her husband.

To make the case fully understood, I will here remark, that Mr. Packard was educated in the Calvinistic faith, and for twenty-nine years has been a preacher of that creed, and would in no wise depart from the religion of his fathers. He is cold, selfish, and illiberal in his views, possessed of but little talent, and a physiognomy innocent of expression. He has large self-will, and his stubbornness is only exceeded by his bigotry.

Mrs. Packard is a lady of fine mental endowments, and blest with a liberal education. She is an original, vigorous, masculine thinker, and were it not for her superior judgment, combined with native modesty, she would rank as a " strong-minded woman." As it is, her conduct comports strictly with the sphere usually occupied by woman. She dislikes parade or show of any kind. Her confidence that Right will prevail, leads her to too tamely submit to wrongs. She was educated in the same religious belief with her husband, and during the first twenty years of married life, his labors in the parish and in the pulpit were greatly relieved by the willing hand and able intellect of his wife.

Phrenologists would also say of her, that her self-will was large and her married life tended in no wise to diminish this phrenological bump. They have been married twenty-five years, and have six children, the issue of their intermarriage, the youngest of whom was eighteen months old when she was kidnapped and transferred to Jacksonville. The older children have maintained a firm position against the abuse and persecutions of their father towards their mother, but were of too tender age to render her any material assistance.

Her views of religion are more in accordance with the liberal views of the age in which we live. She scouts the Calvinistic doctrine of man's total depravity, and that God has fore-ordained some to be saved and others to be damned. She stands fully on the platform of man's free agency and account-ability to God for his actions. She believes that man, and nations, are progressive; and that in his own good time, and in accordance with His great purposes, Right will prevail over Wrong, and the oppressed will be freed from the oppressor. She believes slavery to be a national sin, and the church and the pulpit a proper place to combat this sin. These, in brief, are the points in her religious creed which were combated by Mr. Packard, and were denominated by him as "emanations from the devil," or "the vagaries of a crazed brain."

For maintaining such ideas as above indicated, Mr. Packard denounced her from the pulpit, denied her the privilege of family prayer in the home circle, expelled her from the Bible Class, and refused to let her be heard in the Sabbath School. He excluded her from her friends, and made her a prisoner in her own house.

Her reasonings and her logic appeared to him as the ravings of a mad woman—her religion was the religion of the devil. To justify his conduct, he gave out that she was insane, and found a few willing believers, among his family connections.

This case was commenced by filing a petition in the words following, to wit:

STATE OF ILLINOIS, ⎱ ss.
   KANKAKEE COUNTY. ⎰

To the Honorable CHARLES R. STARR, *Judge of the 20th Judicial Circuit in the State of Illinois.*

William Haslet, Daniel Beedy, Zalmon Hanford, and Joseph Younglove, of said county, on behalf of Elizabeth P. W. Packard, wife of Theophilus Packard, of said county, respectfully represent unto your Honor, that said Elizabeth P. W. Packard, is unlawfully restrained of her liberty, at Manteno, in the county of Kankakee, by her husband, Rev. Theophilus Packard, being forcibly confined and imprisoned in a close room of the dwelling-house of her said husband, for a long time, to wit, for the space of six weeks, her said husband refusing to let her visit her neighbors and refusing her neighbors to visit her; that they believe her said husband is about to forcibly convey her from out the State; that they believe there is no just cause or ground for restraining said wife of her liberty; that they believe that said wife is a mild and amiable woman. And they are advised and believe, that said husband cruelly abuses and misuses said wife, by depriving her of her winter's clothing, this cold and inclement weather, and that there is no necessity for such cruelty on the part of said husband to said wife; and they are advised and believe, that said wife desires to come to Kankakee City, to make application to your Honor for a writ of *habeas corpus*, to liberate herself from said confinement or imprisonment, and that said husband refused and refuses to allow said wife to come to Kankakee City for said purpose; and that these petitioners make application for a writ of *habeas corpus* in her behalf, at her request. These petitioners therefore pray that a writ of *habeas corpus* may forthwith issue, commanding said Theophilus Packard to produce the body of said wife,

2

before your Honor, according to law, and that said wife may be discharged from said imprisonment.

(Signed),

WILLIAM HASLET.
DANIEL BEEDY.
ZALMON HANFORD.
J. YOUNGLOVE.

J. W. ORR, }
H. LORING, } *Petitioners' Attorneys.*

STEPHEN R. MOORE, *Counsel.*

STATE OF ILLINOIS, }
    KANKAKEE COUNTY. } *ss.*

William Haslet, Daniel Beedy, Zalmon Hanford, and Joseph Younglove, whose names are subscribed to the above petition, being duly sworn, severally depose and say, that the matters and facts set forth in the above petition are true in substance and fact, to the best of their knowledge and belief.

WILLIAM HASLET.
DANIEL BEEDY.
ZALMON HANFORD.
J. YOUNGLOVE.

Sworn to and subscribed before me, this }
   11th day of January, A. D. 1864. }

MASON B. LOOMIS, J. P.

Upon the above petition, the Honorable C. R. Starr, Judge as aforesaid, issued a writ of *habeas corpus.* as follows:

STATE OF ILLINOIS, }
    KANKAKEE COUNTY, } *ss.*

The People of the State of Illinois, To THEOPHILUS PACKARD:

WE COMMAND YOU, That the body of Elizabeth P. W. Packard, in your custody detained and imprisoned, as it is said, together with the day and cause of caption and detention, by whatsoever name the same may be called, you safely have before Charles R. Starr, Judge of the Twentieth Judicial Circuit, State of Illinois, at his chambers, at Kankakee City in the said county, on the 12th instant, at one o'clock, P.M., and to do and receive all and singular those things which the said Judge shall then and'there consider of her in this behalf, and have you then and there this writ.

Witness, Charles R. Starr, Judge aforesaid, this 11th day of January, A. D. 1864.

[REVENUE STAMP.]   CHARLES R. STARR, [SEAL.]
Judge of the Twentieth Judicial Circuit of the State of Illinois.

Indorsed: "By the *Habeas Corpus* Act."

To said writ, the Rev. Theophilus Packard made the following return:

The within named Theophilus Packard does hereby certify, to the within named, the Honorable Charles R. Starr, Judge of the Twentieth Judicial Circuit of the State of Illinois, that the within named Elizabeth P. W. Packard is now in my custody, before your Honor. That the said Elizabeth is the wife of the undersigned, and is and has been for more than three years past insane, and for about three years of that time was in the Insane Asylum of the State of Illinois, under treatment, as an insane person. That she was discharged from said Asylum, without being cured, and is incurably insane, on or about the 18th day of June, A. D. 1863, and that since the 23rd day of October, the undersigned has kept the said Elizabeth with him in Manteno, in this county, and while he has faithfully and anxiously watched, cared for, and guarded the said Elizabeth, yet he has not unlawfully restrained her of her liberty; and has not confined and imprisoned her in a close room, in the dwelling-house of the undersigned, or in any other place, or way, but, on the contrary, the undersigned has allowed her all the liberty compatible with her welfare and safety. That the undersigned is about to remove his residence from Manteno, in this State, to the town of Deerfield, in the county of Franklin, in the State of Massachusetts, and designs and intends to take his said wife Elizabeth with him. That the undersigned has never misused or abused the said Elizabeth, by depriving her of her winter's clothing. but. on the contrary, the undersigned has always treated the said Elizabeth with kindness and affection, and has provided her with a sufficient quantity of winter clothing and other clothing: and that the said Elizabeth has never made any request of the undersigned, for liberty to come to Kankakee City, for the purpose of suing out a writ of *habeas corpus.* The undersigned hereby presents a letter from Andrew McFarland, Superintendent of the Illinois State Hospital, at Jacksonville, in this State. showing her discharge. and reasons of discharge, from said institution, which is marked " A." and is made a part of this return. And also presents a certificate from the said Andrew McFarland, under the seal of said hospital, marked " C," refusing to re-admit the said Elizabeth again into said hospital, on the ground of her being incurably insane, which is also hereby made a part of this return.

THEOPHILUS PACKARD.

Dated January 12, 1864.

The Court, upon its own motion, ordered an issue to be formed, as to the sanity or insanity of Mrs. E. P. W. Packard, and ordered a venire of twelve men to aid the Court in the investigation of said issue. And thereupon a venire was issued.

The counsel for the respondent, Thomas P. Bonfield. Mason B. Loomis, and Hon. C. A. Lake, moved the court to quash the venire, on the ground that the court had no right to call a jury to determine the question, on an application to be discharged on a writ of *habeas corpus.* The court overruled the motion; and thereupon the following jury was selected:

John Stiles. Daniel G. Bean, V. H. Young, F. G. Hutchinson, Thomas Muncey. H. Hirshberg. Nelson Jarvais, William Hyer, George H. Andrews, J. F. Mafet, Lemuel Milk, G. M. Lyons.

Christopher W. Knott was the first witness sworn by the
respondent, to maintain the issue on his part, that she was
insane; who being sworn, deposed and said:

I am a practicing physician in Kankakee City. Have been
in practice fifteen years. Have seen Mrs. Packard; saw her
three or four years ago. Am not much acquainted with her.
Had never seen her until I was called to see her at that time.
I was called to visit her by Theophilus Packard. I thought
her partially deranged on religious matters, and gave a certificate to that effect. I certified that she was insane upon the
subject of religion. I have never seen her since.

Cross-examination.—This visit I made her was three or four
years ago. I was there twice—one-half hour each time. I
visited her on request of Mr. Packard, to determine if she was
insane. I learned from him that he designed to convey her to
the State Asylum. Do not know whether she was aware of my
object or not. Her mind appeared to be excited on the subject
of religion; on all other subjects she was perfectly rational.
It was probably caused by overtaxing the mental faculties.
She was what might be called a monomaniac. Monomania
is insanity on one subject. Three-fourths of the religious community are insane in the same manner, in my opinion. Her
insanity was such that with a little rest she would readily have
recovered from it. The female mind is more excitable than
the male. I saw her perhaps one-half hour each time I visited
her. I formed my judgment as to her insanity wholly from
conversing with her. I could see nothing except an unusual
zealousness and warmth upon religious topics. Nothing was
said in my conversation with her, about disagreeing with Mr.
Packard on religious topics. Mr. Packard introduced the subject of religion the first time I was there; the second time, I
introduced the subject. Mr. Packard and Mr. Comstock were
present. The subject was pressed on her for the purpose of
drawing her out. Mrs. Packard would manifest more zeal

than most of people upon any subject that interested her. I take her to be a lady of fine mental abilities, possessing more ability than ordinarily found. She is possessed of a nervous temperament, easily excited, and has a strong will. I would say that she was insane, the same as I would say Henry Ward Beecher, Spurgeon, Horace Greeley, and like persons, are insane. Probably three weeks intervened between the visits I made Mrs. Packard. This was in June, 1860.

Re-examined.—She is a woman of large, active brain, and nervous temperament. I take her to be a woman of good intellect. There is no subject which excites people so much as religion. Insanity produces, oftentimes, ill-feelings towards the best friends, and particularly the family, or those more nearly related to the insane person—but not so with monomania. She told me, in the conversation, that the Calvinistic doctrines were wrong, and that she had been compelled to withdraw from the church. She said that Mr. Packard was more insane than she was, and that people would find it out. I had no doubt that she was insane. I only considered her insane on that subject, and she was not bad at that. I could not judge whether it was hereditary. I thought if she was withdrawn from conversation and excitement, she could have got well in a short time. Confinement in any shape, or restraint, would have made her worse. I did not think it was a bad case; it only required rest.

J. W. Brown, being sworn, said:

I am a physician; live in this city; have no extensive acquaintance with Mrs. Packard. Saw her three or four weeks ago. I examined her as to her sanity or insanity. I was requested to make a visit, and had an extended conference with her; I spent some three hours with her. I had no difficulty in arriving at the conclusion, in my mind, that she was insane.

Cross-examination.—I visited her by request of Mr. Packard, at her house. The children were in and out of the room ; no one else was present. I concealed my object in visiting her. She asked me if I was a physician, and I told her no ; that I was an agent, selling sewing machines, and had come there to sell her one.

The first subject we conversed about was sewing machines. She showed no sign of insanity on that subject.

The next subject discussed, was the social condition of the female sex. She exhibited no special marks of insanity on that subject, although she had many ideas quite at variance with mine, on the subject.

The subject of politics was introduced. She spoke of the condition of the North and the South. She illustrated her difficulties with Mr. Packard, by the difficulties between the North and the South. She said the South was wrong, and was waging war for two wicked purposes : first, to overthrow a good government, and second, to establish a depotism on the inhuman principle of human slavery. But that the North, having right on their side, would prevail. So Mr. Packard was opposing her, to overthrow free thought in woman ; that the despotism of man may prevail over the wife ; but that she had right and truth on her side, and that she would prevail. During this conversation I did not fully conclude that she was insane.

I brought up the subject of religion. We discussed that subject for a long time, and then I had not the slightest difficulty in concluding that she was hopelessly insane.

Question. Dr., what particular idea did she advance on the subject of religion that led you to the conclusion that she was hopelessly insane ?

Answer. She advanced many of them. I formed my opinion not so much on any one idea advanced, as upon her whole conversation. She then said that she was the " Personification of the Holy Ghost." I did not know what she meant by that.

Ques. Was not this the idea conveyed to you in that conversation: That there are three attributes of the Deity—the Father, the Son, and the Holy Ghost? Now, did she not say, that the attributes of the Father were represented in mankind, in man; that the attributes of the Holy Ghost were represented in woman; and that the Son was the fruit of these two attributes of the Deity?

Ans. Well, I am not sure but that was the idea conveyed, though I did not fully get her idea at the time.

Ques. Was not that a new idea to you in theology?

Ans. It was.

Ques. Are you much of a theologian?

Ans. No.

Ques. Then because the idea was a novel one to you, you pronounced her insane.

Ans. Well, I pronounced her insane on that and other things that exhibited themselves in this conversation.

Ques. Did she not show more familiarity with the subject of religion and the questions of theology, than you had with these subjects?

Ans. I do not pretend much knowledge on these subjects.

Ques. What else did she say or do there, that showed marks of insanity?

Ans. She claimed to be better than her husband—that she was right—and that he was wrong—and that all she did was good, and all he did was bad—that she was farther advanced than other people, and more nearly perfection. She found fault particularly that Mr. Packard would not discuss their points of difference on religion in an open, manly way, instead of going around and denouncing her as crazy to her friends and to the church.

She had a great aversion to being called insane. Before I got through the conversation she exhibited a great dislike to me, and almost treated me in a contemptuous manner. She appeared quite lady-like. She had a great reverence for God, and a regard for religious and pious people.

Re-examined. Ques. Dr., you may now state all the reasons you have for pronouncing her insane.

Ans. I have written down, in order, the reasons which I had, to found my opinion on, that she was insane. I will read them.

1. That she claimed to be in advance of the age thirty or forty years.

2. That she disliked to be called insane.

3. That she pronounced me a copperhead, and did not prove the fact.

4. An incoherency of thought. That she failed to illuminate me and fill me with light.

5. Her aversion to the doctrine of the total depravity of man.

6. Her claim to perfection, or nearer perfection in action and conduct.

7. Her aversion to being called insane.

8. Her feeling towards her husband.

9. Her belief that to call her insane and abuse her, was blasphemy against the Holy Ghost.

10. Her explanation of this idea.

11. Incoherency of thought and ideas.

12. Her extreme aversion to the doctrine of the total depravity of mankind, and in the same conversation, saying her husband was a specimen of man's total depravity.

13. The general history of the case.

14. Her belief that some calamity would befall her, owing to my being there, and her refusal to shake hands with me when I went away.

15. Her viewing the subject of religion from the osteric standpoint of Christian exegetical analysis, and agglutinating the polsynthetical ectoblasts of homogeneous ascoticism.

The witness left the stand amid roars of laughter; and it required some moments to restore order in the court room.

JOSEPH H. WAY, sworn, and said:

I am a practicing physician in Kankakee City, Illinois. I made a medical examination of Mrs. Packard a few weeks since at her house; was there perhaps two hours. On most subjects she was quite sane. On the subject of religion I thought she had some ideas that are not generally entertained. At that time I thought her to be somewhat deranged or excited on that subject; since that time I have thought perhaps I was not a proper judge, for I am not much posted on disputed points in theology, and I find that other people entertain similar ideas. They are not in accordance with my views, but that is no evidence that she is insane.

Cross-examined.—I made this visit at her house, or his house, perhaps, at Manteno. I conversed on various subjects. She was perfectly sane on every subject except religion, and I would not swear now that she was insane. She seemed to have been laboring under an undue excitement on that subject. She has a nervous temperament, and is easily excited. She said she liked her children, and that it was hard to be torn from them. That none but a mother could feel the anguish she had suffered; that while she was confined in the Asylum, the children had been educated by their father to call her insane. She said she would have them punished if they called their own mother insane, for it was not right.

ABIJAH DOLE, sworn, and says:

I know Mrs. Packard; have known her twenty-five or thirty years. I am her brother-in-law. Lived in Manteno seven years. Mrs. Packard has lived there six years. I have been sent for several times by her and Mr. Packard, and found her in an excited state of mind. I was there frequently; we were very familiar. One morning early, I was sent for; she was in the west room; she was in her night clothes. She took me by the hand and led me to the bed. Libby was lying in bed, moaning and moving her head. Mrs. Packard now spoke and said, "How pure we are." "I am one of the children of heaven; Libby is one of the branches." "The woman shall bruise the serpent's head." She called Mr. Packard a devil. She said, Brother Dole, these are serious matters. If Brother Haslet will help me, we will crush the body. She said Christ had come into the world to save men, and that she had come to save woman. Her hair was disheveled. Her face looked wild. This was over three years ago.

I was there again one morning after this. She came to me. She pitied me for marrying my wife, who is a sister to Mr. Packard; said, I might find an agreeable companion. She said if she had cultivated amativeness, she would have made a more agreeable companion. She took me to another room and talked about going away; this was in June, before they took her to the State Hospital. She sent for me again; she was in the east room; she was very cordial. She wanted me to intercede for Theophilus, who was at Marshall, Michigan; she wanted him to stay there, and it was thought not advisable for him to stay. We wished him to come away, but did not tell her the reasons. He was with a Swedenborgian.

After this I was called there once in the night. She said she could not live with Mr. Packard, and she thought she had better go away. One time she was in the Bible-class. The question came up in regard to Moses smiting the Egyptian; she thought Moses had acted too hasty, but that all things worked for the glory of God. I requested her to keep quiet, and she agreed to do it.

I have had no conversation with Mrs. Packard since her return from the Hospital; she will not talk with me because she thinks I think she is insane. Her brother came to see her; he said he had not seen her for four or five years. I tried to have Mrs. Packard talk with him, and she would not have anything to do with him because he said she was a crazy woman. She generally was in the kitchen when I was there, overseeing her household affairs.

I was Superintendent of the Sabbath School. One Sabbath, just at the close of the school, I was behind the desk, and almost like a vision she appeared before me, and requested to deliver or read an address to the school. I was much surprised; I felt so bad, I did not know what to do. (At this juncture the witness became very much affected, and choked up so that he could not proceed, and cried so loud that he could be heard in any part of the court-room. When he became calm, he went on and said,) I was willing to gratify her all I could, for I knew she was crazy, but I did not want to take the responsibility myself, so I put it to a vote of the school, if she should be allowed to read it. She was allowed to read it. It occupied ten or fifteen minutes in reading.

I cannot state any of the particulars of that paper. It bore evidence of her insanity. She went on and condemned the church, all in all, and the individuals composing the church, because they did not agree with her. She looked very wild and very much excited. She seemed to be insane. She came to church one morning just as services commenced, and wished to have the church act upon her letter withdrawing from the church immediately. Mr. Packard was in the pulpit. She wanted to know if Brother Dole and Brother Merrick were in the church, and wanted them to have it acted upon. This was three years ago, just before she was taken away to the hospital.

Cross-examined.—I supposed when I first went into the room that her influence over the child had caused the child to become deranged. The child was ten years old. I believed that she had exerted some mesmeric or other influence over the child, that caused it to moan and toss its head. The child had been sick with brain fever; I learned that after I got there. I suppose the mother had considerable anxiety over the child; I suppose she had been watching over the child all night, and that would tend to excite her. The child got well. It was sick several days after this; it was lying on the bed moaning and tossing its head; the mother did not appear to be alarmed. Mr. Packard was not with her; she was all alone; she did not say that Mr. Packard did not show proper care for the sick child. I suppose she thought Libby would die.

Her ideas on religion did not agree with mine, nor with my view of the Bible.

I knew Mr. Packard thought her insane, and did not want her to discuss these questions in the Sabbath School. I knew he had opposed her more or less. This letter to the church was for the purpose of asking for a letter from the church.

Question. Was it an indication of insanity that she wanted to leave the Presbyterian Church?

Answer. I think it strange that she should ask for letters from the church. She would not leave the church unless she was insane.

I am a member of the church—I believe the church is right. I believe everything the church does is right. I believe everything in the Bible.

Ques. Do you believe literally that Jonah was swallowed by a whale, and remained in its belly three days, and was then cast up?

Ans. I do.

Ques. Do you believe literally that Elijah went direct up to Heaven in a chariot of fire—that the chariot had wheels, and seats, and was drawn by horses?

Ans. I do—for with God all things are possible.

Quas. Do you believe Mrs. Packard was insane, and is insane?

Ans. I do.

I never read any of Swedenborg's works. I do not deem it proper for persons to investigate new doctrines or systems of theology.

Re-examined.—I became a Presbyterian eight years ago. I was formerly a Congregationalist; Mr. Packard was a Congregationalist.

Re-cross-examination.—*Ques.* Was it dangerous for you to examine the doctrines or theology embraced in the Presbyterian Church, when you left the Congregationalist Church, and joined it?

Ans. I will not answer so foolish a question.

Witness discharged.

JOSEPHUS B. SMITH, sworn, says:

Am aged fifty years; have known Mrs. Packard seven years. I cannot tell the first appearance of any abnormal condition of her mind. I first saw it at the Sabbath School. She came in and wished to read a communication. I do not recollect everything of the communication. She did not read the letter, but presented it to Brother Dole. She said something about her small children, and left. She seemed to be excited. There was nothing very unusual in her appearance. Her voice was rather excited; it could be heard nearly over the house. I merely recall the circumstance, but recollect scarce anything else. It was an unusual thing for any person to come in and read an address. I do not recollect anything unusual in her manner.

(At this stage of the trial, an incident occurred that for a time stopped all proceedings, and produced quite an excitement in the court-room; and this report would not be faithful if it were passed over unnoticed. Mrs. Dole, the sister of Mr. Packard, came in, leading the little daughter of Mrs. Packard, and in passing by the table occupied by Mrs. Packard and her counsel, the child stopped, went up to her mother, kissed and hugged her, and was clinging to her with all child-like fervor, when it was observed by Mrs. Dole, who snatched the child up—and bid it "come away from that woman;" adding, "She is not fit to take care of you—I have you in my charge;" and thereupon led her away. The court-room was crowded to its utmost, and not a mother's heart there but what was touched, and scarce a dry eye was seen. Quite a stir was made, but the sheriff soon restored order.)

Cross-examined.—I had charge of the Sunday School; am a member of Mr. Packard's church. I knew Mr. Packard had considered her insane; knew they had had difficulties. I was elected Superintendent of the school in place of Brother Dole, for the special purpose of keeping Mrs. Packard straight.

SYBIL DOLE, sworn, and says—

I am Mr. Packard's sister; have known her twenty-five years. Her natural disposition is very kind and sweet. Her education is very good; her morals without a stain or blemish. I first observed a change in her after we came to Manteno. I had a conversation with her, when she talked an hour without interruption; she talked in a wild, excited manner; the subject was partly religion. She spoke of her own attainments; she said she had advanced in spiritual affairs. This was two or three years before she went to the Asylum.

The next time was when she was preparing to go to York State. She was weeping and sick. Her trunk was packed and ready to go, but Mr. Packard was sick. From her voice, and the manner she talked, I formed an opinion of her insanity. She talked on various points; the conversation distressed me very much; I could not sleep. She was going alone; we tried to persuade her not to go alone. She accused Mr. Packard very strangely of depriving her of her rights of conscience—that he would not allow her to think for her-self on religious questions, because they disagreed on these topics. She made her visit to New York. The first time I met her after her return, her health was much improved; she appeared much better. In the course of a few weeks, she visited at my house.

At another time, one of the children came up, and wanted me to go down; I did so. She was very much excited about her son remaining at Marshall. She was wild. She thought it was very wrong and tyrannical for Mr. Packard not to permit her son to remain there. She said very many things which seemed unnatural. Her voice, manner and ways, all showed she was insane.

I was there when Mr. Baker came there, to see about Theophilus remaining at Marshall with him. She was calmer than she was the day before. She said that she should spend the day in fasting and prayer. She said he had come in unexpectedly, and they were not prepared to entertain strangers. She was out of bread, and had to make biscuit for dinner. (One gentleman in the crowd turned to his wife and said, " Wife, were you ever out of bread, and had to make biscuit for dinner ? I must put you into an Insane Asylum! No mistake!") I occupied the same room and bed with her. She went to Mr. Packard's room, and when she returned, she said, that if her son was not permitted to remain at Marshall, it would result in a divorce. She got up several times during the night. She told me how much she enjoyed the family circle. She spoke very highly of Mr. Packard's kindness to her. She spoke particularly of the tenderness which had once existed between them. I did not notice anything very remarkable in her conduct toward Mr. Packard, until just before she was sent to the Hospital.

One morning afterward, I went to her house with a lady; we wanted to go in, and were admitted. She seemed much excited. She said, " You regard me insane. I will thank you to leave my room." This was two or three months before she was sent to Jacksonville. Mr. Packard went out. She put her hand on my shoulder, and said she would thank me to go out too. I went out.

I afterward wanted to take the baby home. One morning I went down to see her, and prepared breakfast for her. She appeared thankful, and complimented me on my kindness. She consented for me to take the child; I did so. In a short time, about ten days after, the other children came up, and said, that she wanted to take her own child. I took the child down. Her appearance was very wild. She was filled with spite toward Mr. Packard. She defied me to take the child again, and said that she would evoke the strong arm of the law to help her keep it.

At another time, at the table, she was talking about religion, when Mr. Packard remonstrated with her; she became angry, and told him she would talk what and when she had a mind to. She rose up from the table, and took her tea-cup, and left the room in great violence.

Cross-examined.—I am a member of Mr. Packard's church, and am his sister. He and I have often consulted together about Mrs. Packard. Mr. Packard was the first to ever suggest that she was insane; after that, I would more carefully watch her actions to find out if she was insane. The religious doctrines she advanced were at variance with those entertained by our church. She was a good, neat, thrifty, and careful housekeeper. She was economical; kept the children clean and neatly dressed. She was sane on all subjects except religion. I do not think she would have entertained these ideas, if she had not been insane. I do not think she would have wanted to have withdrawn from our church, and unite with another church, if she had not been insane. She said she would worship with the Methodists. They were the only other Protestant denomination that held service at Manteno at the time. I knew when she was taken to Jacksonville Hospital. She was taken away in the morning. She did not want to go; we thought it advisable for her to go.

Sarah Rumsey, sworn, and says:

Have lived one week in Mrs. Packard's house. I was present at the interview when Mrs. Packard ordered us to leave the room. Mrs. Packard was very pale and angry. She was in an undress, and her hair was down over her face. It was 11 o'clock in the forenoon—I staid at the house; Mrs. Packard came out to the kitchen. She was dressed then. She said she had come to reveal to me what Mr. Packard was. She talked very rapidly; she would not talk calm. She said Mr. Packard was an arch deceiver; that he and the members of his church had made a conspiracy to put her into the Insane Asylum; she wanted me to leave the Conspirators. Soon after dinner she said, " Come with me, I have something to tell you." She said she had a new revelation; it would soon be here; and that she had been chosen by God for a particular mission. She said that all who decided with her, and remained true to her, would be rewarded in the millennium, and if I would side with her, that I would be a chief apostle in the millennium. She wanted to go to Batavia, but that Mr. Packard would give her no money to take her there; that Mr. Packard called her insane. She started to go out, and Mr. Packard made her return; took her into Mr. Comstock's, and Mr. Comstock made her go home.

I saw her again when Libby had the brain fever. She was disturbed because the family called her insane. She and Libby were crying together; they cried together a long time. This was Tuesday. She would not let me into the room. The next morning while at breakfast Mr. La Brie passed the window and came in. He said that Georgie had been over for him, and said that they were killing his mother. She acted very strangely all the time; was wild and excited.

Cross-examined.—Knew Mr. Packard two years before I went

there to live. He was the pastor of our church. I am a member of the church. I did not attend the Bible-class. Brother Dole came to me and said somebody of the church should go there, and stay at the house, and assist in packing her clothes and getting her ready to take off to the Hospital, and stay and take care of the children. I consented to go; I heard that Brother Packard requested Brother Dole to come for me. I never worked out before. They had a French servant, before I went there; Mr. Packard turned her off when I came, the same day. I did not want to take Mrs. Packard away. I did not think she exhibited any very unusual excitement, when the men came there to take her away. Doctors Merrick and Newkirk were the physicians who came there with Sheriff Burgess. She did not manifest as much excitement, when being taken away, as I would have done under the same circumstances; any person would have naturally been opposed to being carried away.

The church had opposed her, in disseminating her ideas in the church; I was opposed to her promulgating her religious ideas in the church; I thought them wrong, and injurious. I was present at the Sabbath School when she read the paper to the school; I thought that bore evidence of insanity. It was a refutation of what Mrs. Dixon had written; I cannot give the contents of the paper now.

I was present when she read a confession of her conduct to the church; she had had her views changed partially, from a sermon preached upon the subject of the sovereignty and immutability of God. I did not think it strange conduct that she changed her views; and never said so. This was in the spring before the June when they took her away.

The article she read in the school was by the permission of the school.

I was present when she presented a protest against the church for refusing to let her be heard; I have only an

indistinct recollection of it; it was a protest because they refused to listen to her.

Mr. Dole was the only person who came to the house when
she was taken away, except the men with Burgess.

She said that Mr. Packard had deprived her of the liberty
of conscience in charging her to be insane, when she only
entertained ideas new to him.

I thought it was an evidence of insanity, because she maintained these ideas. I do not know that many people entertain similar ideas; I suppose a good many do not think the
Calvinistic doctrine is right; they are not necessarily insane
because they think so.

When she found I was going to stay in the house, and that
the French servant had been discharged, she ordered me into
the kitchen; before that she had treated me kindly as a visitor.

I thought it was an evidence of insanity for her to order me
into the kitchen; she ought to have known that I was not an
ordinary servant. The proper place for the servant is in the
kitchen at work, and not in the parlor; I took the place of
the servant girl for a short time.

She wanted the flower beds in the front yard cleaned out,
and tried to get Mr. Packard to do it; he would not do it.
She went and put on an old dress and went to work, and
cleaned the weeds out, and worked herself into a great heat.
It was a warm day; she staid out until she was almost melted
down with the heat.

Question. What did she do then?

Ans. She went to her room, took a bath and dressed herself,
and then lay down exhausted. She did not come down to dinner.

Ques. And did you think that was an evidence of insanity?

Ans. I did—the way it was done.

Ques. What would you have done under similar circumstances? Would you have set down in the clothes you had
worked in?

Ans. No.

Ques. Probably you would have taken a bath and changed your clothes too. And so would any lady, would they not?

Ans. Yes.

Ques. Then would you call yourself insane?

Ans. No. But she was angry and excited, and showed ill-will. She was very tidy in her habits; liked to keep the house clean, and have her yard and flowers look well. She took considerable pains with these things.

I remained there until she was taken away. I approved taking her away; I deemed her dangerous to the church; her ideas were contrary to the church, and were wrong.

The baby was eighteen months old when she was taken away. She was very fond of her children, and treated them very kindly. Never saw her misuse them. Never heard that she had misused them. Never heard that she was dangerous to herself or to her family. Never heard that she had threatened or offered to destroy anything or injure any person.

JUDGE BARTLETT was next called to the stand.

Am acquainted with Mrs. Packard. Had a conversation with her on religious topics. We agreed very well in most things. She did not say she believed in the transmigration of souls; she said, some persons had expressed that idea to her, but she did not believe it. It was spoken of lightly. She did not say ever to me, that Mr. Packard's soul would go into an ox. She did not say anything about her being related to the Holy Ghost. I thought then, and said it, that religious subjects were her study, and that she would easily be excited on that subject. I could not see that she was insane. I would go no stronger than to say, that her mind dwelt on religious subjects. She could not be called insane, for thousands of people believe as she does, on religion.

MRS. SYBIL DOLE, recalled.

At the time she got up from the table she went out. She said, " I will have no fellowship with the unfruitful works of darkness. No! not so much as to eat with them."

Re-cross-examined.—Question. Did you deem that an evidence of Insanity?

Answer. I did.

Ques. She called Mr. Packard the unfruitful works of darkness?

Ans. I suppose so.

Ques. Did she also include you?

Ans. She might have done so.

Ques. This was about the time that her husband was plotting to kidnap her, was it not?

Ans. It was just before she was removed to the Asylum.

Ques. He had been charging her with insanity, had he not, at the table?

Ans. He had.

The prosecution now wished to adjourn the court for ten days, to enable them to get Dr. McFarland, Superintendent of the State Hospital, who, they claimed, would testify that she was insane. Counsel stated, he had been telegraphed to come, and a reply was received, that he was in Zanesville, Ohio, and would return in about ten days. They claimed his testimony would be very important. This motion the counsel of Mrs. Packard opposed, as it was an unheard-of proceeding to continue a cause after the hearing was commenced, to enable a party to hunt up testimony.

The matter was discussed on each side for a considerable length of time, when the court held that the defense should go on with their testimony, and after that was heard, then the court would determine about continuing the case to get Dr. McFarland, and perhaps he could be got before the defense was through, and if so, he might be sworn; and held that the defense should go on now.

The counsel for Mrs. Packard withdrew for consultation, and in a brief time returned, and announced to the court that they would submit the case without introducing any testimony, and were willing to submit it without argument. The counsel for Mr. Packard objected to this, and renewed the motion for a continuance ; which the court refused.

The counsel for Mr. Packard then offered to read to the jury a letter from Dr. McFarland, dated in the month of December, 1863, written to Rev. Theophilus Packard ; and also a certificate, under the seal of the State Hospital at Jacksonville, certifying that Mrs. Packard was discharged from the institution in June, 1863, and was incurably insane, which certificate was signed by Dr. McFarland, the Superintendent. To the introduction of this to the jury, the counsel for Mrs. Packard objected, as being incompetent testimony, and debarred the defense of the benefit of a cross-examination. The court permitted the letter and certificate to be read to the jury.

These documents were retained by Rev. Theophilus Packard, and the reporter has been unable to obtain copies of them. The letter is dated in December, 1863, at the State Hospital, Jacksonville, Illinois, and written to Rev. Theophilus Packard, wherein Dr. McFarland writes him that Mrs. Packard is hopelessly insane, and that no possible good could result by having her returned to the Hospital ; that the officers of the institution had done everything in their power to effect a cure, and were satisfied she could not be cured, and refused to receive her into the institution.

The certificate, under the seal of the Hospital, was a statement, dated in June, 1863, at Jacksonville, Illinois, setting forth the time (three years) that Mrs. Packard had been under treatment, and that she had been discharged, as beyond a possibility of being cured.

The above is the import of these documents, which the reporter regrets he cannot lay before the public in full.

The prosecution now announced that they closed their case.

Defense.

J. L. Simington was the first witness called for the defense. Being sworn, he said:

I live in Manteno; lived there since 1859, early in the spring. Knew Rev. Mr. Packard and Mrs. Packard. First became acquainted with them in 1858; I was then engaged in the ministry of the Methodist Church. I have practiced medicine eleven years.

I was consulted as a family physician by Mrs. Packard in 1860. Was quite well acquainted with Mrs. Packard, and with the family. Lived fifty or sixty rods from their house. Saw her and the family almost daily. I did not see anything unusual in her, in regard to her mind. I never saw anything I thought insanity with her. So far as I know she was a sane woman. I have seen her since she came from the Hospital; have seen nothing since to indicate she was insane. My opinion is, she is a sane woman.

No cross-examination was made.

Dr. J. D. Mann, sworn, and says:

I live in Manteno; have lived there nine years. Practiced medicine there six years. I am not very intimately acquainted with either Mr. or Mrs. Packard. Mr. Packard invited me to go to his house to have an interview with Mrs. Packard. I went at his request. He requested me to make a second examination, which I did. There had been a physician there before I went. The last time he wanted me to meet Dr. Brown, of this city, there. This was late in November last. He introduced me to Mrs. Packard. I had known her before she was taken to the Hospital, and this was the first time I had seen her since she had returned. I was there from one to two hours. I then made up my mind, as I had made up my mind from the first interview, that I could find nothing that indicated insanity. I did not go when Dr. Brown was there. Mr. Packard had told me she was insane, and my prejudices were, that she was insane. He wanted a certificate of her insanity, to take East with him. I would not give it.

The witness was not cross-examined.

JOSEPH E. LA BRIE, sworn, and says:

Have known Mrs. Packard six years; lived fifteen or twenty rods from their house. Knew her in spring of 1860. Saw her nearly every day—sometimes two or three times a day. I belong to the Catholic Church. Have seen her since her return from Jacksonville. I have seen nothing that could make me think her insane. I always said she was a sane woman, and say so yet.

Cross-examined.—I am not a physician. I am not an expert. She might be insane, but no common-sense man could find it out.

Re-examined.—I am a Justice of the Peace, and Notary Public. Mr. Packard requested me to go to his house, and take an acknowledgment of a deed from her. I went there, and she signed and acknowledged the deed. This was within the past two months.

Re-cross-examined.—I was sent for to go to the house in the spring of 1860. My wife was with me. It was about taking her to Jacksonville. Mrs. Packard would not come to the room where I was. I stayed there only about twenty minutes.

Have been there since she returned from the Hospital. The door to her room was. locked on the outside. Mr. Packard said, he had made up his mind to let no one into her room.

The counsel for Mrs. Packard offered to read to the jury the following paper, which had been referred to by the witnesses, as evidence of Mrs. Packard's insanity, and which Deacon Smith

3

refused to hear read. The counsel for Mr. Packard examined the paper, and admitted it was the same paper.

The counsel for Mrs. Packard then requested permission of the court for Mrs. Packard to read it to the jury, which was most strenuously opposed. The court permitted Mrs. Packard to read it to the jury. Mrs. Packard arose, and read in a distinct tone of voice, so that every word was heard all over the court-room.

How Godliness is Profltable.

Deacon Smith.—A question was proposed to this class, the last Sabbath Brother Dole taught us, and it was requested that the class consider and report the result of their investigations at a future session. May I now bring it up? The question was this:

"Have we any reason to expect that a Christian farmer, as a Christian, will be any more successful in his farming operations, than an impenitent sinner—and if not, how is it that godliness is profitable unto all things? Or, in other words, does the motive with which one prosecutes his secular busi ness, other things being equal, make any difference in the pecuniary results?"

Mrs. Dixon gave it as her opinion, at the time, that the motive did affect the pecuniary results.

Now the practical result to which this conclusion leads, is such as will justify us in our judging of Mrs. Dixon's true moral character, next fall, by her success in her farming operations this summer.

My opinion differs from hers on this point; and my reasons are here given in writing, since I deem it necessary for me, under the existing state of feeling toward me, to put into a written form all 1 have to say, in the class, to prevent misrepresentation.

Should I be appropriating an unreasonable share of time, as

a pupil, Mr. Smith, to occupy four minutes of your time in reading them? I should like very much to read them, that the class may pass their honest criticism upon them.

An Answer to the Question.

I think we have no intelligent reason for believing that the motives with which we prosecute our secular business, have any influence in the pecuniary results.

My reasons are common sense reasons, rather than strictly Bible proofs, viz.: I regard man as existing in three distinct departments of being, viz., his physical or animal, his mental or intellectual, his moral or spiritual; and each of these three distinct departments are under the control of *laws*, peculiar to itself; and these different laws do not interchange with, or affect each other's department.

For instance, a very immoral man may be a very healthy, long-lived man; for, notwithstanding he violates the moral department, he may live in conformity to the physical laws of his animal nature, which secure to him his physical health—and on the other hand, a very moral man may suffer greatly from a diseased body, and be cut off in the very midst of his usefulness by an early death, in consequence of having violated the physical laws of his animal constitution. But on the moral plane he is the gainer, and the immoral man is the loser.

So our success in business depends upon our conformity to *those laws* on which success depends—not upon the motives which act only upon the moral plane.

On this ground, the Christian farmer has no more reason to expect success in his farming operations, than the impenitent sinner. In either case, the foundation for success must depend upon the degree of fidelity with which the natural laws are applied, which cause the natural result—not upon the motives of the operator; since these moral acts receive their penalty and reward upon an entirely different plane of his being.

Now comes in the question, how then is it true, that " godliness is *profitable* unto all things," if godliness is no guarantee to success in business pursuits?

I reply, that the profits of godliness cannot mean, simply, pecuniary profits, because this would limit the gain of godliness to this world, alone; whereas, it is profitable not only for this life, but also for the life to come. Gain and loss, dollars and cents, are not the coins current in the spiritual world.

But happiness and misery are coins which are current in both worlds. Therefore, it appears to me, that *happiness* is the profit attendant upon godliness, and for this reason, a practically godly person, who lives in conformity to all the various laws of his entire being, may expect to secure to himself, as a natural result, a greater amount of happiness than the ungodly person.

So that, in this sense, " Godliness is profitable unto all things," to every department of our being.

Manteno, March 22, 1860.   E. P. W. Packard

Mrs. Packard then stated that the above was presented to the class, the 15th day of the following April, and was rejected by the teacher, Deacon Smith, on the ground of its being irrelevant to the subject, since she had not confined herself to the Bible alone for proof of her position.

As she took her seat a murmur of applause arose from every part of the room, which was promptly suppressed by the sheriff.

Daniel Beedy sworn, and says:

I live in Manteno. Have known Mrs. Packard six years; knew her in the spring of 1860. I lived a mile and a half from them. Have seen her very frequently since her return from Jacksonville. Had many conversations with her before she was taken away, and since her return. She always appeared to me like a sane woman. I heard she was insane, and my wife and I went to satisfy ourselves. I went there soon after the difficulties in the Bible-class.

She is not insane. We talked about religion, politics, and various matters, such as a grey-haired old farmer could talk about, and I saw nothing insane about her.

Mr. BLESSING, sworn, and says:

I live in Manteno; have known Mrs. Packard six years; knew her in the spring of 1860; lived eighty rods from their house. She visited at my house. I have seen her at church. She attended the Methodist church for a while after the difficulties commenced, and then I saw her every Sunday. I never thought her insane.

After the word was given out by her husband that she was insane, she claimed my particular protection, and wanted me to obtain a trial for her by the laws of the land, and such an investigation she said she was willing to stand by. She claimed Mr. Packard was insane, if any one was. She begged for a trial. I did not then do anything, because I did not like to interfere between man and wife. I never saw anything that indicated insanity. She was always rational. Had conversations with her since her return. She first came to my house. She claimed a right to live with her family. She considered herself more capable of taking care of her family than any other person.

I saw her at Jacksonville. I took Dr. Shirley with me to test her sanity. Dr. Shirley told me she was not insane.

Cross-examination waived.

Mrs. BLESSING, sworn, and says:

Have known Mrs. Packard seven years; knew her in 1860. Lived near them; we visited each other as neighbors. She first came to our house when she returned from Jacksonville. I did not see anything that indicated that she was insane. I saw her at Jacksonville. She had the keys, and showed me around. I heard the conversation there with Dr. Shirley; they talked about religion; did not think she talked unnatural. When I first went in, she was at work on a dress for Dr. McFarland's wife. I saw her after she returned home last fall, quite often, until she was locked in her room. On Monday after she got home, I called on her; she was at work; she was cleaning up the feather beds; they needed cleaning badly. I went there afterward; her daughter let me in. On Saturday before the trial commenced, I was let into her room by Mr. Packard; she had no fire in it; we sat there in the cold. Mr. Packard had a handful of keys, and unlocked the door and let me in. Mrs. Hanford was with me. Before this, Mrs. Hanford and myself went there to see her; he would not let us see her; he shook his hand at me, and threatened to put me out.

Mrs. HASLET, sworn, and said:

Know Mrs. Packard very well; have known her since they lived in Manteno; knew her in the spring of 1860; and since she returned from Jacksonville, we have been on intimate terms. I never saw any signs of insanity in her. I called often before she was kidnapped and carried to Jacksonville, and since her return.

I recollect the time Miss Rumsey was there; I did not see anything that showed insanity. I called to see her in a few days after she returned from Jacksonville; she was in the yard, cleaning feather beds. I called again in a few days; she was still cleaning house. The house needed cleaning; and when I again called, it looked as if the mistress of the house was at home. She had no hired girl. I went again, and was not admitted. I conversed with her through the window; the window was fastened down. The son refused me admission. The window was fastened with nails on the inside, and by two screws, passing through the lower part of the upper sash and the upper part of the lower sash, from the outside. I did not see Mr. Packard this time.

Cross-examination.—She talked about getting released from her imprisonment. She asked if filing a bill of complaint would lead to a divorce. She said she did not want a divorce; she only wanted protection from Mr. Packard's cruelty. I advised her to not stand it quietly, but get a divorce.

Dr. DUNCANSON, sworn, and said:

I live here; am a physician; have been a clergyman; have been a practicing physician twenty-one years. Have known Mrs. Packard since this trial commenced. Have known her by general report for three years and upwards. I visited her at Mr. Orr's. I was requested to go there and have a conversation with her and determine if she was sane or insane. Talked three hours with her, on political, religious and scientific subjects, and on mental and moral philosophy. I was educated at and received diplomas from the University of Glasgow, and Anderson University of Glasgow. I went there to see her, and prove or disprove her insanity. I think not only that she is sane, but the most intelligent lady I have talked with in many years. We talked religion very thoroughly. I find her an expert in both departments, Old School and New School theology. There are thousands of persons who believe just as she does. Many of her ideas and doctrines are embraced in Swedenborgianism, and many are found only in the New School theology. The best and most learned men of both Europe and this country, are advocates of these doctrines, in one shape or the other; and some bigots and men with minds of small calibre may call these great minds insane; but that does not make them insane. An insane mind is a diseased mind. These minds are the perfection of intellectual powers, healthy, strong, vigorous, and just the reverse of diseased minds, or insane. Her explanation of woman representing the Holy Ghost, and man representing the male attributes of the Father, and that the Son is the fruit of the Father and the Holy Ghost, is a very ancient theological dogma, and entertained by many of our most eminent men. With every topic I introduced, she was perfectly familiar, and discussed them with an intelligence that at once showed she was possessed of a good education, and a strong and vigorous mind. I did not agree with her in sentiment on many things, but I do not call people insane because they differ from me, nor from a majority, even, of people. Many persons called Swedenborg insane. That is true; but he had the largest brain of any person during the age in which he lived; and no one now dares call him insane. You might with as much propriety call Christ insane, because he taught the people many new and strange things; or Galileo; or Newton; or Luther; or Robert Fulton; or Morse, who electrified the world; or Watts, or a thousand others I might name. Morse's best friends for a long time thought him mad; yet there was a magnificent mind, the embodiment of health and vigor.

So with Mrs. Packard. There is wanting every indication of insanity that is laid down in the books. I pronounce her a sane woman, and wish we had a nation of such women.

This witness was cross-examined at some length, which elicited nothing new, when he retired.

The defense now announced to the court that they had closed all the testimony they wished to introduce, and inasmuch as the case had occupied so much time, they would propose to submit it without argument. The prosecution would **not** consent to this arrangement.

The case was argued ably and at length, by Messrs. Loomis and Bonfield for the prosecution, and by Messrs. Orr and Loring on the part of the defense.

It would be impossible to give even a statement of the arguments made, and do the attorneys justice, in the space allotted to this report.

On the 18th day of January, 1864, at 10 o'clock, P. M., the jury retired for consultation, under the charge of the sheriff. After an absence of seven minutes, they returned into court, and gave the following verdict:

STATE OF ILLINOIS, } ss.
  KANKAKEE COUNTY.

We, the undersigned, Jurors in the case of Mrs. Elizabeth P. W. Packard, alleged to be insane, having heard the evidence in the case, are satisfied that said Elizabeth P. W. Packard is SANE.

JOHN STILES, *Foreman.*	H. HIRSHBERG.
DANIEL G. BEAN.	NELSON JERVAIS.
F. G. HUTCHINSON.	WILLIAM HYER.
V. H. YOUNG.	GEO. H. ANDREWS.
G. M. LYONS.	J. F. MAFIT.
THOMAS MUNCEY.	LEMUEL MILK.

Cheers rose from every part of the house; the ladies waved their handkerchiefs, and pressed around Mrs. Packard, and extended her their congratulations. It was sometime before the outburst of applause could be checked. When order was restored, the counsel for Mrs. Packard moved the court, that she be discharged. Thereupon the court ordered the clerk to enter the following order:

STATE OF ILLINOIS, } ss.
  KANKAKEE COUNTY,

It is hereby ordered that Mrs. Elizabeth P. W. Packard be relieved from all restraint incompatible with her condition as a sane woman.

C. R. STARR,
Judge of the Twentieth Judicial District
of the State of Illinois.

January 18, 1864.

Thus ended the trial of this remarkable case. During each
day of the proceedings the court-room was crowded to excess
by an anxious audience of ladies and gentlemen, who are seldom in our courts. The verdict of the jury was received with
applause, and hosts of friends crowded upon Mrs. Packard to
congratulate her upon her release.

During the past six weeks, Mr. Packard had locked her up
in her own house, fastened the windows outside, and carried
the key to the door, and made her a close prisoner. He was
maturing a plan to immure her in an Asylum in Massachusetts,
and for that purpose was ready to start on the Thursday before the writ was sued out, when his plan was disclosed to
Mrs. Packard by letters he accidentally left in her room, one of
which was written by his sister in Massachusetts, telling him
the route he should take, and that a carriage would be ready
at the station to put her in and convey her to the Asylum.

Vigorous action became necessary, and she communicated
this startling intelligence through her window to some ladies
who had come to see her, and were refused admission into the
house.

On Monday morning, and before the defense had rested their
case, Mr. Packard left the State, bag and baggage, for parts
unknown, having first mortgaged his property for all it is
worth to his sister and other parties.

We cannot do better than close this report with the following
editorial from the Kankakee *Gazette*, of January 21, 1864:

Mrs. Packard.

The case of this lady, which has attracted so much attention
and excited so much interest for ten days past, was decided on
Monday evening last, and resulted, as almost every person
thought it must, in a complete vindication of her sanity. The
jury retired on Monday evening, after hearing the arguments

of the counsel; and after a brief consultation, they brought in a verdict that Mrs. Packard is a *sane* woman.

Thus has resulted an investigation which Mrs. Packard has long and always desired should be had, but which her cruel husband has ever sternly refused her. She has always asked and earnestly pleaded for a jury trial of her case, but her relentless persecutor has ever turned a deaf ear to her entreaties, and flagrantly violated all the dictates of justice and humanity.

She has suffered the alienation of friends and relatives—the shock of a kidnapping by her husband and his posse when forcibly removed to the Asylum—has endured three years incarceration in that Institution—upon the general treatment in which there is severe comment in the State, and which, in her special case, was aggravatingly unpleasant and ill-favored—and when at last returning to her home found her husband's saintly blood still congealed; a winter of perpetual frown on his face, and the sad, dull monotony of "Insane! Insane!" escaping his lips in all his communications to and concerning her—her children, the youngest of the four at home being less than four years of age, over whose slumbers she had watched, and whose wailings she had hushed with all a mother's care and tenderness—taught to look upon her as insane, and not to respect the counsels or heed the voice of a maniac just loosed from the Asylum, doom sealed by official certificates.

Soon her aberration of mind led her to seek some of her better clothing carefully kept from her by her husband, which very woman-like act was seized by him as an excuse for confining her in her room, and depriving her of her apparel, and excluding her lady friends. Believing that he was about to again forcibly take her to an asylum, four responsible citizens of that village made affidavit of facts which caused the investigation as to her sanity or insanity. During the whole of the trial she was present, and counseled with her attorneys in the management of the case.

Notwithstanding the severe treatment she has received for nearly four years past, the outrages she has suffered, the wrong to her nature she has endured, she deported herself during the trial as one who is not only not insane, but as one possessing intellectual endowments of a high order, and an equipoise and control of mind far above the majority of human kind.

The heroic motto: " suffer and be strong," is fairly illustrated in her case. While many would have opposed force to his force, displayed frantic emotions of displeasure at such treatment, or sat convulsed and " maddened with the passion of her part," she meekly submitted to the tortures of her bigoted tormentor, trusting and believing in God's Providence the hour of her vindication and her release from thraldom would come. And now the fruit of her suffering and persecution has all the autumn glory of perfection.

> "One who walked
> From the throne's splendor to the bloody block,
> Said : ' This completes my glory' with a smile
> Which still illuminates men's thoughts of her."

Feeling the accusations of his guilty conscience, seeing the meshes of the net with which he had kept her surrounded were broken, and a storm-cloud of indignation about to break over his head in pitiless fury, the intolerant Packard, after encumbering their property with trust deeds, and despoiling her of her furniture and clothing, left the country. Let him wander! with the mark of infamy upon his brow, through far-off states, where distance and obscurity may diminish till the grave shall cover the wrongs it cannot heal.

It is to be hoped Mrs. Packard will make immediate application for a divorce, and thereby relieve herself of a repetition of the wrongs and outrages she has suffered by him who for the past four years has only used the marriage relation to persecute and torment her in a merciless and unfeeling manner.

Note to the Reader.

It is but justice to myself to say, that the testimony of the two great Conspirators, Deacon Abijah Dole and Deacon Josephus B. Smith, ought to be taken by my readers at a discount, since those who were present during the whole trial saw the fact demonstrated, that both of these Deacons perjured themselves openly, upon the witness stand, while giving in their manufactured testimony against my moral character.

A part of the time of the five days trial was consumed in taking testimony from these two witnesses while making a most malign attack upon my moral character, by *manufactured testimony*, which, when tested by cross-examination, would not hold together—in fact, was so plainly contradictory and absurd, that I was strongly urged, by my friends, to enter a prosecution, at once, against them both, for perjury.

This part of the trial was not reported by Mr. Moore, because, as he said, this attack was entirely foreign to the question at issue. My moral character was not the question the jury were called upon to consider—but whether I was insane or not.

This most wanton and cruel attack, made at Packard's dictation, was shown to be merely an act of desperation on their part to save their sinking cause; but as it proved, these weapons of cruel slander and defamation were most signally turned against themselves, by forcing the conviction upon the jury, and all who heard it, that their testimony, as witnesses against my sanity, was of no account whatever. In fact the remark was often made to me :

"We do not believe a word that Deacon Dole or Deacon Smith have spoken against your sanity, now that they have so plainly proved themselves to be lying witnesses against your virtue."

E. P. W. P.

CHAPTER III.

Mr. Packard takes My Children and Property and Flees His Country.

When this trial terminated, I returned to my home in Manteno, where five days previous I had bestowed the parting kiss upon my three youngest children, little thinking it would be the last embrace for years I should be allowed to bestow upon these dear objects of my warmest affections.

But alas! so it proved!

Mr. Packard had fled with them to Massachusetts, leaving me in the court-room a childless widow. He could not but see that the current of popular indignation was concentrating against him, as the revelations of the Court ventilated the dreadful facts of this conspiracy, and he " fled his country," a fugitive from justice!

He, however, left a letter for me which was handed me before I left the Court-house, wherein he stated that he had moved to Massachusetts, and extended to me an invitation to follow him, with the promise that he would provide me a suitable home.

But I did not feel much like trusting either to *his* humanity or judgment in providing me another home. Indeed, I did not think it safe to follow him, knowing that the laws of Massachusetts as well as those of Illinois then gave him the absolute custody of my person.

He went to South Deerfield, Massachusetts, and sought shelter for himself and his children in the family of his sister, Mrs. Severance, his co-conspirator. Here he found willing ears to credit his tale of abuses he had suffered in this interference with his right to do as he pleased with his lawful wife—and in representing the trial as a "mock trial," an illegal interference with his rights as head of his own household, and a "mob triumph,"—in short, he was an innocent victim of a persecution against his legally constituted rights as a husband, to protect his wife in the way his own feelings of bigotry and intolerance should dictate!

This was the region of his nativity and former pastorate, which he had left about eleven years previously, with an unblemished external character, and sharing, to an uncommon degree, the entire confidence of the public as a Christian man and a minister. Nothing had occurred, *to their knowledge*, to disturb this confidence in his present integrity as an honest reporter, and the entire community credited his testimony as perfectly reliable, in his entire misrepresentations of the facts in the case, and the character of the trial.

His view was the only view the community were allowed to hear, so far as it was in his power to prevent it. The press also lent him its aid, as his organ of communication.

He met his old associates in the ministry, and by his artfully arranged web of lies, and his cunning sophistries, he deluded them also into a belief of his views, so that they, unanimously, gave him their certificate of confidence and fraternal sympathy!

This certificate served as a passport to the confidence of Sunderland people in Mr. Packard as a man and a minister, and procured for him a call to become their minister in holy things. He was accordingly hired, as stated supply, and paid fifteen dollars a Sabbath for one year and a half, and was boarded by my father in his family, part of the time, free of charge.

The condition in which Mr. Packard left me I will now give in the language of another, by inserting here a quotation from one of the many Chicago papers which published an account of this trial with editorial remarks accompanying it. The following is a part of one of these Editorial Articles, which appeared under the caption :

"A Heartless Clergyman."

Chicago, March 6, 1864.

" We recently gave an extended account of the melancholy case of Mrs. Packard, of Manteno, Ill., and showed how she was persecuted by her husband, Rev. Theophilus Packard, a bigoted Presbyterian minister of Manteno.

Mrs. Packard became liberal in her views, and as her husband was unable to answer her arguments, he thought he could silence her tongue, by calling her insane, and having her incarcerated in the Insane Asylum at Jacksonville, Illinois.

He finally succeeded in finding one or two orthodox physicians, as bigoted as himself, ready to aid him in his nefarious work, and she was confined in the asylum, under the charge (?) of Dr. McFarland, who kept her there three years.

She at last succeeded in having a jury trial, and was pronounced *sane.*

Previous, however, to the termination of the trial, this persecutor of his wife mortgaged his property, took away his children from the mother, and left her penniless and homeless, without a cent to buy food, or a place where to lay her head ! And yet he pretended to believe that she was insane !

Is this the way to treat an insane wife ?

Abandon her, turn her out upon the world without a morsel .. bread, and no home ?

Her husband calls her insane. Before the case is decided by the jury, he starts for parts unknown.

Was there ever such a case of heartlessness ?

If Mr. Packard believed his wife to be hopelessly insane, why did he abandon her ? Is this the way to treat a companion afflicted with insanity ?

If he believed his own story, he should, like a devoted husband, have watched over her with tenderness, his heart full of love should have gone out towards the poor, afflicted woman, and he should have bent over her and soothed her, and spent the last penny he had, for her recovery!

But instead of this, he gathers in his funds, " packs up his duds," and leaves his poor insane wife, as *he* calls her, in the court-room, without food or shelter. He abandons her, leaving her homeless, penniless and childless!"

CHAPTER IV.

Return to my Home—Married woman a Slave!

After my acquittal from the court at Kankakee, I, of course, turned my attention and thoughts towards my dear children, whom I had left five days previous in my own dear home in Manteno.

But alas! Upon arriving at the spot I once called my home, I found there was no home left for me! Mr. Packard had left the court-room on the previous Saturday evening, spent the night in removing my furniture to the house of his brother-in-law, Deacon Dole, then rented the place to Mr. Wood, who had taken possession; and taking my wardrobe, money, notes, and children, had fled, Sabbath morning, to parts unknown.

Ignorant of this purpose of Mr. Packard, on my return from my trial this Saturday evening previous to my acquittal on the Monday evening following, I had fortunately arrived prior to Mr. Packard, on account of the extra fleetness of Mr. Hanford's team to that of Mr. Dole's. Indeed, our merry sleigh-bells were soon lost in the distance as we flew past Mr. Dole's sleigh load including Mr. Packard, for we had an especial object in seeking an arrival before them, hoping thus to be able to remove my trunk without interference.

At about eleven o'clock at night we arrived at the door of my house, to find it unoccupied—but locked—both doors and windows.

" How shall we enter?" was the question to be solved.

"Shall my men force an entrance and thus expose themselves to a prosecution for larceny? or, shall I introduce them into my own house by opening the door myself with my own key?"

The latter policy prevailed, for neither Mr. Packard, nor any other person had seen fit to disturb the locality where I had chosen to place the keys two months before. Therefore, instead of directing my men, as Mr. Packard had directed his children to look where the keys were *not*, I simply told them to look where they were, in the " right place," for, of course, that was the only place in which to find them! And, although the snow and ice had buried them a trifle deeper than my own hands had done, under the sod beneath my window, yet, by the aid of the identical axe by which Packard had broken into my window three years and a half before, my men easily found the keys, so that we could unlock the door and enter quietly and peaceably into my own house, when I directed my men to take my trunk, already packed with my Asylum wardrobe, and remove it to their sleigh, and thus it was transported with myself to Mr. Hanford's house, where I quietly rested until Monday morning, while Mr. Packard was robbing me and my house and fleeing from justice.

Thus robbed of all my life·earnings, and bereaved of my children, in addition to my three years of ' false imprisonment,' as the decision of the jury proved it to have been, I now appealed to the laws for protection, as a married woman, when, alas! I found I had no laws to appeal to!

My counsel assured me, that before the law, I was merely a " nonentity," and therefore, as I had no rights, I had no protection in the law, except in a divorce.

I replied, " Gentlemen, I cannot conscientiously get a divorce, as I am a Bible woman, and cannot claim that I have any Bible cause for a divorce. Besides, I claim the right to be a married woman, therefore I claim protection, as a married woman."

My counsel replied, " As a married woman, you have no protection in law. Your 'husband is the only protector you have."

"But he has become my persecutor! can't you protect me against my persecutor?"

"There is no way, but by a divorce, that we can extend to you the protection of any law to shield you from marital usurpation; for on the principle of common law, whatever is yours is his—your property is his—your earnings are his—your children are his—and you are his. Whatever you hold in common with him, in his own name, you have no more right to than any other woman, while your husband lives. But should you outlive him, you have a ' right of dower' in his real estate, which you have a right to use during your life-time. But while he lives, you have not a right even to the hat on your head."

"But, Sir, I have bought and paid for my hat with my own money!"

"That is of no consequence. If you did not hold this money you purchased it with in your own name, as a single woman, independent of himself, you have no more legal right to use it, as your own, than any other woman."

"I had supposed that I was his partner, in law, as I am in society."

"No indeed! there is your grand mistake. There is no such thing as a partnership relation in the marriage union. The man and wife become one, but that one is the man! for the rights of the married woman are all ' suspended during coverture,' while all the rights of the married man remain established and protected by law, just as they were before marriage."

"But why do you not allow married woman a right to an existence as before, also? Can't she, as a woman, be as well protected while she is married, as he is as a man, while he is married?"

"No. For married woman is a slave! and we cannot protect slaves, except through their masters."

" Slave!" said I, " Why, I have always been an abolition-
ist, and I never before knew that I was a slave. I supposed
I was the partner and companion of my husband. I never
suspected or thought I was his *slave!*"

" You are his companion and partner socially; but legally,
you are his slave."

" Why is this? Why don't our legal and social condition
correspond more nearly?"

" Because married woman has never been legally emancipated from the slavish social position she occupied in the un-
civilized state of society in the dark ages. Society then made
married woman a slave to her husband, and in order to make
her legal position to correspond to this her social position, the
law-makers of that age inaugurated this common law as
their basis of the marriage union. Thus married woman
became a ' nonentity,' by a legal suspension of her rights
during coverture. And a person whose rights are all suspended is a mere chattel before the law. Then this legal
position corresponded with her social position. But now her
social and legal position do not correspond; for civilization
has elevated woman from this slavish social position, so that
she is now the companion and partner of her husband. She
is not now his slave socially, but legally she is still in the
position of a slave.

" True her slavish position has been somewhat modified by
statute law, still she is not yet emancipated; for her position
of ' nonentity' still excludes her from becoming in law a companion or partner of her husband."

" But why don't you emancipate married women? You
have emancipated the negro slave, and we think our claim to
' life, liberty, and the pursuit of happiness' is equal, at least,
to that of the colored men."

" 'Tis true, it ought to be done," my counsel replied, " but
as men generally protect their wives, as public sentiment, and

her social position both demand she should be, and as it is not generally known that married woman is a slave in law, there has been no special call for the agitation of this question. But your case demonstrates the fact that she *ought* to be emancipated, for since you insist upon the right to be a married woman, there is no possible way to protect even your personal liberty from this marital usurper so long as you claim a right to your individual conscience and opinions in religious matters. Certainly her present condition not only encourages divorce or disunion of the married pair, but it makes the laws of divorce an imperative necessity.

"Besides this is only substituting one evil to supplant another. It is not removing any evil. The great underlying cause of the evils of our social system as yet remains unremoved and unmolested by legislation. Until this relic of barbarism is expunged from the laws of our Christian government, and woman is allowed to be an·individualized partner or companion of her husband in law, as she now is in society, there can be no legal remedy for the constantly increasing and momentous evils of our social system. So long as this legalized usurpation of human rights exists, these social evils must necessarily increase—they cannot diminish under the fostering influence of injustice."

From one more stand point allow me to portray married woman's legal disabilities for my readers' consideration.

Finding, as I had, that my property rights—my rights of conscience and opinion—and my personal liberty—were at the mercy of my legal usurper, I inquired with the most intense anxiety how it was with my children. "Can I not have children protected to me while I am a married woman?"

"No! The children are all the husband's after the 'tender age.' You can have no legal right to your children without you get a divorce, and then the Judge will give you children and alimony."

" Then your laws do protect children to the single woman, while they do not protect them to the married woman ? "

" Yes, the laws do respect the right of maternity in the single woman, but in the married woman this right, like all her other rights, is ignored by this suspension of rights during coverture."

Now, we married women claim that the time has fully come to have our natural rights, as women, established and protected by law, equally, at least, to those of the single woman, for by such laws as these the government is offering a premium on infidelity, and encourages divorce. Whereas, the best interests of society demand that the sacred institution of marriage be based on the principle of right and justice to both parties, so that neither party can ignore or usurp the inalienable rights of the other.

Until this is done, the children of this Republic have only half their rights, in law. They can claim a legal right to a father's training, but none to a mother's care !

Inasmuch as the law of manliness did not influence my husband to respect my rights, I had no tribunal whatever to appeal to, since this law did not recognize any separate interest or identity in the married woman.

The law of manliness is the only law the married woman has to depend upon for protection under the common law.

This I at once recognized as an all-sufficient refuge in most cases ; for doubtless this law is based upon the almost universal fact that man will defend his own wife even before he would himself. Therefore, laws for the wife's protection seem almost to ignore this principle of manhood.

Yet, in such cases as my own, that is—exceptional cases— where the higher law is not a sufficient guarantee for the protection of the wife, there seems to be a necessity for the lower law of **human** enactments to enforce the dictates of the higher law. **In** such cases, and in these alone, there docs seem to be a necessity for some laws to ensure the safety of the married woman.

But at that date the common law in Illinois had not been modified by statute law as it has since been. Thus Mr. Packard's course was sustained and is still sustained under common law, wherever it exists unmodified by statute law.

And it is hoped that this delineation of its injustice to married woman may have its influence in securing its modification still farther, where justice to woman requires it, so that no other married woman may be compelled to go without protection, for want of laws to shield her from marital injustice.

Under these painful circumstances I found that Mr. Packard had only been telling me the simple truth when he said, that:

"For twenty years I have given you a home to live in—and also allowed you the privilege of taking care of *my own* children in it—and to me alone are you indebted for these privileges—as by law you have no legal right to my home, my property, or my children *while I live !*"

Finding I could not prosecute my husband for doing a legal act, and also that he had put his property out of his own hands to prevent his paying any bills I might contract, I found that necessity was laid upon me to become my own protector.

CHAPTER V.

Defense of my Right to Property.

I therefore went to Kankakee to get out "·a replevy" to get possession of my own things at Deacon Dole's, or at least, so many of them as would furnish me a room decently for my accommodation.

But, to my sorrow, I found that a married woman could not even replevy her own stolen property—that I was literally *outlawed*, so far as legal rights and self-protection were concerned, as much so as an " infant, idiot, insane or criminal."

And these rights were not denied on the plea that I was an insane person, for a jury of my country had just pronounced me sane, and entitled to all the rights and privileges of a sane person ; but the right of citizenship was denied me simply, because I was a *married* woman, and therefore I was no longer an individual before the law.

With equal propriety, as it seemed to me, might I have been informed :

" You have no right to eat or sleep now that you are a married woman, for you are no longer an individual before the law!"

If the married woman has no right to her home, no right to her food, or property to buy food with, and no right to her children, what right has she to be hungry or to be cold, or to desire offspring, if she is a " nonenity" or a chattel, as is the case while she is a married woman, under the common law ?

As the laws of my country denied me the right to my own property, as this furniture ·was bought with my own patrimony, I concluded I would use the law of justice as my claim to my own things, in defiance of human enactments by which justice was denied me.

4

As my furniture was too heavy for me to lift without assistance, and as I had no team to transport it from Mr. Dole's to my room, a distance of about two miles, I was obliged to hire help to get it for me, and therefore engaged six men with three teams to help me, and we proceeded to Deacon Dole's for the purpose of quietly taking my own things into my own possession.

Upon arriving there, and finding no one in the house except his daughter, I led my men quietly into the room where I found my best furniture snugly packed, and told them to carry it to their wagons as fast as possible.

Meeting no opposition except the protest of his daughter, Laura, we soon cleared that room, and I went up stairs for my bedding, when I heard Mr. Dole's voice below stairs demanding what this meant. My men, of course, directed him to me, and we met on the stairs, while I was helping one of my men carry down one of my feather beds.

He stopped us, and said:

"What are you doing?"

"I am getting my own things."

"Show me your papers!"

"I did not come to show papers—I simply came to get my own things."

Adding:

"Mr. Holden, carry my bed to your wagon!"

Mr. Dole closed the front door against him, and locked it, and put the key into his own pocket, while Mr. Holden looked to me for directions. Said I:

"Mr. Holden, pass out the back-door with your load!"

He did so, while I retreated to the chamber in pursuit of more articles. Finding a pile of my own bedclothes, I took them and threw them over the banister, down stairs to my men, who were there to take them, while Mr. Haslet detained Mr. Dole, by an argument in defense of their act.

I then went into his pantry and took articles from thence which belonged to me and gave them to my men to put into their wagons.

Mr. Dole headed them again, and said:

"You shall not take them!"

"Go ahead with the things, gentlemen!" said I.

Which they did.

I then looked overhead in his back-kitchen and saw some of my bedsteads, and said:

"Gentlemen, I must have one bedstead to sleep upon. Take down one of these bedsteads and I will not ask you to get anything more."

They tried to do so, but Mr. Dole interfered, and in the struggle one light of glass was broken in Mr. Dole's window.

I apologized to Mr. Dole, adding:

"I will repair it."

And accordingly sent a glazier the next day to replace it, but Mr. Dole would not allow him to do it.

After another short but lively contest about some boxes of books which Mr. Dole said did not belong to him, and which Mr. Haslet said he would therefore claim for my benefit, we left, but not until I had, in the hearing of all the witnesses, which, with Mr. Dole's hired men and his wife, in addition to my own men, now formed quite a company, distinctly stated:

"I wish to say in the presence of you all, that this is *my* act—I, alone, assume all the responsibility of it—these men are merely my agents carrying out my orders, therefore the acts are my own acts, not theirs, and upon me rests the entire responsibility of getting this portion of my own things. Those that I have not taken I claim as my own things, and shall take them when I think proper."

We then left the premises unimpeded; but had not gone far before we were overtaken by Mr. Dole on horseback, who was going in hot haste for a Sheriff to arrest us. But he could find no one, either in Manteno or Kankakee, who were willing to undertake such a prosecution!

But by his persistency in going several times, and at last with his wife to Kankakee, and threatening to prosecute the officer who should refuse to act when called upon, he succeeded in finding one, whom he almost impressed into service, who did prosecute my men for riot and trespass!

I claimed the right to be prosecuted for my *own acts*, and protested against prosecuting my agents instead of the one who employed them, but:

" No, we can't prosecute *you*, for you are a married woman, and *therefore are a nonentity*, or nobody before the law!

" Does not the law hold me responsible for my own acts? "

"Not in such a case—your husband is responsible for your actions, but you are not responsible for your own! You must remember, Mrs. Packard, you have no legal right to hold any kind of property, while you are a married woman, therefore you have no right to defend any kind of property. For this reason you cannot be prosecuted, while your men can be, as they are regarded as responsible individuals before the law, while you are not."

My men were prosecuted before a Justice, both for "riot" and "trespass," and bound over for trial before the court the next fall term—about six months from date.

I instructed my men to be sure and not compromise in any manner, but to stand their ground like men, and I would stand between them and all harm—that I had received voluntary offers from two of the most influential lawyers in Illinois, one of whom then stood candidate for Congress, that they would defend any case of mine free of cost to me—that I wished the case to come to trial as a test case, to ventilate the laws for married women—that a trial of this kind might do more for the enlightenment of public sentiment on this subject, than any series of lectures could do.

I told them in addition, that before the time for the trial I hoped to get my book into print, and by its sale I should raise money to pay their costs and fines if they had any to pay, so that in the end they should suffer no harm, if *they stood their ground like men.*

I did as I proposed, printed my book and sold enough above all my expenses to pay my three lawyers at Kankakee, in full, for their defense of my case six months previously, and was fast laying up money for these men, when to my surprise I was informed that their fears had triumphed over their courage and manliness and they had agreed to return all my furniture to Mr. Dole and pay him two hundred dollars in addition!

This they did without my knowledge or consent.

While I was in Boston prosecuting my business, about a year from this time, I received a letter from one of these men, stating what they had done, and that Mr. Dole, acting as Mr. Packard's agent, demanded the two hundred dollars to be paid at once. They therefore wished me to send them the money as I had agreed.

Following my impressions I counted out the money and found it took every cent I then had outside of my business, and then lacked fifty cents of being two hundred dollars. I accordingly wrote a letter acknowledging the debt as being one of honor, and saying:

"Enclosed you will find a draft of two hundred dollars to meet it, &c."

And took my money and letter and went to the bank to get my draft, hoping to sell a book on the way to get the fifty cents needed.

At the door of the bank I met a gentleman waiting for the door to be opened, and I improved the opportunity by introducing my book to his notice, and as an inducement for him to purchase, I mentioned the pressing emergency which had brought me out in such a rainy morning and my lack of fifty cents to meet it.

As it proved the banks did not open on this New Year's Day, and therefore we both seemed to have leisure for quite a lengthy discussion, which finally ended with these remarks from this stranger :

"Mrs. Packard, I will buy your book," adding as he handed me the fifty cents :

"I think I comprehend the case. Now, will you allow me to give you a little advice! I am capable of doing so. I am a lawyer of some note in this city, and have just returned from Washington where I have been sent on official business. My advice is, that you do not send this money to these men. It is neither a debt of honor or of justice. Your men have not complied with your conditions to stand a trial, and thereby help on the cause of married woman, for which you willingly would spend your hard earnings. But without your consent, they have done just what you had forbid their doing—compromised—and thereby have defeated your purpose to ventilate the laws. By so doing, I think they have forfeited all their claims on you to stand between them and all harm, since they have broken the terms of the contract themselves. Therefore, it is not a debt of honor.

"Neither is it a debt of justice. You are the injured party. This money and the goods go into the hands of your husband. You are doing yourself injustice by giving him two hundred dollars more of your own money, by your own act. And this very act he may employ as a precedent to claim the whole of your earnings, on some other false pretext.

"Again. Your men are not guilty either of riot or trespass. You had a just and a moral right to your own things, and no jury of our country would have convicted them of riot or trespass, for assisting you, as they did, under the circumstances. You would not have had one cent of fine to pay for them, had they possessed the moral courage of men to stand the trial. But they did not. And the money they claim from you now does not help married woman's cause, nor your own either. Therefore I advise you to keep it, and go directly to your boarding place and write another letter and tell them who has advised you to take this course."

I did so, and soon came a response upbraiding me seriously for allowing my own impressions of duty to be supplanted by the sophistry of a pretended Lawyer, or a pretended Congressman!

I then decided it was not my duty to distress or incommode myself greatly to meet this demand, but let the matter rest for the present.

About two years after, when my earnings had so accumula-- ted as to render it no inconvenience for me to part with a few hundred dollars, I concluded I would make these men a present of two hundred dollars; and as an act of self-defense against slanderous reports which were in circulation respecting my conduct in this transaction, I decided that the following cer- tificate must be signed by each before receiving this money, namely :

"I do hereby certify that in the year 1864, while Mrs. Packard was absent from her home, attending her trial at Kankakee City, Mr. Abijah Dole took from her house, in the night, her household furniture without her knowledge or consent, and deposited it in his own house.

"That Mrs. Packard claims that she had bought this furni- ture with her own money. That Mrs. Packard was at this time in a penniless and defenseless condition.

"That at Mrs. Packard's request, I went, with five other men, in company with Mrs. Packard, to Mr. Dole's house, and in his absence, quietly took a portion of this furniture, without Mr. Dole's knowledge or consent, to supply Mrs. Packard's wants and necessities.

"That Mrs. Packard voluntarily promised to stand between us and all harm in case of a prosecution, if we would stand a fair jury trial, like men.

"That Deacon Dole entered a prosecution against us, both for riot and trespass, at Rev. Mr. Packard's especial request.

"That instead of standing these trials, as Mrs. Packard wished us to, we settled with Mr. Dole, by returning all of Mrs. Packard's furniture, and paid him in addition two hundred dollars.

"That we made this settlement in the absence of Mrs. Packard, and without her knowledge or consent.

"That we have asked Mrs. Packard to pay us this two hundred dollars from her own earnings—and she has refused to pay it, on the ground of its not being either a debt of honor or justice. But she now presents us this amount of money as a free, voluntary gift on her part, for this act of gallantry to a dependent and defenseless woman; and as such, I accept my share of the money from her."

I sent each man a copy of the above, with the assurance that I would send him his share, in a draft, by return of the mail on condition that he return me this certificate signed and with his Post-Office address.

The certificates were all returned without a single signature, and I have never sent or offered them another present.

These facts are delineated, not for the purpose of injuring the feelings or reputation of any of the parties concerned, but that the public may see how exceedingly difficult it is for an *outlawed* person to be protected in her natural rights; hoping it may force conviction upon the hearts of law-makers that the time has fully come, to restore to married woman her right of citizenship which the common law denies her.

The Government does with eminent propriety establish and protect the rights of married men, and it is equally proper that it should establish and protect the rights of married women also. As the mother produces all the men who compose this great American Government, therefore she—the mother—should be protected by that Government. These sons should shield the mother who bore them, in all her rights, as a woman, equally at least, with the father, in all his rights, as a man.

CHAPTER VI.

An Incident.

In the winter of 1868, while on board the train from Chicago to Aurora, my attention was arrested by the very earnest conversation of two ministerial looking gentlemen, who sat directly opposite me, but each in a seat by himself, so they were obliged to speak in quite an elevated tone of voice to be understood.

By what I overheard I soon perceived they were talking about a certain woman, with whom I was quite intimately acquainted, and thereby my curiosity became so dominant, as to draw my attention to their remarks about her, without seeming to notice them.

I found the knowing gentleman on the front seat was instructing his uninformed listener on the back seat into the details of Mrs. Packard's persecution. And I soon became satisfied that he was the defender of Mr. Packard, and therefore clothed facts with such a fictitious drapery that the truth became too distorted to be even recognized by his listener.

He seemed determined to defend the position that this lady was insane, and in making out his proof he used lies and misrepresentations as his evidence.

"Did I understand you she had a trial of her sanity?" asked the inquirer.

"Yes, she had a trial before a jury of twelve men."

"What was their decision?"

"After hearing all the evidence in the case, strange to say! they decided she was sane."

"Indeed! What did Mr. Packard do then?"

"He, for some unaccountable reason, fled his country."

"What became of his wife?"

" She returned to Manteno, made quite a fuss about his robbing her of her things, and got some men to assist her in getting them, promising them she would stand between them and all harm, and then fled, without paying them as she had promised."

" Indeed! then she showed herself out at last! didn't she?"

At this point my indignation could no longer be repressed—I could hear that woman slandered no longer, without rushing to the defense of the injured one. I arose from my seat, stepped across the car, and thus addressed them:

" Gentlemen, excuse me for interrupting you, but I am too staunch a defender of truth and justice, to allow a falsehood to pass unnoticed. I know the facts in relation to the lady of whom you speak to be a little different from what you state. I think you stated she left her men without paying them as she promised—the fact is she *offered* each one of them the money they asked and they would not accept it."

" That does give a different view to the case. Are you acquainted with Mrs. Packard?" inquired the listener.

" Yes, I am somewhat acquainted, and am very familiar with the facts in the case?"

" Will you please sit down and inform us, for I have become interested in her case."

As I did so, he inquired:

" Do you think Mrs. Packard a sane woman?"

" There is a difference of opinion on that point," I replied.

" What do *you* think about it?"

" I am inclined to think the decision of the jury was correct, for had there been even any evidence of insanity I think it would have been presented to the jury. But they failed to produce the slightest evidence."

Here the knowing minister remarked, for they both told me they were ministers: " I hear Dr. Sturtevant, and all the ministers in Jacksonville, are down upon her!"

" Yes, so are the Calvinists generally, as she is fearless in exposing their system as an anti-Christian one. But I don't think they have any right to call her insane for this reason alone. But they do."

Thus he asked and I answered questions for about one-half hour about this lady they had been so long slandering, and I gave her such a good defense as led the uninformed minister to change his opinion of her, and even to express sympathy for her in these words:

" I do feel some pity for that woman after all. She may have been a much injured woman ! "

I retraced the whole ground gone over by his informant, who now evidently quailed before the truth when divested of its false habiliments, and I think, when the cars stopped at Aurora, he did not regret to hear me say :

" I stop here."

But the blank look of astonishment which overspread his countenance, I shall not soon forget, as I arose to leave and introduced myself in these words :

" Gentlemen, before leaving, allow me to introduce myself as Mrs. Packard ! Good morning, gentlemen ! "

CHAPTER VII.

How to Commence Business Without Capital.

The sad lesson was now learned, by my own experience, that as the laws then were, married woman could hold no legal right to either her own or her husband's property, *while he lived,* and as there was no prospect of my coming into possession of my " right of dower " by becoming his widow, and as my principles forbade my seeking protection under the divorce laws, by alimony, I seemed driven to the alternative of either following Mr. Packard to Massachusetts, to be imprisoned by him, for life, in an Insane Asylum, or to keep out of his reach and support myself.

This last I chose, inasmuch as I preferred personal liberty, on a self-supporting basis, rather than imprisonment with my food and clothing provided at public expense.

. " Yes, give me liberty and want, rather than imprisonment and plenty."

" But what need is there of my suffering want in this free country, with health and education for my capital?"

" None at all! "

" But how shall I commence a lucrative business without money ? " is the question now to be solved.

I left the Asylum prison with a book written, ready for publication, which would cost two thousand five hundred dollars to print one thousand copies.

This sum I could not, of course, borrow, neither could I get a publisher to print it, at his own risk.

I therefore concluded to publish only an Introductory volume, of about one hundred and fifty pages, trusting that by the sale of this I might raise enough in time to print the entire volume.

" But how could I print even this, without one dollar for a capital to work upon ? "

This was a problem which cost me much study before I found its solution. But I did, at last, find a satisfactory solution in the following devise.

I found, in the judgment of Chicago publishers, it would cost me five hundred dollars to print one thousand copies ; but did not close a contract until I was sure my plan to raise this money would succeed, which was, to sell tickets for the unpublished book, on the promise that I would redeem these tickets in a specified time, by exchanging each ticket for a book worth the price of the ticket. A week's trial convinced me it would take just about three months to raise this money at the rate of my present sales.

My tickets were printed and read thus :

"The Bearer is Entitled to the first Volume of Mrs. Packard's Book, Entitled 'The Great Drama, or The Millennial Harbinger.' Price fifty cents. None are genuine without my signature."

E. P. W. Packard.

To cover all expenses, I found I must raise seven hundred dollars, by the sale of one thousand four hundred tickets, in three months. To sell these tickets for money was no easy task.

I must first inspire in my patron sufficient confidence in my veracity, ability, and perseverance, to induce him to pay out fifty cents for a ticket, simply upon the promise of a stranger, that it should be redeemed in three months by a book as yet unprinted—and that the publication of this book must depend upon the sale of fourteen hundred tickets.

I sold these mostly in country villages, on the railroads. Upon arriving, my first business would be to secure a reliable agent, who would engage to receive my books when published, and deliver them to the ticket holders, who would call there for them. I would then seek for patrons, telling them that at such a time the books would be in the hands of this agent, who would give them a book on the presentation of their ticket. The Post-master, or some prominent Bookseller were usually employed as my agents.

After I had canvassed one place I would go to another and pursue the same course there, and so on, until I had sold four-teen hundred tickets.

My board, car fare, and all other expenses, I paid from the money realized from the sale of my tickets and small books. Never in these days of struggle did I ask for charity, neither would I receive it, by way of free car rides, or a night's lodging, or food, or money. I almost invariably stopped at hotels instead of private boarding houses. I sometimes had offers of money, as a gift, instead of buying tickets, which was always indig-nantly refused, claiming that I was not an object of charity, but was doing business on a business basis, and was, therefore, very grateful for patronage, but not for gifts, as an object of charity.

I felt an invincible determination to demonstrate my self-supporting capacities by actual proof—that of stubborn facts.

Encouraged by my sales, and sure of ultimate success, I re-turned to Chicago to contract for the printing of my book—but to my surprise found there had been a great and sudden inflation in the price of paper and labor, since giving their former estimates, so that it would be impossible now to get it done for much less than seven hundred dollars instead of five hundred dollars.

Finding the book would now cost me seventy-five cents in-stead of fifty cents, I was in quite a sad dilemma not knowing how to meet it, since I had promised my patrons the book for fifty cents, and could not forfeit my word.

Upon inquiry, I found the next edition could be printed for about one-third the cost of this after the stereotyped plates were paid for. I therefore continued to sell my tickets for the same price, depending upon the profits of the second edition to compensate for the losses of the first. Thus, by selling two thousand tickets I was not only free from debt, but had my capital—my stereotyped plates—paid for.

Thus I redeemed every ticket and had my book paid for in three months, having raised a capital of seven hundred dollars by the sale of one thousand four hundred tickets.

Besides my tickets, I sold small books of my own, from ten to twenty-five cents in value, which about covered my traveling expenses. Fifteen months from this date I had sold twelve thousand books.

But selling these tickets and books was but a small part of the obstacles and difficulties to be overcome and surmounted in order to establish my business. Delay in commencing my book according to agreement, caused me much solicitude lest I should not meet my promise to my patrons. After three weeks delay I was therefore greatly relieved when the mail brought me my first proof-sheets at Bloomington.

But upon examining them I found them so very defective and in such bad taste and in short brevier type instead of long primer, as the agreement stipulated, that I sent a message back at once to stop their work, as I should not accept such work at all, as it was not according to agreement. As soon as possible I returned to Chicago and found the business entirely suspended. Upon inquiry, I found I had engaged an incompetent firm; they did not understand book-making, as their specialty was job and paper printing. Neither could I instruct them, as this was not my trade, although they volunteered to follow my directions.

I accordingly sought and found a publisher at the *Tribune* office, who engaged to do the work in three weeks, which was the time the tickets were to be redeemed. I engaged my stereotyper, engraver, and binder, and set them all at work and left the city to sell tickets. But imperfect proofs and delays would bring me often back to the city to find my work-men were waiting for some money as an assurance I should succeed, as they seemed to feel it unsafe to trust to my selling tickets for their pay.   So in order to keep all these wheels running, I was often compelled to oil them with greenbacks, or they would stop running altogether.

These journeys greatly increased my expenses of travel as well as of board, as my day board at Hotels in Chicago amounted to seventeen dollars and a half a week. Yet my book would not be done unless I thus urged it on, and as I had no partner I had every department of business to attend to my-self, besides earning the money the business required.

But solicitude from another source and cause outweighed all others ; for energy, courage and perseverance combined could not remove this obstruction out of my onward path ; for I was constantly liable to have all my business plans thwarted by Mr. Packard's interference.   As this danger is clearly eluci-dated by my interview with Mayor Sherman about this time, I will here narrate it, since it not only discloses one of the dan-gers and difficulties I had to encounter in prosecuting my en-terprise, but it also serves as another exemplification of that marital power which is legally guaranteed to the husband, leaving the wife utterly helpless and legally defenseless.

I called upon him at his office in the court house, and was received with respectful, manly courtesy.   After introducing myself as the Mrs. Packard whose case had recently acquired so much notoriety through the Chicago press, and after briefly recapitulating the main facts of the persecution, I said to him:

" Now, Mr. Sherman, as the Mayor of this city, I appeal to you for protection, while printing my book in your city. Will you protect me here ? "

" Why, Mrs. Packard, what protection do you need ? What dangers do you apprehend ?

" Sir, I am a married woman, and my husband is my persecutor, therefore I have no legal protection. The husband is, you probably know, the wife's only protector in the law, therefore, what I want now, Sir, is *protection against my protector!*"

" Is he in this city ? "

" No, Sir ; but his agents are, and he can delegate his power to them, and authorize them what to do."

" What do you fear he will do ? "

" I fear he may intercept the publication of my book ; for you probably know, Sir, he can come either himself, or by proxy, and with his Sheriff, can demand my manuscript of my printer, and neither the printer, nor you, Sir, have any legal power to defend it. He can demand it, and burn it, and I am helpless in legal self-defense. For, Sir, my identity was legally lost in his, when I married him, leaving me nothing and nobody in law ; and besides, all I have is his in law, and, of course, no one can prosecute him for taking his own things. My manuscript is his, and entirely at his disposal. I have no right in law even to my own thoughts, either spoken or written—he has even claimed the right to superintend my written thoughts, as well as post-office rights. I can not claim these rights—they are mine only as he grants them as *his gifts* to me ! ' "

" What does your printer say about it ? "

" He says if the Sheriff comes to him for the book he shall tell him he must get the book where he can find it, *I* shall not find it for him." I then said to my printer, " supposing he should come with money, and offer to buy the manuscript, what then ? " " I say, it will take more money than there is in Chicago to buy that manuscript of us," replied my printer.

" I think that sounds like protection, Mrs. Packard. I think you have nothing to fear."

" No, Mr. Sherman, I have nothing to fear from the manliness of my printer, for this is my sole and only protection— but as one man to whom I trusted even myself, has proved a traitor to his manliness, is there not a possibility another may? I should not object to a double guard, since the single guard of manliness has not even protected me from imprisonment!"

"Well, Mrs. Packard, you shall have my protection; and I can also assure you the protection of my counsel, also. If you get into trouble, apply to us, and we will give you all the help the laws will allow."

"I beg you to consider, Sir, the laws do not allow you to interfere in such a matter. Are you authorized to stop a man from doing a *legal* act?"

"No, Mrs. Packard, I am not. I see you are without any legal protection. Still I think you are safe in Chicago."

"I hope it may so prove, Sir. But one thing more I wish your advice about; how can I keep the money I get for my book from Mr. Packard, the legal owner of it?"

"Keep it about your person, so he can't get it."

"But, Sir; Mr. Packard has a right to my person in law, and can take it anywhere, and put it where he pleases; and if he can get my person, he can take what is on it."

"That's so—yours is a sad case, truly,—I must say, I never before knew that any one under our government was so utterly defenseless as you are. Your case ought to be known. Every soldier in our army ought to have one of your books, so as to have our laws changed."

Soldiers of our army! receive this tacit compliment from Mayor Sherman. *You* are henceforth to hold the reins of the American Government. And it is my candid opinion, they could not be in better or safer hands. And in your hands would I most confidently trust my sacred cause—the cause of Married Woman—for, so far as my observation extends, no class of American citizens are more manly than our soldiers. I am inclined to cherish the idea, that gallantry and patriotism are identified; at least, I find they are almost always associated in the same manly heart.

CHAPTER VIII.

Visit to my Father in Massachusetts. Mr. Packard Forbids my Seeing my Children.

When I had sold about half of my twelve thousand books, I resolved to visit my relatives in Massachusetts, who had not seen me for about twelve years.

I felt assured that my dear father, and brothers, and my kind step-mother, were all looking at the facts of my persecution from a wrong stand-point; and I determined to risk my exposure to Mr. Packard's persecuting power again, so far as to let my relatives see me once for themselves; hoping thus the scales might drop from their eyes, so far at least as to protect me from another kidnapping from Mr. Packard.

I arrived first at my brother Austin Ware's home in South Deerfield, who then lived about two miles from Mr. Severance, where were my three youngest children, and where Mr. Packard spent one day of each week.

I spent two days with my brother and his new wife, who both gave me a very kind and patient hearing; and the result was, their eyes were opened to see their error in believing me to be an insane person, and expressed their decided condemnation of the course Mr. Packard had pursued towards me. Brother became at once my gallant and manly protector, and the defender of my rights.

"Sister," said he, "you have a right to see your children, and you shall see them. I will send for them to-day."

He accordingly sent a team for them twice, but was twice refused by Mr. Packard, who had heard of my arrival.

Still, he assured me I should see them in due time. He

carried me over to Sunderland, about four miles distant, to my father's house, promising me I should meet my dear children there; feeling confident that my father's request joined with his own, would induce Mr. Packard to let me once more see my own dear offspring.

As he expected, my father at once espoused my cause, and assured me I should see my children; "for," added he:

"Mr. Packard knows it will not do for him to refuse me."

He then directed brother to go directly for them himself, and say to Mr. Packard:

"Elizabeth's father requests him to let the children have an interview with their mother at his house."

But, instead of the children, came a letter from brother, saying, that Mr. Packard had refused, in the most decided terms, to let sister see her own children; or, to use his own language, he said:

"I came from Illinois to Massachusetts to protect the children from their mother, and I shall do it, in spite of you, or father Ware, or any one else!"

Brother adds, "the mystery of this dark case is now solved, in my mind, completely. Mr. Packard is a monomaniac on this subject; there is no more reason in his treatment of sister, than in a brute."

These facts of his refusal to let me see my children, were soon in circulation in the two adjacent villages of Sunderland and South Deerfield, and a strongly indignant feeling was manifested against Mr. Packard's defiant and unreasonable position; and he, becoming aware of the danger to his interests which a conflict with this tide of public sentiment might occasion, seemed forced, by this pressure of public opinion, to succumb; for, on the following Monday morning, (this was on Saturday, P. M.,) he brought all my three children to my father's house, with himself and Mrs. Severance, as their body-guard, and with both as my witnesses, I was allowed to talk with them an hour or two. He refused me an interview with them alone in my room.

Of course it was a great satisfaction to me to be allowed once more to look upon these dear objects of my tenderest affections, yet his refusal to allow me to see them alone, almost paralyzed the joyful emotions their presence had inspired; and when my Arthur left my embrace for his father's lap, in obedience to his authority, I felt the utter helplessness of my position to such a degree that the joy of meeting was almost superseded by the thought of another, and, perhaps, a final parting.

Since the common law of marriage deprives the married woman of her individual identity, she has therefore no chance, while her husband lives, to defend her inalienable rights from his usurpation.

Even her right of self-defense on the plane of argument is denied her, for when she *reasons*, then she is insane! and if her reasons are wielded potently, and with irresistible logic, she is then exposed to hopeless imprisonment, as the response of her opponent.

This is now her legalized penalty for using her own reason in defense of her identity! This is the modern mode of persecuting married women!

My husband has not only accepted of my identity as the law gives it to him, but he has also usurped all the minor gifts included in it. The gift from God, which I prize next to that of my personal identity, is my right of maternity—my right to my own offspring—which he claims is his exclusively, by separating me entirely from them, with no ray of hope from him or the law, that I shall ever be allowed to exercise a mother's care or control over them again.

Bereft of six lovely children by the will of my husband, and no one to dare defend this right for me—for the law extends protection to such kidnappers—indeed to me is a living death of hopeless bereavement!

Yes, any husband can kidnap all of his own children, by forcibly separating them from the mother who bore them, and the laws defend the act!

The mother of the illegitimate child is protected by the law, in her right to her own offspring, while the lawfully married wife is not. Thus the only shield maternity has under the common law, is in prostitution!!

Again my property is all shipwrecked, and legally claimed by this usurper. And as I did not hold it in my own name, as the statute laws now allow, I am, on the principle of common law, legally robbed of every property right. The husband does not expose all his rights to usurpation when he marries ; why should he make laws to demand this exposure to his wife and daughter ? Are women in less need of protection than men, simply because they are weaker, and therefore more liable to usurpation? Nay, verily, the weakest demand the strongest protection, instead of none at all. When will man look upon woman as his partner, instead of dependent?

Oh, I do need the protection of law to shield my rights from my usurper! but I have none at all, so long as I am a married woman.

And Dr. McFarland assured me, too, that so long as I claim my right of opinion and conscience, no church will extend fellowship to me.

Therefore, my attempt to follow Christ by holding myself as a responsible moral agent, rather than an echo or a parasite, has cast me out of the protection of the law, and also out of the pale of the Christian church, if what the Doctor tells me is true.

Well, be it so! I am determined to ever *deserve* the love, respect, confidence, and protection of my husband. And I am equally determined to secure a rightful claim to the fellowship of *all* Christian churches, by living a life of practical godliness.

I remained at my father's house a few days only, knowing that even in Massachusetts the laws did not protect me from another similar outrage, if Mr. Packard could procure the certificate of two physicians that I was insane ; for, with these alone, without any chance for self-defense, he could force me into some of the Private Asylums here, as he did into a State Asylum in Illinois.

I knew that, as I was Mr. Packard's wife, neither my brother nor father could be my legal protectors in such an event, as they could command no influence in my defense, except that of public sentiment or mob-law.

CHAPTER IX.

My Successful Appeal to the Massachusetts Legislature for Protection.

I therefore felt forced to leave my father's house in self-defense, to seek some protection of the Legislature of Massachusetts, by petitioning them for a change in their laws on the mode of commitment into Insane Asylums.

As a preparatory step, I endeavored to get up an agitation on the subject, by printing and selling about six thousand books relative to the subject; and then, trusting to this enlightened public sentiment to back up the movement, I petitioned Massachusetts' Legislature to make the needed change in the laws.

Hon. S. E. Sewall, of Boston, drafted the petition, and I circulated it, and obtained between one and two hundred names of men of the first standing and influence in Boston, such as the Aldermen, the Common Council, the High Sheriff, and several other City Officers; besides, Judges, Lawyers, Editors, Bank Directors, Physicians and Merchants.

Mr. Sewall presented this petition to the Legislature, and they referred it to a committee, who convened seven special meetings on the subject.

I was invited to meet with them each time, and did so, as were also Mrs. Phelps and Mrs. Denny, two ladies of Boston who had suffered a term of false imprisonment in a private institution at Sommersville, without any previous trial.

Hon. S. A. Sewall and Mr. Wendell Phillips both made a plea in its behalf before this committee, who kindly allowed me a hearing of several hours time in all, besides allowing me to present the two following bills of which they afterwards requested a copy in writing.

The three Superintendents, Dr. Walker, Dr. Jarvis, and Dr. Tyler, represented the opposition. And my reply to Dr. Walker constituted the preamble to my bills.

GENTLEMEN OF THE COMMITTEE:

I feel it my duty to say one word in defense of the petitioners, in reply to Dr. Walker's statement, that:

"In my opinion, nineteen-twentieths of the petitioners did not know nor care what they petitioned for, and that they signed it out of compliment to the lady."

I differ from Dr. Walker in opinion on this point, for this reason. I obtained these names by my own individual appeals, except from most of the members of the "Common Council," who signed it during an evening session, by its being passed around for their names. I witnessed their signing, and saw them read it, carefully, before signing it. And I think they signed it intelligently, and from a desire for safer legislation. The others I know signed intelligently, and for this reason. And I could easily have got one thousand more names, had it been necessary; for, in selling my books, I have conversed with many thousand men on this subject, and among them all, have only found one man who defends the present mode of commitment—that of leaving it all to the physicians.

I spent a day in the Custom House, and a day and a half in the Navy Yard, and these men, like all others, defend our movement.

I have sold one hundred and thirty-nine books in the Navy Yard within the last day and a half, by conversing personally with gentlemen in their counting-rooms on this subject, and they are carefully watching your decision on this question.

Now, from this stand-point of extensive observation, added to my own personal experience, I feel fully confident these **two** bills are needed to meet the public demand at this crisis.

5

BILL No. 1.

No person shall be regarded or treated as an Insane person, or a Monomaniac, simply for the *expression of opinions*, no matter how absurd these opinions may appear to others.

My Brief in Defense of the bill.

1st. This law is needed for the personal safety of Reformers. We are living in a Progressive Age. Everything is in a state of transmutation, and as our laws now are, the Reformer, the Pioneer, the Originator of any new idea is liable to be treated as a Monomaniac with imprisonment.

2d. It is a *Crime* against human progress to allow Reformers to be treated as Monomaniacs; for who will dare to be true to the inspirations of the divinity within them, if the Pioneers of truth are thus liable to lose their personal liberty for life by so doing?

3d. It is *Treason* against the principles of our Government to treat opinions as Insanity, and to imprison for it, as our present laws allow.

4th. There always are those in every age who are opposed to everything new, and if allowed, will persecute Reformers with the stigma of Insanity. This has been the fate of all Reformers, from the days of Christ—the Great Reformer—until the present age.

5th. Our Government, of all others, ought especially to guard, by legislation, the vital principle on which it is based, namely: *individuality*, which guarantees an individual right of opinion to all persons.

Therefore, gentlemen, *Protect your Thinkers!* by a law against the charge of Monomania, and posterity shall bless our Government, as a Model Government, and Massachusetts as the Pioneer State, in thus protecting individuality as the vital principle on which the highest development of humanity rests.

BILL No. 2.

No person shall be imprisoned and treated as an insane person except for *irregularities of conduct,* such as indicate that the individual is so lost to reason as to render him an unaccountable moral agent.

My Brief in Defense of the Bill.

Multitudes are now imprisoned without the least evidence that reason is dethroned, as indicated by this test. And I am a representative of this class of prisoners; for when Dr. McFarland was driven to give his reasons for regarding me as insane, on this basis, the only reason which he could name, after closely inspecting my conduct for three years, was that I once " fell down stairs ! "

I do insist upon it, gentlemen, that no person should be imprisoned without a just cause ; for personal liberty is the most blessed boon of our existence, and ought therefore to be reasonably guarded as an inalienable right. But it is not reasonably protected under our present legislation, while it allows the simple opinion of two doctors to imprison a person for life, without one proof in the conduct of the accused, that he is an unaccountable moral agent. We do not hang a person on the simple opinion that he is a murderer, but proof is required from the accused's own actions, that he is guilty of the charge which forfeits his life. So the charge which forfeits our personal liberty ought to be proved from the individual's *own conduct*, before imprisonment.

So long as insanity is treated as a crime, instead of a misfortune, as our present system practically does thus treat it, the protection of our individual liberty imperatively demands such an enactment. Many contend that every person is insane on some point. On this ground, all persons are liable to be legally imprisoned, under our present system ; for intelligent physicians are everywhere to be found, who will not scruple to give a certificate that an individual is a Monomaniac on that point where he differs from him in opinion! This Monomania in many instances is not insanity, but individuality, which is the highest natural development of a human being.

Gentlemen, I know, and have felt, the horrors—the untold soul agonies—attendant on such a persecution. Therefore, as philanthropists, I beg of you to guard your own liberties, and those of your countrymen, by recommending the adoption of these two bills as an imperative necessity.

The above bills were presented to the Committee on the Commitment of the Insane, in Boston State-House, March 29, 1865.

The result was, the petition triumphed, by so changing the mode of commitment, that, instead of the husband being allowed to enter his wife at his simple request, added to the certificate of two physicians, he must now get ten of her nearest relatives to join with him in this request; and the person committed, instead of not being allowed to communicate by writing to any one outside of the Institution, except under the censorship of the Superintendent, can now send a letter to each of these ten relatives, and to any other two persons whom the person committed shall designate. This the Superintendent is required to do within two days from the time of commitment.

This Law is found in Chapter 268, Section 2, of the General Laws of Massachusetts.

I regard my personal liberty in Massachusetts now as not absolutely in the power of my husband; as my family friends must now co-operate in order to make my commitment legal. And since my family relatives are now fully satisfied of my sanity, after having seen me for themselves, I feel now comparatively safe, while in Massachusetts.

CHAPTER X.

My Father Becomes my Protector.

I therefore returned to my father's house in Sunderland, and finding both of my dear parents feeble, and in need of some one to care for them, and finding myself in need of a season of rest and quiet, I accepted their kind invitation to make their house my home for the present. At this point my father indicated his true position in relation to my interests, by his self-moved efforts in my behalf, in writing and sending the following letter to Mr. Packard.

"*Sunderland, Sept.* 2, 1865.

"REV. SIR : I think the time has fully come for you to give up to Elizabeth her clothes. Whatever reason might have existed to justify you in retaining them, has, in process of time, entirely vanished. There is not a shadow of excuse for retaining them. It is my presumption there is not an individual in this town who would justify you in retaining them a single day.

Elizabeth is about to make a home at my house, and I must be her protector. She is very destitute of clothing, and greatly needs all those articles which are hers.

I hope to hear from you soon, before I shall be constrained to take another step. Yours, Respectfully,

REV. T. PACKARD.   SAMUEL WARE."

The result of this letter was, that in about twenty-four hours after the letter was delivered, Mr. Packard brought the greater part of my wardrobe and delivered it into the hands of my father.

In a few weeks after this event, Mr. Packard's place in the pulpit in Sunderland was filled by a candidate for settlement, and he left the place.

The reasons why he thus left his ministerial charge in this place, cannot perhaps be more summarily given than by transcribing the following letter which my father requested me to write for him, in answer to Rev. Dr. Pomeroy's letter, inquiring of my father *why* Mr. Packard had left Sunderland.

Sunderland, Oct. 28, 1865.

DR. POMEROY, DEAR SIR: I am sorry to say that my dear father feels too weak to reply to your kind and affectionate letter of the twenty-third instant, and therefore I cheerfully consent to reply to it myself.

As to the subject of your letter, it is as you intimated. We have every reason to believe that my father's defense of me, has been the indirect cause of Mr. Packard's leaving Sunderland; although we knew nothing of the matter until he left, and a candidate filled his place.

Neither father, mother, nor I, have used any direct influence to undermine the confidence of this people in Mr. Packard.

But where this simple fact, that I have been imprisoned three years, is known to have become a demonstrated truth, by the decision of a jury, after a thorough legal investigation of five days' trial, it is found to be rather an unfortunate truth for the public sentiment of the present age to grapple with.

And Mr. Packard and his persecuting party may yet find I uttered no fictitious sentiment, when I remarked to Dr. Mc-Farland in the Asylum that, " I shall yet *live down* this slander of Insanity, and also live down my persecutors! "

And Mr. Packard is affording me every facility for so doing, by his continuing strenuously to insist upon it, that I am now just as insane as when he incarcerated me in Jacksonville Insane Asylum. And he still insists upon it, that an Asylum Prison is the only suitable place for me in which to spend the residue of my earth-life.

But, fortunately for me, my friends judge differently upon seeing me for themselves. Especially fortunate is it for me, that my own dear father feels confident that his house is a more suitable home for me, notwithstanding the assertion of Mrs. Dickinson, the widow with whom Mr. Packard boards, that:

"It is such a pity that Mrs. Packard should come to Sunderland, where Mr. Packard preaches!"

Mr. Johnson replied, in answer to this remark, that:

"I think Mrs. Packard has a right to come to her father's house for protection, and also that her father has an equal right to extend protection to his only daughter, when thrown adrift and penniless upon the cold world without a place to shelter her defenseless head."

Mr. Packard has withdrawn all intercourse with us all since he was called upon by my father to return my wardrobe to me. Would that Mr. Packard's eyes might be opened to see what he is doing, and repent, so that I might be allowed to extend to him the forgiveness my heart longs to bestow, upon this gospel condition.

Thankful for all the kindness and sympathy you have bestowed upon my father and mother, as well as myself, I subscribe myself your true friend,   E. P. W. PACKARD.

I remained six months a member of my father's family, and found this period one of the brightest oases of my existence. For during this period my dear father manifested a tenderness of feeling transcending anything he had ever before exhibited towards me.

His fatherly conduct, thus manifested, said to me, more forcibly than any words could have done:

"I am sorry I have been so deluded by Mr. Packard as to leave you to suffer so long, so intensely, so unjustly, without appearing in your defense, and rescuing you from your tormentors. But as it is, the only atonement I can possibly make shall be made! I shall shield you from all future harm, so far as a father's love and care can extend."

In speaking of my children, he once said :

" My Daughter, you ought to have the care of your children, for you have been the best mother to them I ever knew, and were it in my power you should now have them all, and never be separated from them again. But, my Daughter, I am as helpless as you are in this matter. The strong arm of law shields Mr. Packard in his course, and I cannot remove this obstacle in the way of your taking them under your custody. You must submit to the inevitable, and try to take all the comfort you can without them."

Another act of fatherly confidence in my sanity was, that he changed his will for my benefit, and by this change, he not only gave me a much larger portion of his property, but also gave it to me directly, instead of giving it " in trust" to my brother, as he had by the will he had before made when under the delusion of Mr. Packard, that I was insane—for, said he, to this brother :

" Elizabeth is just as capable of taking care of property as you are or any other person, therefore I shall leave her portion to her independent of all supervision."

He also gave to the public a certificate of my sanity, for the purpose of counteracting the influence of those he had before given in defense of Mr. Packard, at his request, thus making restitution for this wrong he had innocently done his daughter as far as lay in his power thus to do. Although this certificate is given to my readers in the first volume, yet, I will here insert it again, not only as an evidence of his confidence in my sanity, but as proof of his repentance in having ever been induced to call it in question.

" This is to certify, that the certificates which have appeared in public in relation to my daughter's sanity, were given upon the conviction that Mr. Packard's representations respecting her condition were true, and were given wholly upon the authority of Mr. Packard's own statements. I do, therefore, hereby certify, that it is now my opinion that Mr. Packard has had no cause for treating my daughter Elizabeth, as an insane person.   Samuel Ware.

South Deerfield, Aug. 2, 1866.   *Attest,* { Olive Ware, Austin Ware."

When this was done he felt that he could die in peace. But not before.

At the expiration of this six months' sojourn with my father in Massachusetts—he died.   And as I looked upon his peaceful corpse, as he lay in his coffin dressed for the tomb, I could not but exclaim :

Peace to thy memory ! Dear Father ! Your work is done ! Now, well done ! for you have not only repented of the wrongs you have so innocently done your daughter, but have also made restitution, so far as lay in your power so to do in this life.   Blessed be thy memory ! My Honored Father !

My own dear Mother had at this time been in her grave about twenty years.   Had this most affectionate and devoted mother been alive during these days of my persecution, a mother's love would have surmounted and overcome every obstacle which human ingenuity could devise to effect my deliverance from the power of this cruel conspiracy.

But a wise Providence had otherwise ordered the events of this sad drama.   For some purpose, hitherto unrevealed, this malign plot must have been executed just as it has been, and this dear mother could not be allowed to be where she might have intercepted its progress.

But there is one mystery attending this plot which no ingenuity or skill has yet been able to fathom.   It is this :

A few weeks prior to my incarceration, a stranger stopped at Mr. Blessing's hotel for two days and one night.   He claimed to be the " Brother of Mrs. Packard," that he had been sent by her mother to deliver her out of the hands of her cruel and unfeeling husband—that he had just arrived in port at Boston, Mass., and had there been told to " Go to your sister at once ! for she is in most imminent peril, and there is no power to rescue her from her impending doom." · And he added :

" I have come to deliver her out of the hands of her husband, and I shall do so! even if· I have to resort to the aid of this six-barrelled revolver to do it ! " at the same time showing his pistol.

Crowds collected at the Hotel to hear his strange story and the revelations he had to make of Mr. Packard's private character. Among other witnesses was my son, Isaac, then about sixteen years of age. In reporting this interview to me he said :

" Mother, I never saw any one who could relate family incidents with more accuracy and in minute detail than he did, and he even narrated events which no one knew outside of our family. Indeed, had he been in our family for ten years past, he could not have described our family scenes more accurately and promptly. In detailing father's treatment of you, he would often burst into tears and exclaim : " No one can know what that kind, patient woman has suffered from him—her relentless tormentor."

The community set a guard about our house to defend Mr. Packard's life, thus threatened, for about one week, after the disappearance of this stranger from the place.

Who this stranger was—by whom sent—how he received his information about the secret incidents of our family— and whither he went, is all unknown.

But to me, who can realize the intensity of my dear mother's love for her only daughter, it seems like a plot of desperation, similar to what the devoted love of a true mother might be driven to resort, rather than have the object of her tenderest love uncared for—unpitied—and unprotected.

CHAPTER XI.

Mr. Packard a Beggar.

Fidelity to the truth requires me to add one more melancholy fact, in order to make this narrative of events complete, and that is, Mr. Packard has made merchandise of this stigma of Insanity with which he has branded me, and used it as a lucrative source of gain to himself, in the following manner:

He has made most pathetic appeals to the sympathies of the public for their charities to be bestowed upon him, on the plea of his great misfortune in having an insane wife to support—one who is incapable of taking care of herself or her six children—and on this false premise he has based a most pathetic argument and appeal to their sympathies for pecuniary help, in the form of boxes of clothing for himself and his destitute and defenseless children!

These appeals have been most generously responded to from the American Home Missionary Society.

When I returned to my home from the Asylum, I counted twelve boxes of such clothing, some of which were very large, containing the spoils he had thus purloined from this benevolent society, by entirely false representations.

My family were not destitute. But on the contrary, were plentifully supplied with a superabundant amount of such missionary gifts, which had been lavished upon us, at his request, before I was imprisoned. I had often said to him, that I and my children had already more than a supply for our wants until they were grown up.

Now, what could he do with twelve more such boxes!

My son, Isaac, then in Chicago, and twenty-one years of age, told me he had counted fifty new vests in one pile, and as many pants and coats, and overcoats, and almost every thing else, of men's wearing apparel, in like ratio.

He said a pile of dress patterns had accumulated intended for my use from these boxes, to one yard in depth in one solid pile. And this was only one sample of all kinds of ladies' apparel which he had thus accumulated, by his cunningly-devised begging system.

Still, to this very date, he is pleading want and destitution as a basis for more charities of like kind.

He has even so moved the benevolent sympathies of the widow Dickinson with whom he boarded, as to make her feel that he was an honest claimant upon their charities in this line, on the ground of poverty and destitution. She accordingly started a subscription to procure him a suit of clothes, on the ground of his extreme destitution, and finally succeeded in begging a subscription of one hundred and thirteen dollars for his benefit, and presented it to him as a token of sympathy and regard.

Another fact, he has put his property out of his hands, so that he can say he has nothing. And should I sue him for my maintainance, I could get nothing.

His rich brother-in-law, George Hastings, did then support the three youngest children, mostly, and as Mr. Packard had so disposed of his wife and children, as to render them entirely independent of him for their support, scarcely any claimants were left upon his own purse, except his own personal wants.

And it is my honest opinion, that had the Sunderland people known of these facts in his financial matters, they would not have presented him with one hundred and thirteen dollars, as a token of their sympathy and esteem. Still, looking at the subject from their stand-point, I have no doubt they acted conscientiously in this matter.

I have never deemed it my duty to enlighten them on this

subject, except as the truth was sought for from me, in a few individual isolated cases. I seldom associated with the people, and had sold none of my books among them. For, self-defense did not require me to seek the protection of enlightened public sentiment now that the laws protected my personal liberty, while in Massachusetts.

But fidelity to the cause of humanity, especially the cause of "Married Woman," requires me to make public the facts of this notorious persecution, in order to have her true legal position known and fully apprehended.

And since my case is a practical illustration of what the law is on this subject—showing how entirely destitute she is of any legal protection, except what the will and wishes of her husband secures her—and also demonstrates the fact, that the common-law, everywhere, in relation to married woman, not only gravitates towards an absolute despotism, but even protects and sustains and defends a despotism of the most arbitrary and absolute kind—therefore, in order to have her social position changed legally, the need of this change must first be seen and appreciated by the common people—the law-makers of this Republic.

And this need or necessity for a revolution on this subject can be made to appear in no more direct manner, than by a practical case, such as my own furnishes.

As the need of a revolution of the law in relation to negro servitude was made to appear, by the practical exhibition of the Slave Code in "Uncle Tom's" experience, showing that all slaves were *liable* to suffer to the extent he did; so my experience, although like "Uncle Tom's," an extreme case, shows how all married women are *liable* to suffer to the same extent that I have.

Now justice to humanity claims that such liabilities should not exist in any Christian government. The laws should be so changed that such another outrage could not possibly take place under the sanction of the laws of a Christian government.

As Uncle Tom's case aroused the indignation of the people against the slave code, so my case, so far as it is known, arouses the same feeling of indignation against those laws which protect married servitude. Married woman needs legal emancipation from married servitude, as much as the slave needed legal emancipation from his servitude.

Again, all slaves did not suffer under negro slavery, neither do all married women suffer from this legalized servitude. Still, the principle of slavery is wrong, and the principle of emancipation is right, and the laws ought so to regard it. And this married servitude exposes the wife to as great suffering as negro servitude did.

It is my candid opinion, that no Southern slave ever suffered more spiritual agony than I have suffered ; as I am more developed in my moral and spiritual nature than they are, therefore more capable of suffering. I think no slave mother ever endured more keen anguish by being deprived of her own off-spring than I have in being legally separated from my own.

God grant! that married woman's emancipation may quickly follow in the wake of negro emancipation!

CHAPTER XII.

Why I Do Not Get a Divorce.

Because, in the first place, I do not want to be a divorced woman : but on the contrary, I wish to be a married woman, and have my husband for my protector ; for I do not like this being divorced from my own home. I want a home to live in, and I prefer the one I have labored twenty-one years myself to procure, and furnished to my own taste and mind.

Neither do I like this being divorced from my own children. I want to live with my dear children, whom I have borne and nursed, reared and educated, almost entirely by my own unwearied, indefatigable exertions ; and I love them, with all the fondness of a mother's undying love, and no place is home to me in this wide world without them.

And again, I have done nothing to deserve this exclusion from the rights and privileges of my own dear home ; but on the contrary, my untiring fidelity to the best interests of my family for twenty-one years of healthful, constant service, having never been sick during this time so as to require a doctor's bill to be paid for me or my six children, and having done all the housework, sewing, nursing, and so forth, for my entire family for twenty-one years, with no hired help, except for only nine months, during all this long period of constant toil and labor. I say, this self-sacrificing devotion to the best interests of my family and home, deserve and claim a right to be protected in it, at least, so long as my good conduct continues, instead of being divorced from it, against my own will or consent.

In short, what I want is, *protection in my home*, instead of a divorce from it. I do not wish to drive Mr. Packard from his own home, and exclude him from all its rights and privileges—neither do I want he should treat me in this manner, especially so long as he himself claims that I have always been a most kind, patient, devoted wife and mother. He even claims as his justification of his course, that I am so good a woman, and he loves me so well, that he wants to save me from fatal errors!

It is my opinions—my religious opinions—and those alone, he makes an occasion for treating me as he has. He frankly owned to me, that he was putting me into an Asylum so that my reputation for being an insane person might destroy the influence of my religious opinions; and I see in one letter which he wrote to my father, he mentions this as the chief evidence of my insanity. He writes:

"Her many excellences and past services I highly appreciate; but she says she has widely departed from, or progressed beyond, her former religious views and sentiments—and I think it is too true !!"

Here is all the insanity he claims, or has attempted to prove.

Now comes the question: Is this a crime for which I ought to be divorced from all the comforts and privileges of my own dear home?

To do this, that is to get a divorce, would it not be becoming an accomplice in crime, by doing the very deed which he is so desirous of having done, namely: banishment from the family circle for fear of the contaminating influence of my new views? Has a married woman no rights at all? Can she not even think her own thoughts, and speak her own words, unless her thoughts and expressions harmonize with those of her husband?

I think it is high time the merits of this question should be practically tested on a proper basis, the basis of truth—of facts. And the fact, that I have been not only practically divorced from my own home and children, but also incarcerated for three years in a prison, simply for my religious belief, by the arbitrary will of my husband, ought to raise the question as to what are the married woman's rights, and what is her protection ?

And it is to this practical issue I have ever striven to force this question. And this issue I felt might be reached more directly and promptly by the public mind, by laying the necessities of the case before the community, and by a direct appeal to them for personal protection, instead of getting a divorce for my protection. I know that by so doing, I have run a great risk of losing my liberty again. Still, I felt that the great cause of married woman's rights might be promoted by this agitation ; and so far as my own feelings were concerned, I felt willing to suffer even another martyrdom in this cause, if my sisters in the bonds of marital power might be benefited thereby.

I want and seek protection *as a married woman*, not divorce, in order to escape the abuses of marital power—that is, I want protection from the abuse of marital power, not a divorce from it. I can live in my home with my husband, if he will only let me do so ; but he will not suffer it, unless I recant my religious belief. Cannot religious bigotry under such manifestations, receive some check under our government, which is professedly based on the very principle of religious tolerance to all ?

Cannot there be laws enacted by which a married woman can stand on the same platform as a married man, that is, have an equal right, at least, to the protection of her inalienable rights ? And is not this our petition for protection founded in justice and humanity ?

Is it just to leave the weakest and most defenseless of these two parties wholly without the shelter of law to shield her, while the strongest and most independent has all the aid of the legal arm to strengthen his own ?

Nay, verily, it is not right or manly for our man government thus to usurp the whole legal power of self-protection and defense, and leave confiding, trusting woman wholly at the mercy of this gigantic power. For perverted men will use this absolute power to abuse the defenseless, rather than protect them; and abuse of power inevitably leads to the contempt of its victim.

A man who can trample on all the inalienable rights of his wife, will by so doing come to despise her as an inevitable consequence of wrong doing. Woman, too, is a more spiritual being than a man, and is therefore a more sensitive being, and a more patient sufferer than a man; therefore she, more than any other being, needs protection, and she should find it in that government she has sacrificed so much to uphold and sustain.

Again, I do not believe in the divorce principle. I say it is a "Secession" principle. It undermines the very vital principle of our Union, and saps the very foundation of our social and civil obligations.

For example. Suppose the small, weak, and comparatively feeble States in our Union were not protected by the Government in any of their State rights, while the large, strong, and powerful ones had their State rights fully guaranteed and secured to them. Would not this state of the Union endanger the rights of the defenseless ones? and endanger the Union also? Could these defenseless States resort to any other means of self-defense from the usurpation of the powerful States than that of secession? But secession is death to the Union—death to the principles of love and harmony which ought to bind the parts in one sacred whole.

Now, I claim that the Marriage Union, as our laws now stand, rests on just this principle. The woman has no alternative of resort from any kind of abuse from her partner, but divorce or secession from the Marriage Union.

Now the weak States have rights as well as the strong ones,

and it is the rights of the weak which the Government are especially bound to respect and defend, to prevent usurpation and its legitimate issue—secession from the Union.

What we want of our Government is to prevent this usurpation, by protecting us equally with our partners, so that a divorce need not become a necessity.

By equality of rights, I do not mean that woman's rights and man's rights are one and the same. By no means; we do not want the man's rights, but simply our own, natural, womanly rights. There are man's rights and woman's rights. Both different, yet both equally inalienable. There must be a head in every firm; and the head in the Marriage Firm or Union is the man, as the Bible and nature both plainly teach.

We maintain that the senior partner, the man, has rights of the greatest importance, as regards the interests of the marriage firm, which should not only be respected and protected by our Government, but also enforced upon them as an obligation, if the senior is not self-moved to use his rights practically—and one of these his rights, is a *right to protect* his own wife and children.

The junior partner also has rights of equal moment to the interests of the firm, and one of these is her right *to be protected* by her senior partner. Not protected in a prison, but in her own home, as mistress of her own house, and as a God appointed guardian of her infant children. The Government would then be protecting the Marriage Union, while it now practically ignores it.

To make this matter still plainer, suppose this government was under the control of the female instead of the male influence, and suppose our female government should enact laws which required the men when they entered the Marriage Union to alienate their right to hold their own property—their right to hold their future earnings—their right to their own homes —their right to their own offspring, if they have any—their right to their personal liberty—and all these rights be passed over into the hands of their wives for safe keeping, and so long as they chose to be married men, all their claims on our womanly government for protection should be abrogated entirely by this marriage contract. Now, I ask, how many men would venture to get married under these laws? Would they not be tempted to ignore the marriage laws of our Woman Government altogether?

Now, gentlemen, we are sorry to own it, this is the very condition in which your Man Government places us. We, women, looking from this very stand-point of sad experience, are tempted to exclaim:

"Where is the manliness of our Man Government!'

Divorce, I say, then, is in itself an evil—and is only employed as an evil to avoid a greater one, in many instances. Therefore, instead of being forced to choose the least of two evils, I would rather reject both evils, and choose a good thing —that of being protected in my own dear home from unmerited, unreasonable abuse—a restitution of my rights, instead of a continuance of this robbery, sanctioned by a divorce.

In short, we desire to live under such laws as will *oblige* our husbands to treat us with decent respect, so long as our good conduct merits it, and then will they be made to feel a decent regard for us as their companions and partners, whom the laws protect from their abuse.

CHAPTER XIII.

The Opinions which Caused this Family Rupture.

The question is often asked, " what are your religious opinions, Mrs. Packard, which have caused all this rupture in your once happy family ? "

My first impulse prompts me to answer, pertly, it is no one's business what I *think* but my own, since it is to God alone I am accountable for my thoughts.

Whether my thoughts are right or wrong, true or false, is no one's business but my own. It is my own God given right to superintend my own thoughts, and this right I shall never delegate to any other human being—for God himself has authorized me to "judge ye not of your own selves what is right ? "

Yes, I do, and shall judge for myself what is right for me to think, what is right for me to speak, and what is right for me to do—and if I do wrong, I stand amenable to the laws of society and my country ; for to human tribunals I submit all my actions, as just and proper matter for criticism and control.

But my thoughts, I shall never yield to any human tribunal or oligarchy, as a just and proper matter for arbitration or discipline. It is my opinion that the time has gone by for thoughts to be chained to any creeds or oligarchies ; but on the contrary, these chains and restraints which have so long bound the human reason to human dictation, must be broken, for the reign of individual, spiritual freedom is about dawning upon our progressive world.

Yes, I insist upon it, that it is my own individual right to superintend my own thoughts; and I say farther, it is not my right to superintend the thoughts or conscience of any other developed being.

It is none of my business what Mr. Packard, my father, or any other developed man or woman believe or think, for I do not hold myself responsible for their views. I believe they are as honest and sincere as myself in the views they cherish, although so antagonistic to my own; and I have no wish or desire to harass or disturb them, by urging my views upon their notice.

Yea, further, I prefer to have them left entirely free and unshackled to believe just as their own developed reason dictates. And all I ask of them is, that they allow me the same privilege. My own dear father did kindly allow me this right of a developed moral agent, although we differed as essentially and materially in our views as Mr. Packard and I did. We, like two accountable moral agents, simply agree to differ, and all is peace and harmony.

My individuality has been naturally developed by a life of practical godliness, so that I now know what I do believe, as is not the case with that class in society who dare not individualize themselves. This class are mere echoes or parasites, instead of individuals. They just flow on with the tide of public sentiment, whether right or wrong; whereas the individualized ones can and do stem or resist this tide, when they think it is wrong, and in this way they meet with persecution. It is my misfortune to belong to this unfortunate class.

Therefore I am not afraid or ashamed to avow my honest opinions even in the face of a frowning world. Therefore, when duty to myself or others, or the cause of truth requires it, I willingly avow my own honest convictions. On this ground, I feel not only justified, but authorized, to give the question under consideration, a plain and candid answer, knowing that this narrative of the case would be incomplete without it.

Another thing is necessary as an introduction, and that is, I do not present my views for others to adopt or endorse as their own. They are simply my individual opinions, and it is a matter of indifference to me, whether they find an echo in any other individual's heart or not.

I do not arrogate to myself any popish right or power to enforce my opinions upon the notice of any human being but myself. While at the same time, I claim that I have just as good a right to my opinions as Scott, Clark, Edwards, Barnes, or Beecher, or any other human being has to his. And furthermore, these theologians have no more right to dictate to me what I must think and believe, than I have to dictate to them what they must think and believe. All have an equal right to their own thoughts.

And I know of no more compact form in which to give utterance to my opinions, than by inserting the following letter I wrote from my prison, to a lady friend in Mount Pleasant, Iowa, and sent out on my "under ground railroad."

The only tidings I ever had from this letter, was a sight of it in one of the Chicago papers, following a long and minute report of my jury trial at Kankakee. I never knew how it found its way there; I only knew it was my own identical letter, since I still retain a true copy of the original among my Asylum papers.

The following is a copy of the original letter, as it now stands in my own hand-writing. The friend to whom it was written has requested me to omit those portions of the letter which refer directly to herself. In compliance with her wishes, I leave a blank for such omissions. In other respects it is a true copy.

The candid reader can judge for himself, whether the cherishing of such radical opinions is a crime of sufficient magnitude to justify all my wrongs and imprisonment! Is my Persecutor guiltless in this matter?

Jacksonville, Ill., Oct. 23, 1861.

MRS. FISHER. MY DEAR OLD FRIEND:

My love and sympathy for you is undiminished. Changes do not sever our hearts. I cannot but respect your self-reliant, independent, and therefore progressive efforts to become more and more assimilated to Christ's glorious image. I rejoice whenever I find one who dares to rely upon their own organization, in the investigation of truth. In other words, one who dares to be an independent thinker.   *   *   *

Yes, you, Mrs. Fisher, in your individuality, are just what God made you to be. And I respect every one who respects himself enough not to try to pervert his organization, by striving to remodel it, and thus defile God's image in him.

To be natural, is our highest praise. To let God's image shine through our individuality, should be our highest aim. Alas, Mrs. Fisher, how few there are, who dare to be true to their God given nature!

That terrible dogma that our natures are depraved, has ruined its advocates, and led astray many a guileless, confiding soul. Why can we not accept of God's well done work as perfect, and instead of defiling, perverting it, let it stand in all its holy proportions, filling the place God designed it to occupy, and adorn the temple it was fitted for? I for one, Mrs. Fisher, am determined to be a woman, true to my nature. I regard my nature as holy, and every deviation from its instinctive tendency I regard as a perversion—a sin. To live a natural, holy life, as Christ did, I regard as my highest honor, my chief glory.

I know this sentiment conflicts with our educated belief—our Church creeds—and the honestly cherished opinions of our relatives and friends. Still I believe a " thus saith the Lord " supports it. Could Christ take upon himself our nature, and yet know no sin, if our natures are necessarily sinful? Are not God's simple, common sense teachings, sufficient authority for our opinions?

Indeed, Mrs. Fisher, I have become so radical, as to call in question every opinion of my educated belief, which conflicts with the dictates of reason and common sense. I even believe that God has revealed to his creatures no practical truth, which conflicts with the common instincts of our common natures. In other words, I believe that God has adapted our natures to his teachings. Truth and nature harmonize. I believe that all truth has its source in God, and is eternal.

But some perceive truth before others, because some are less perverted in their natures than others, by their educational influences, so that the light of the sun of righteousness finds less to obstruct its beams in some than in others. Thus they become lights in the world, for the benefit of others less favored.

You preceded me in bursting the shackles of preconceived opinions and creeds, and have been longer basking in the liberty wherewith Christ makes his people free, and have therefore longer been taught of him in things pertaining to life and godliness. Would that I had had the moral courage sooner to have imitated you, and thus have broken the fetters which bound me to dogmas and creeds. Oh, Mrs. Fisher, how trammeled and crippled our consciences have been! Oh, that we might have an open Bible, and an unshackled conscience!

And these precious boons we shall have, for God, by His providence, is securing them to us. Yes, Mrs. Fisher, the persecutions through which we are now passing is securing to us spiritual freedom, liberty, a right, a determination to call no man master, to know no teacher but the Spirit, to follow no light or guide not sanctioned by the Word of God and our conscience, to know no " ism " or creed, but truthism, and **no** pattern but Christ. ·

6

Henceforth, I am determined to use my own reason and conscience in my investigation of truth, and in the establishment of my own opinions and practice I shall give my own reason and conscience the preference to all others. * * *

I know, also, that I am a sincere seeker after the simple truth—not willful, but conscientious in my conduct. And notwithstanding others deny this, I know their testimony is false. The Searcher of hearts knows that I am as honest with myself as I am with others. And, although like Paul, I may appear foolish to others in so doing, yet my regard for truth transcends all other considerations.

God's good work of grace in me shall never be denied by me, let others defame it and stigmatize it as insanity, as they will. They, not I, are responsible for this sacrilegious act. God himself has made me dare to be honest and truthful, even in defiance of this heaven-daring charge, and God's work will stand in spite of all opposition. " He always wins, who sides with God."

Dear Mrs. Fisher, I am not now afraid or ashamed to utter my honest opinions. The worst that my enemies can do to defame my character, they have done, and I fear them no more. I am now free to be true and honest, for this persecution for opinion and conscience's sake, has so strengthened and confirmed me in the free exercise of these inalienable rights in future, that no opposition can overcome me. For I stand by faith in what is true and right. I feel that I am born into a new element—freedom, spiritual freedom. And although the birth throes are agonizing, yet the joyous results compensate for all.

How mysterious are God's ways and plans! My persecutors verily thought they could compel me to yield these rights to human dictation, when they have only fortified them against human dictation. God saw that suffering for my opinions was necessary to confirm me in them. And the work is done, and well done, as all God's work always is. No fear of any human oligarchy will, henceforth, terrify me, or tempt me to succumb to it.

I am not now afraid of being called insane if I avow my belief that Christ died for all mankind, and that this atonement will be effectual in saving all mankind from endless torment—that good will ultimately overcome all evil—that God's benevolent purposes concerning his creatures will never be thwarted—that no rebellious child of God's great family will ever transcend his ability to discipline into entire willing obedience to his will. Can I ever believe that God loves his children less than I do mine ? * * * And has God less power to execute his kind plans than I have ?

Yes, I do and will rejoice to utter with a trumpet tongue, the glorious truth that God is infinitely benevolent as well as infinitely wise and just.

Mrs. Fisher, what can have tempted us ever to doubt this glorious truth ? And do we not practically deny it, when we endorse the revolting doctrine of endless punishment ?

I cannot but feel that the Bible, literally interpreted, teaches the doctrine of endless punishment ; yet, since the teachings of nature, and God's holy character and government, seem to contradict this interpretation, I conclude we must have misinterpreted its holy teachings. For example, Jonah uses the word everlasting with a limited meaning, when he says, "thine everlasting bars are about me." Although to his view his punishment was everlasting, yet the issue proved that in reality there was a limit to the time he was to be in the whale's belly.

So it may be in the case of the incorrigible ; they may be compelled to suffer what *to them* is endless torment, because they see no hope for them in the future. Yet the issue will prove God's love to be infinite, in rescuing them from eternal perdition.

Again, Mrs. Fisher, my determination and aim is, to become

a perfect person in Christ's estimation, although by so doing
I may be numbered among the filth and off-scouring of all
perverted humanity. What consequence is it to us to be
judged of man's judgment, when the cause of our being thus
condemned by them as insane, is the very character which
entitles us to rank among the archangels in heaven ?

Again, I am calling in question my right to unite myself to
any Church of Christ militant on earth ; fearing I shall be
thereby entrammelled by some yoke of bondage—that the
liberty wherewith Christ makes his people free may thus be
circumscribed.   There is so much of the spirit of bigotry and
intolerance in every denomination of Christians now on
earth, that they do not allow us an open Bible and an unshackled conscience.   Or, in other words, there are some to
be found in almost every church, to whom we shall become
stumbling blocks or rocks of offence, if we practically use
the liberty which Christ offers us.   Now what shall I do ?   I
do want to obey Christ's direct command to come out from
the world and be separate, while at the same time I feel that
there is more Christian liberty and charity out of the Church
than in it.   I am now waiting and seeking the Spirit's aid in
bringing this question to a practical test and issue.

And, Mrs. Fisher, I fully believe, from God's past care of
me, that he will lead me to see the true and living way in
which I ought to walk.   I will not hide my light under a
bushel, but put it upon a candlestick, that it may give light to
others.   I will also live out, practically, my honestly cherished
opinions, believing " that they that do his commandments
shall know of the doctrine."

I also fully believe that the more fully and exclusively I
live out the teachings of the Holy Spirit, the more persecution
I shall experience.   For they that will live godly, in Christ's
estimation, " shall suffer persecution."

Mrs. Fisher, I fully believe that Christ's coming cannot be

far distant. His coming will restore all things, which we have lost for his sake. Our cause will then find an eloquent pleader in Christ himself, and through our Advocate, the Judge, Himself, will acknowledge us to be his true, loyal subjects, and we shall enter into the full possession of our promised inheritance.

With this glorious prospect in full view to the eye of faith, let us " gird up the loins of our mind." In other words, let us dare to pursue the course of the independent thinker, and let us run with patience the race set before us.

Let us carry uncomplainingly the mortifying cross which is laid upon us, so long as God suffers it to remain ; remembering that it is enough for the servant that he be as his Master. For " as they have persecuted me, they will persecute you also." " Be of good cheer." " I have overcome the world." Blessed consolation !

Mrs. Fisher, the only response I expect to get from this letter, is your silent, heart-felt sympathy in my sorrows. No utterance is allowed for my alleviation. And the only way that I am allowed to administer consolation through the pen is by stratagem. I shall employ this means so far as lies in my power, so that when the day of revelation arrives, it may be said truthfully of me, " she hath done what she could."

Impossibilities are not required of us.

Please tell Theophilus, my oft repeated attempts to send him a motherly letter have been thwarted. And he, poor persecuted boy ! cannot be allowed a mother's tender, heartfelt sympathy. Oh, my God, protect my precious boy ! and carry him safely through this pitiless storm of cruel persecution. Do be to him a mother and a sister, and God shall bless you. Please deliver this message, charged to overflowing with a mother's undying love. Be true to Jesus. Ever believe me your true friend and sympathizing sister,

E. P. W. PACKARD

CHAPTER XIV.

Progression the Law of our Being.– "Seeing Eye to Eye."

On the distant hill-top stands the Observatory—the observed of all observing—Christ—"the Model Man."

Each human heart pulsates in sympathy more or less strong, to gain that eminence. At various stand-points on the hill-side, are seen the individual, the sects, the tribes, the nations of the earth, all, all moving onward,—upward.

At the base stands the Conservative, the Presbyterian, the Calvinist, whom no entreaties, no prospective views, can induce to try the ascending slope. Friends urge—enemies deride—but all in vain. Immovable he stands, confident he sees, from his low stand-point, all there is to be seen of the vast landscape of eternal truth spread out before him.

Henry Ward Beecher leaps from their ranks and rises one step above his cotemporaries. He reports his views from his new stand-point to those below him. But, alas! The spring was unpropitious.

"Our confidence in your firmness and inflexibility of purpose is shaken."

Beecher has lost the confidence of some of his former friends: but in losing old friends he has found new and untried ones, who gladly extend to him the welcome hand. Upward they all move in company; and as they rise, new and more extended views of the surrounding country break upon their pleased and excited vision.

Again they report to the conservatives at the base

"Nay, verily, we will not heed thy tales of new truths. Our Bibles confidently say, there is nothing new under the sun."

" But come and see for yourselves."

" No, no.   We are satisfied—Trouble us not."

Onward and upward the ascending party go, until they behold on the right side, the Methodist creed—on the left, the Baptist creed in view.   On they go in a winding course, and they see the Unitarian view.   Onward they move to the Universalist stand-point, and they see the Universalist view.   Onward they see the Christian view.   Again, the Swedenborgian view, the Episcopalian, the Puseyite, and at length, the Catholic position.   All and each presenting a distinctly different view of the same landscape below.

The further they ascend the more friends they find in the great human family, all equally intent to reach the Observatory above them all.

At length one man from the summit shouts out :

" *You are all right !* "

The Presbyterian, the Methodist, the Baptist, the Unitarian, the Universalist, the Christian, the Swedenborgian, the Episcopalian, the Puseyite, the Catholic, each and all, from your own stand-point have reported correctly.

He ascends to the top of the Observatory and takes the footprints of his Master—he and Christ " see eye to eye," for they see from the same stand-point.

One by one the travelers after holiness or likeness to Christ arrive at his stand-point upon the pinnacle of the Observatory. All see now, as Christ sees : and all " see eye to eye." Their charity is now God-like.   It embraces all races, all sects, all men :   and as they ascended through distinct paths, each being true to himself, has safely arrived at his destined goal.

But no one can see just as another saw ; for his angle of vision, his organization, differs from each and all others, and yet he is true to himself—and true to God.

So, can we but start the conservative, we shall at length all

" see eye to eye." But I fear some will compel us to pul them with a lasso up to a higher stand-point before we can convince them there is one! But let us try chafing them before hanging them; rub their feet—give a start to the circulation, by tempting even a retaliatory passion, rather than let them become pillars of salt, or die of dyspepsia, for we cannot have an universal jubilee until the last tardy conservative has attained the pinnacle of the Observatory.

Oh, Conservative! For the sake of the world above you, if not for your own sake, be persuaded to try one advance movement. And let not the consummate age of righteousness be longer retarded by your obstinate, inflexible determination never to know any more than you do at present!

Again—from the sunny side of this vast hill, enlightened by the sun of civilization, can be seen the cultivated farm, the verdant stream whose banks are studded with the mill, the factory—and from the peaceful, quiet village stands out in bold relief the school-house, the academy, the college, the university—and above all is seen the church-spire, pointing heavenward to the fount and source of all the blessings of cultivated life.

And from the shady side, which the sun of civilization has not yet reached, is seen the unbroken forest, where the wild man roams, hunting his forest prey. And from India's vast plains may be seen the heathen temple, the car of Juggernaut, the Mahommedan paradise, bounded by the Ganges, upon whose banks may be seen the devoted conscientious mother sacrificing the object dearer than her own life, to the crocodile and the flood, to propitiate the favor of her deity.

But as the sun of civilization moves onward in its westward course, leaving the sunny plains of civilization eclipsed by the principles of Calvinism, it is only to chase away the darkness of ignorance by which the conscience of the Pagan has been hitherto darkened and eclipsed.

Day of judgment! Day of wonders!

Again—on the side of this hill stand the different trees of God's great unbroken forest—each perfect—because true to the respective functions with which God has endowed it. And being true to itself, each perfects its own appropriate fruit—the walnut, the chestnut, the butternut, the hazelnut— all perfect—yet all different; all unlike, yet all right. All good, that have life enough in the nut to sprout another like it: all bad, that have not vitality enough to rise again.

But, from whence comes the mouldy, rotten, shriveled nut?

From the gnarly, old, decayed, rotten and crumbling trees of Calvinism!

Let the woodman's axe level *it*, and prepare it for the flames.

But let the fair young twigs of nature's verdant soil remain, to fill the welcome vacuums with the fragrant foliage, and spreading boughs, and teeming fruits of the perfected Christianity of nature.

So, in God's great family of human trees—the sects, tribes, races, nations of men—each and all, have a shell, and a nut, peculiar to itself. For God has made us to differ.

How shall we perfect ourselves?

Shall the butternut try to be a walnut?

Shall the chestnut strive to be a hazelnut?

No. Be what God has made you to be—a good butternut, a good chestnut.

Some like chestnuts best. Some like walnuts best. Be good in your sphere, and you will be sure to find some to admire and appreciate you.

But the mongrel all rejects. It is not a native-born plant; nature perfects her own fruit on a self-reliant base. It is bad cultivation that makes nature's prodigies.

God made man a democrat; society makes him an aristocrat. Let not the aristocracy of the Presbyterian Church boast of their being God's workmanship.

No! aristocracy is the fruit of Calvinism, not of Christianity. It is the true man, the true woman, which God makes. And those only are good men and good women who are natural—who bring forth the fruits of righteousness. "He that feareth God, and worketh righteousness, is accepted of him," whether Jew or Gentile, bond or free.

Be a good slave, and try to wait as patiently as you can for your freedom, for it is certain *God* will free you before long if your government does not.

Be a good slaveholder, if God's providence has made you one; but don't trust to Providence to be responsible for your continuing to be one; for to be a good slaveholder *now*, you must and will emancipate your slaves forthwith: for God says you must do it, or he will do it for you.

Be a good Catholic, if God has made you a Catholic; and to be a good Catholic you must not believe that Protestants are all heretics, for they are not all heretics. It is only the bigoted Calvinist that is a heretic—a tyrant—a despot. It is the Calvinist alone who reflects your image; or rather, it is you who reflects his image.

Be generous to your impulses. Be a free, independent thinker, standing on the self-reliant base of a whole true man.

Be equally generous to others. Let them be as true to themselves as you are to yourself, and all will be harmony and peace.

It is the Christians, the *practical* Christians, who are alike —not the creeds or sects. In every man behold a brother and a friend—one endued with equal rights and privileges with yourselves.

Remember, there is a well in every rock. Moses did not well to be impatient to see the waters of humanity gush out at the first drill stroke. The drill of perseverance does wonders in tunneling the rock.

Remember, too, that iron is melted by the furnace of affliction.

Remember, too, that God thought that one Niagara was enough for one world. But not so with the verdant rill, the babbling brook, the heavy moving stream, the pond, the lake, the sea. Each has his own office to fill, and none can fill another's.

The foaming cataract is the world's wonder—but the mountain spring is the world's blessing.

" One Lord, one Faith, one Baptism."

CHAPTER XV.

An Asylum Incident—A Spiritual Conquest.

On the afternoon of October 16, 1863, as I was preparing to copy my first volume for the press, Dr. McFarland came to my room to inspect the business.

I saw by the eye of my instinct, rather than by the eye of my natural vision, that he had not come alone, as usual, but brought that most unwelcome guest, the *bad* Dr. McFarland, or, the " old Adam," rather, with him.

I knew I must now be as wise as a serpent, in dealing with the serpent, or I should be bit by it!   So I put on my " charming" powers to quiet his asperities and control his reason. And choosing, as I thought, the most unexceptionable manuscript, my " Dedication," I offered to read it to him, for him to offer his criticism upon, before copying it for the press.

I had read about two-thirds of it, with rather a palpitating heart, when he suddenly interrupted me by saying:

" I should like to remark here, that I don't like your calling this place a *prison*, so much ; for it isn't so.   And as I'm to superintend these manuscripts for the press, I'm not willing you should call it a prison.   You may call it a place of *confinement*, if you choose, but not a prison.   It is only a notion you have taken up, to call it a prison, by your choosing voluntarily to confine yourself to it, as if it were a prison.   But you have no occasion for so doing.   I am just as willing you should have your liberty, as I am to let Mrs. Chapman have hers.   And she goes about just where she pleases ; and so could you, if you chose to."

Here he paused for a reply.   A silence ensued.

I saw he was in the possession of his "evil spirit," and I dared not to contradict him, or even to assert my rights of opinion, lest, by so doing, I tempt him to commit himself still more strongly on the wrong or Calvinistic side of truth; for I have found that opposition is apt to give the "old man" strength.

But at length, with the innocent fearlessness and composure of truth, I took part in the discussion, hitherto so unsatisfactory to me, by remarking:

"It is a prison *to me*, and I have based all my book upon this truth. I do not intend to exaggerate or overstep the bounds of truth in what I say, but I intend to clothe truth in its own drapery, and to call things by their true names, as I apprehend them. I profess to report no one's opinions but my own; and I do say, that Mrs. Chapman is as much a prisoner as Mrs. Packard is; and Mrs. Packard is no more a prisoner *now* than she was when she first came, when she used her parole of honor as Mrs. Chapman now does. When I took the patients to ride fourteen times, and took a dollar from your own hands, and went up town and expended it alone or according to my own judgment, I was as much the State's prisoner as I have been for the last eighteen months, though I have not stepped my foot out of this house, as my protest forbids my doing so. I am not your prisoner, nor the trustees' prisoner, but the State's or the *Government's* prisoner."

"But you will acknowledge, Mrs. Packard, that the penitentiary inmates are on a different plane as prisoners, from what you are?"

"As to our both being prisoners, we are on one and the same plane. The inmates in each institution are alike prisoners under keepers, who hold our personal liberty entirely under subjection to bolts, grates, bars, and keys. Those in each, whom their keepers can trust, are allowed their paroles of honor, extending from the liberty of the yard, to the furlough of a conditional absence upon mutual terms of agreement. But should either prisoners use their furloughs or paroles of honor as a means of escape from their place of involuntary confinement, each are alike sought as a fugitive from justice, and the laws uphold the keepers in pursuing the fugitive, and forcing his return to his place of "involuntary confinement," which expression, according to Webster, means a prison.

"In these respects we are alike, but in another respect we are unlike. The convicts are imprisoned in the penitentiary for doing wrong; the afflicted, persecuted, oppressed and innocent, are here imprisoned for doing right.

"The penitentiary is our government's place of punishing the guilty; insane asylums are our government's place of punishing the innocent—for to me it is capital punishment to be thus hopelessly imprisoned.

"This general rule has its exceptions. Some innocent ones are punished there; some guilty ones are punished here. Insane Asylums are the "*Inquisitions*" of the American government. My imprisonment is as hopeless as is my sinning to escape from it.

"I report opinions from the stand-point of a patient—a victim of this Inquisition; and not from the stand-point of a governmental officer, appointed as guardian of this institution. It is the government, not its officers, who are responsible for the basis on which our Inquisitions are placed.

"I, for one, should altogether prefer to be a penitentiary prisoner, to being an insane prisoner; for there my *accountability* is recognized, but here it is not, by the laws of the institution. It is in defiance of these laws, that you recognize it in me. And besides, my sense of justice would not be so outraged by a false imprisonment there, as here. And as to treatment, no criminals ought to be treated *worse* than the insane are treated here, and it would not hurt them to be treated even better!

" For to be lost to reason, is a greater misfortune than to be lost to virtue; and the contumely and scorn which the world attaches to the former are greater; just in proportion as the slander is more deadly to the moral influence of the injured party."

" You would not, in writing a dictionary, describe each as alike, would you ? "

" I should say they are one and the same thing, as to being *prisoners.*"

Another pause ensued:

" Shall I read on ? "

" Yes."

I finished it, and he remarked:

" It is very good."

I responded to this opinion. On this point we agreed as strongly as we differed on the point under discussion !

The subject was not again alluded to.

I felt, after he left, that something was wrong. I could not put up with this interference, or dictation of the contents of my book.

But what could be done that would not make the matter worse ?

I knew too well, that to *beg* of Dr. McFarland was not the way to succeed. For he is almost as hard to be entreated as he is to be driven. Neither is it right for me to beg for my liberty to write my thoughts. It would degrade my self respect to do so.

But to reprove him, and assert my rights, might so exasperate him as to rashly lead to the destruction of my labored manuscripts.

I cannot conscientiously submit to dictation—I therefore will not !

So I must either suspend my project indefinitely, or seek a settlement of the thing on the basis of justice.

I concluded to *dare to do right*, and risk the consequences to the overruling providence of God. For I have always found this to be the only safe and expedient course. I claim that it is always expedient to do right, and always inexpedient to do wrong.

So after having sought the moral courage and wisdom needed, for the discharge of this responsible duty, I penciled the following note and sent it to Dr. McFarland, by my attendant, Miss Trion.

To the GOOD *Dr. McFarland:*

SIR: I deem it my painful duty to report to you, my now spiritual protector, the insulting conduct I received from one of your employees, in this institution, yesterday afternoon.

It was from a man, an old, and almost superannuated man; although I think he has sense enough left to be responsible for his own actions. He came, unbidden, to my room, and having seated himself, began to upbraid me about my book—my pet—my pride, and, if you believe me, he even threatened, in spite of your proffered protection, to intercept its appearance in print, unless I heeded his suggestions in relation to it!

Now, I appeal to you to say if it is not too bad to be thus trifled with. Ought not this old, bad man (whose name looks so much like your own that I don't like to write it!) to be discharged, and never again to be allowed to enter my presence?

Dr. McFarland if you don't discharge him I shall report you to the trustees; and, if that don't answer, I shall report you to the synod; and if that don't answer, I shall report you up higher. I shall tell no lies to God, for you, nor about you.

God is preparing to summon you to his tribunal, to settle matters with you, and I'm a sworn witness, to testify, on trust to my integrity, candor, truthfulness and loyalty. I shoot evil, whether found in friend or foe, as God's enemy. And I trust to God's providence, alone, for my protection, in fighting these his spiritual battles.

Dr. McFarland, have not I a right to write my own thoughts, as well as to think them, under our constitution, even if I am a woman?

Has any man a right to interfere with this right?

Did not you say it was *my* book, not *our* book?

It is *our* country, *our* government, but it is *my* book.

And can I claim it as my own book unless I indorse its contents?

Can I indorse what, to me, are lies, and expect the blessing of God upon it?

Are not my reason and my conscience to be the sole agents in dictating my book?

My conscience is God's secretary within me, and I shall not insult its dictations, by a proffered compromise with falsehood or error. My opinions and my conscience are my personal capital, which I can, by no means, consent to barter away.

If I cannot be protected in these rights under your guardianship, I must defer the publication of my book until God raises up for me a protector, who will not dare to trample upon the sacred, inalienable rights of my God-given nature.

I ask you, kind sir, will you be the protector of the inalienable rights of my womanly nature? Or, must I suspend my contemplated project until God's providence prepares the way for my spiritual freedom to be so secured to me that I can write a book true to God, and also true to my own truthful nature?

God offers you the honor of being my protector in this act, and he longs to confer it upon you. So do I.

But there is one, and only one condition, on which it can be conferred upon you; and that is, to dare to trust your interests, and the interests of this institution, and the interests of the country, on the immovable principles of truth and justice.

I shall venture to take my stand on the immutable rock of eternal truth, regardless of the foaming billows which dash at its base, and here shall I wield the sword of truth, regardless of my own interests, and those of all others.

I stand or fall with God alone.

Your true friend,
E. P. W. PACKARD.

In about one hour after the above note was delivered, Dr. McFarland came to the door of my room, with a face radiant with smiles, and at the same time giving my hand a most perceptible grasp, inquired:

"Who is that 'old man' who has ventured to insult you so about that precious book? He shall not be tolerated here on any account. You tell me his name and he shall be discharged forthwith. The name of that 'old, bad, superannuated man,' you just give me, and I shall see to his insulting you any more!"

"The good, new, Dr. McFarland is always welcome to my room—most welcome! But that old, bad man, I do not want to see any more."

"No, he shan't disturb you any more. Just give me his name, and I'll see to his discharge!"

"You are doing right, Dr. McFarland! You are treating the 'old man' as he deserves to be treated."

Soon after, Mrs. McFarland came to my room, with a tumbler of her jelly, the second red sacrifice she had presented me, for an atonement for her husband's sins! and gave me a pleasant visit besides. I read to her my "Dedication," and she very sensibly remarked:

"It is so very strange and mysterious why your friends should have all deserted you so. I cannot understand it—how friends can treat their friends in this manner. They put them in here, and then seem to desert them, as if they were not worth caring for afterwards. I am sure I could not desert my friends in this manner."

"No, Mrs. McFarland, I don't think you could, for you are

too true to your womanly nature to do such an unnatural act. But Mrs. McFarland, this is a perverted age. Christianity is almost totally eclipsed by Calvinism. The sun, moon and stars are all under this eclipse. Men, women and children are all more or less perverted by it. This is the culminating age of Calvinism. Its deadly principles must be exposed and abandoned, before Christianity can exert its benign and legitimate influence over the character and destiny of the present age. Mrs. McFarland, we are now passing through the very nadir of the eclipse. It is not midnight. It is a noon-day eclipse of the world's luminary, and when this awful shadow shall have once passed across its disk, it is forever descending to its no distant tomb; while Christianity, dismantled of its false habiliments will shine out with meridian splendor, and the natural and spiritual reign of Christ will have fully commenced. Until then, we must grope our way in darkness, not knowing at what we stumble."

Mrs. McFarland is a very kind woman; none could fill her place as our matron, better than she does. She has repeatedly remarked to me:

"We should be glad to cure you all of your diseases, if we could."

But, alas! mine is one of their "hopeless cases!" My Christianity is incurable! And all the treatment of this American inquisition cannot induce me to abandon it for Calvinism.

I told her how her husband was going to let me have my book all my own way, and how he would be rewarded if "he endures to the end" in his well begun course—that of allowing an American woman her right of opinion during this great eclipse. For he, like all others, must stand on his own actions, and if they exalt and promote him, no influence can dethrone him. And he has as good a right to plume his cap with his own, well-earned feathers, as Mrs. Packard has her bonnet;

for the fortitude of Honesty in enduring his chastisement so martyr-like, is as truly his rightful claim as the innocent fear-lessness of Truth in inflicting the chastisement is Mrs. Pack-ard's rightful claim.

It is my private opinion, that Dr. McFarland's conscience dictated to him the fate which he assigned to the " old man of sin," that " Nathan's " wife had exerted her share of influence in convincing this modern king, that the pet book of the pau-per ought not to be sacrificed to the cupidity of the rich man.

It is also my fondly cherished opinion, that the good Dr. McFarland will never let the " bad man " crowd his ewe lamb again ; since he has found, that a lamb can even crowd a lion, if self-defense demands the pressure of truth upon the lion's conscience, to quicken it into healthful action !

He may, too, be compelled to admit the truth, however un-welcome, of Mrs. Timmons' compliment, viz :

" That two hard heads meet when Mrs. Packard and Dr. McFarland meet," on the arena of discussion ; and it is by no means certain which head would be the most exposed by a collision !

I have volunteered both my manuscripts and myself to Dr. McFarland as a burnt offering, on condition that he can detect a single lie in all my manuscripts.   I shrink not on this condi-tion, to be burnt alive, as God's appointed portion for the liar ; for whether I choose it or not, I know it is God's invincible purpose, to make me stand on my own deserts : and if I am a liar, I know hell is my portion.

I make no claim to infallibility.   I am finite in knowledge and intelligence, and liable to prejudices, prepossessions, and springs of error from educational influences ; yet not from an imperfect organization, since God has endowed me with a good female development ; and am true to my own convictions of truth and duty—and am no " respecter of persons " in dealing with wrong, or evil, in any form.

God grant I may always be loyal to God's government, and disloyal to every other government which interferes with this; and the test of my loyalty is found in my being true to my conscience—God's secretary within me.

My conscience is not a standard for any human being, except myself. I grant every human being an equal right to differ from me in opinion, that I have to differ from them, in relation to my views of truth and duty. God is the only dictator of my inalienable rights; and whoever dares to trespass upon them, does it at their own peril, not mine.

Dr. McFarland has no right guaranteed to him, from any intelligence in God's universe, to dictate to, or interfere with, the utterance of a single expression found in my book. And if he dares to attempt it, he dares to trespass on God's authority, not mine—and God, not I, will be his judge of the act.

I am happy to add that Dr. McFarland never attempted to dictate what I should write after this. This was a complete victory over my spiritual foe—the dictator to my conscience. My rights of conscience have ever since basked in the realm of spiritual freedom. This " Spiritual Conquest" thus obtained confirmed me in the position I had determined to maintain in reference to my efforts to promote the spiritual welfare of Dr. McFarland, for I thought there was more hope in making my appeals to his honor, as a handle by which to lead him to repentance, than to make him feel that I expected no good of him. In order to lead him by his honor, I must feel a degree of confidence in the efficiency of this principle, or I shall be acting a double part myself. I cannot make him feel that I have hopes of him, while I have none, without being a hypocrite. I feel that the secret of true love lies in winning rather than in driving the soul to Christ. By patient continuance in well doing, I wait for the bright fruition of the sustaining hope that he will yet repent sincerely; that he will turn from this wickedness and live a different life.

CHAPTER XVI.

A Dream and its Interpretation.

On the December following my incarceration, I dreamed the following dream, which with its interpretation, may serve a valuable purpose, as an illustration of several important principles.

Mrs. Hosmer, who helped me to its interpretation, has superintended the sewing room for four years and a half there. She has one of the most striking peculiarities of temperament I ever met with—in that her eccentric nature combines the extremes of good and evil, in their most glaring features. This trait she exhibited, for about one year and a half, in being my best friend, and also, my worst enemy—in that she was the medium of some of my choicest social blessings, as well as the source of my keenest sorrows.

I dreamed that it was put upon me to draw a stage coach across a bridge spanning a broad, deep river, and that in order to get the coach upon the bridge, I was compelled to draw it up five stone steps each about five inches high.

I looked upon my appointment at first as an impossibility; but recollecting that " I'll try " has done wonders, I determined to see what I could do by trying.

The stage was prepared for me by substituting a rope, instead of the neap or thills, which encircled my body, so that the greatest pressure came across my breast. Thus prepared I put forth a most herculean effort, when, to my great surprise and joy, the stage came up upon the bridge.

Stimulated by my seemingly miraculous success, I started at full speed across the bridge ; and found, to my joy, that by the momentum acquired by the velocity, the effort to draw it along became correspondingly diminished. Thus running at the top of my speed with my head down, I found, to my surprise, that before I was aware of it, I had run off from the bridge on to a piece of slitwork about four inches wide; which was the only medium of communication between the termination of the bridge, and the opposite shore—the distance being two tiers and a half.

The termination of each tier was marked by a high beam extending from the water, up many feet above the level of the string-piece across the river. The half-tier was nearest the bridge, so that the first support to lean upon was not far distant from my present stand-point.

I stopped and considered what was to be done.

I thought that to draw the stage on to this narrow slitwork, and balance it exactly, so as to drag it over in this way, would plainly be an impossibility; and that the capsizing of the stage into the river, would necessarily drag me with it, by the rope around my body. I therefore determined to drop the rope and step out of the traces ; and thus disentangled, walk on to the standing support. I did so, and then considered what to do.

To return seemed impossible : for the stage presented an insuperable barrier to my getting on to the bridge.

To go forward seemed too hazardous, for the two remaining reaches seemed very long, when looking at the deep river far below me ; and the very narrow path I had to walk upon, appeared still more precarious as it neared the opposite shore— for the extreme end of the last string-piece was so raised on one side of the mortice, as to render the upper surface quite an inclined plane. On this I should not dare to expose myself, for fear I should slip off, and besides, I saw it would be likely to slip down into the mortice by my weight upon it ; and the jar would be very likely to cause me to fall off.

I looked about for help. But no one was within speaking distance.

On the shore I had left, far down below the bridge, I could

see one man standing, solitary and alone, looking with a vacant stare upon the broad, bridgeless, boatless stream before him. I saw distinctly it was my husband, apparently cogitating his own means of crossing the fathomless deep, regardless of my perilous, exposed condition. Cold, selfish indifference marked his appearance. I knew he cared not for me, or my deliverance, or safety.

I turned from this granite statue, and cast a look upon the opposite bank.

My courage revived at the prospect. I could distinctly see a company of men, who seemed to be consulting what to do for me, for I could see they had a rope in their hands. Life, motion, interest the most intense, marked their energetic movements.

But I considered—how can the rope be extended to me, and if it were, how could it help me in sustaining my footing, on the narrow string-piece I had to pass over upon? To look down, my head would swim. To look up, it was clear. Still, then I could not see where to place my feet.

I concluded to hold on to my standing beam, and wait awhile, thinking, there will be doubtless some amongst the by-standing witnesses whose gallantry will prompt them to even expose their own lives, to rescue a defenseless female from her hazardous position.

I therefore, for a time, trusted my deliverance, with all the trustful confidence of my womanly nature, to the care of manhood, whose God-like development instinctively volunteers help to the helpless—protection to the unprotected.

But upon a reconsideration of the difficulties in the case, I found a new one, which had before escaped my notice. I saw that the river below me was covered with empty chairs—large armed office chairs—all upright, but empty! These chairs so obstructed the passage that boats could not be sent to my aid from beneath. I thought, Oh! that the public officers had not vacated these chairs, and I would venture to drop into their arms! But no—instead of these officers being at their posts to help the helpless, their fixtures only serve as an impediment, to obstruct other sources of help.

I therefore concluded, that since I was out of the reach of all human help, the only alternative left me, was to run the risk of *saving myself* by my own unaided exertions, by going forward, risking all the hazards of a progressive movement. I concluded my way must be to look constantly upward, and move my feet forward, with most careful, cautious steps.

Having fully settled upon this course, I stooped down to remove my shoes, and drop them into the stream, so that being thus disencumbered, I might with stocking feet move forward, with less danger of slipping off.

While in the act of removing my shoes, I awoke, happy to find myself in a dormitory bed in an insane asylum, instead of being a fifth of the way across the string-piece.

The next day I told Mrs. Hosmer of my dream; and the interpretation she put upon it, was in her own laconic style, as follows:

"Mrs. Packard, you must leave public opinion behind you, until the bridge is built. You must just go on alone. You are now called to walk through Gethsemane's garden alone, as your Master did, depending upon no human sympathy for support. You may expect God's angel will be sent to sustain you, when your accumulated sorrows become too great for human fortitude to endure. Mrs. Packard, we must all pass to heaven in the same steps our Master trod—like Him, we must all pass through Gethsemane's garden—and like His, the path leading to the consummation of our sanctification is constantly narrowing, and attended with increasing difficulties as we approach its termination. It is then too narrow for two to go abreast. Alone! alone!! we must tread the wine-press of God's wrath, even while under the eclipse of God's countenance—for so God

7

appoints. No other road terminates in eternal day. This promise must sustain you: 'If ye *suffer* with me, ye shall also *reign* with me.' "

" Oh thanks ! ten thousand thanks, Mrs. Hosmer, for these words of comfort to my sorrowing soul ! "

After being strengthened by this angel-visitant, my sinking soul could say with my Master, " Yes, the cup which my Father hath given me, I will drink," uncomplainingly. Yes, " Not my will but thine, O God, be done " concerning me. Henceforth, my highest purpose shall be not to get out of this asylum to be with my precious children—not to convince the world that I am not an insane person—but it shall henceforth be my chief purpose to become a perfect person in Christ Jesus' estimation, regardless of the estimation of perverted humanity.

Yes, God is my witness that hitherto this purpose in me has not been broken.

But O ! the persecution, the sorrows, the agony I have endured in carrying out this purpose into a practical one, God only knows. For He only knows who has been misunderstood, misrepresented, maligned and persecuted unto death, how to feel for those who are.

Yes, when I think how good and kind my Saviour was to all—how innocent he was of the least trespass upon other's rights, and then think how no cruel tyrant was ever hated with a more deadly hate than was my loving Master, I feel like saying, " it is enough for the servant that he be as his master."

Yes, alone ! single-handed and alone, I have dared to expose and condemn as guilty, those laws and those practices which treat insanity as a crime ! To imprison a person for being insane—to cut them off from all communication with outside influences that they may thus punish these helpless, innocent sufferers, with less danger of interference from abroad, thus to expose the most dependent creatures of God's government

to unmerited abuse, is a heaven-daring crime, which well
merits the indignation of an incensed God, sure to follow such
outrages, bestowed upon His children—upon Himself—personified in human form.

Alone have I stood between the laws of my country and my
God, and been a single-handed defender of the Divine code,
in defiance of the human code.

I have dared to be thus true to Jesus, even while in the
absolute power of legalized despotism, and that too, when
I felt this despotic power in full force to crush me beneath
its iron foot. I knew this despotic power could destroy all my
earthly joys—hopes—rights—privileges—interests—my papers—my witnesses and my natural life! And I knew too,
full well, that the Superintendent could be protected by the
laws of our government in so doing!

I knew too, that he had power to destroy himself—but I
knew it was as certain as the decrees of God, that he could
not destroy me, or the mind which dictated these papers.

Therefore in my spiritual might I have moved forward with
a dauntless, inflexible purpose, that Christ's cause should not
suffer here, for want of one faithful advocate—one loyal
witness in defense of truth and righteousness.

The bloodless but terribly painful conflict has ended! The
strong man, armed with all the burnished armory of the American statutes, could not defend himself against a stronger than
he—personified in the form of a legally insane female pauper!

Again—My position on the string-piece illustrates another
point. I have been alone in my position to never again return to my husband. The advocates of my so doing have
argued that the laws placed me there—that no place of refuge
from his legal claims upon me could be found, outside of this
asylum—that here, amongst maniacs as my almost sole companions, I must linger out a most hopeless, wretched existence,
excluded from all communication with my children, or any

other earthly friends, except through the strictest censorship
—that my active habits of body and mind would here be so
restricted and limited, that the inevitable consequence must
ultimately be loss of both health and spirits, however elastic
at present—and therefore it was wholly a suicidal act on my
part, to refuse to go to my husband, as the only alternative
allowed me by individual or legal favor.

I have felt the full force of this logic, Oh, how keenly!
Still, a higher logic has prevailed over my decisions. A simple
"Thus saith the Lord," has forbidden it. My conscience
dictated, with unquestioning distinctness, it is morally wrong
for you to trust yourself again in the legal, absolutely despotic
power of one, who has proved himself to be, to me, a most
unrelenting persecutor. Self-defense forbids it. It is for me
to obey conscience. It is for God to work out the consequences or results of obedience.

Helpless and alone, I have thus moved my frail bark on the
tempestuous sea of human destiny—with God alone for my
pilot. My frail bark has not yet foundered, even amidst the
dashing breakers of cruelly disappointed hopes, of insults
heaped on abuses; by the cold and chilling gusts of ridicule,
scorn, derision, contumely and contempt.

No, all, all combined, have not overmatched the skill of my
faithful Pilot, who has moved my frail bark safely through
them all, to a haven of rest. Thanks! thanks! to Thee,
alone, my Pilot, for thy superior skill and restraining power.
Peacefully I now lie in this haven of rest, trustfully waiting
my Captain's orders for the next voyage.

Again—I was alone in protesting against my illegal imprisonment. Scarcely a single individual has given me the
shadow of approval of this stand—but, instead, I have been
sneered at, ridiculed, and my "tyrant conscience" has been
reproached as being an usurper! But after more than nine-
teen long months of unsympathizing imprisonment Miss

Martha Mills, my intelligent and strong-minded attendant, has, within a few days, assured me that "she should have done just so herself under similar circumstances."

Oh, how grateful is such a response from a human tongue, to one whose love of approbation is so very large as my own. It is this love of approbation which has led me to suffer so cheerfully the loss of all things to secure the approval of my final Judge at last. And when I plainly saw that I must either sacrifice his approbation or that of perverted humanity; I unhesitatingly chose to lose the latter—for I esteem it no great honor to be popular amongst perverted men and women!

Again—I seemed to be alone upon the connecting link between the natural and spiritual worlds. The bridge connecting them is nearly completed. But who dares to step out beyond the limits of popular opinion and sentiment, and let himself be cut loose from all things tangible, to gain the hidden treasures of knowledge laid up in God's vast storehouse ready for distribution to any applicant? Who dares to stand alone in his opinion, and face a frowning world?

Again, how strikingly has my subsequent experience developed the fact that the "empty office chairs"—the laws—have been the chief obstacle in the way of my deliverance. These "empty chairs," or in other words, the "dead letters" on the Statute Books, were the most potent influences used in perpetuating injustice to me and my children. The popular influence of public sentiment stood ready and anxious to help me. But alas! the "empty office chairs" filled the stream below me, so that no boats could be sent to my rescue.

But when the bridge connecting the natural and spiritual worlds is constucted, and the few remaining tiers are built, the public will easily be transported over the river of doubt and uncertainty, which now surrounds the incipient developments of a new spiritual science. In other words, the great truth underlying the agitation of the subject of Magnetism,

Electricity, Psychology, and Spiritualism is being developed into a spiritual science, the laws of which, future generations may be able to apply with as much certainty as to the result, as the present age depends upon steam as a locomotive power. When these remaining tiers are built, or these secret spirit laws are generally understood, the age will pass as readily into the realm of spirit forces for help, as we now pass from continent to continent by the help of steam power.

CHAPTER XVII.

A Prophecy and its Fulfillment.

On my recruiting tour to my friends in New York State, about two years and a-half before my incarceration, I then and there saw for the first time in my life a manifestation of modern Spiritualism.

One evening, at the house of my cousin, Dr. Fordice Rice, of Cazenovia, N. Y., while sitting with his family around the table, sewing and listening to his reading, one of our party, a very intelligent minister's wife, interrupted us by suddenly dropping her needle, and with a very perceptible shiver of her whole frame, exclaiming:

"There is a spirit here wishing to communicate some message!"

This announcement not only astonished, but frightened me to such a degree as led me to exclaim with a trembling voice and deep emotion:

"What does this mean?"

My cousin, Mrs. Laura P. Rice, replied:

"There is nothing to fear, cousin Elizabeth, this is nothing new to us. I will get aunt Sophronia a pencil and paper and she will write out the message sent to us."

While getting the stationery, the table around which we were sitting, commenced tipping towards me, and in the gentlest manner actually tipped so far as to rest lightly upon my lap. At this point my fears so triumphed, I burst into tears. The table quietly assumed its former position, when the medium wrote the following sentence:

"Don't be frightened! My Daughter! We are your friends, come to communicate with you, and help you."

Said I, "Please carry out your programme. I have no desire or wish to interrupt you."

A silence ensued, while the medium proceeded to write, as follows:

"My Daughter, you did right to come this journey. You needed the rest of body and refreshment of spirit it is to impart. I accompanied you here—was with you on your journey. And I approve of your seeking council of Hon. Gerrit Smith, as is your intention to do next Saturday. Your purpose and spirit will be strengthened by communion with his capacious soul. And, my Daughter, you need all these helps to fit and prepare you for the great work God in his providence has assigned you.

"You are living in a very dark, benighted community. You are to become a light to this community and a blessing to many others.

"But my child, prepare for Persecution! Persecution! *Persecution! !*

"For it must come. No power can prevent it. But, fear not! We stand by you. You will be sustained by these unseen powers, who are using you as their chosen instrument for great good to humanity. Be careful to 'try the spirits' —'Prove all things—hold fast that which is good.'

LUCY STRONG PARSONS WARE."

Not a person in the room knew my mother's name, except myself, and although I recollected always seeing her signature, "Lucy S. Ware," I could not have told what the "S" meant. Parsons was her family name before marriage.

On the following Saturday afternoon, while in conversation with Mr. and Mrs. Smith in their parlor, in Peterborough, New York, a similar interruption took place. Here another and a different medium took a pencil, and while writing her message I continued, in a very low, quiet tone of voice, to converse with Mrs. Smith, and as I made the remark, "I think it unfortunate for me that the light of new truths should dawn upon my mind prior to that of Mr. Packard's, for it seems to me a reversion of God's order, for the weaker vessel to lead the stronger," the medium laughed outright, and remarked:

" I have made a strange episode!" reading: " Weaker vessel! When you pass from this to the spirit world, then you will see which is the *Weaker vessel!* "

Upon reading what preceded this exclamation, we found the following: " Sister, prepare for Opposition! Opposition!! Opposition!!! for it will come.

· " Brother's mind is in darkness. His spirit gropes in regions where the light cannot enter. His Theology is the snare into which he has been taken captive by false doctrines. Entrenched as he is by false theories and insane dogmas he cannot extricate himself. Therefore, pity him! but fear not to expose the errors of his creed, for these false doctrines must be overthrown to prepare the way for the teachings of Christ.

" Sister, you have a great work to do, but Persevere! Persevere! *Persevere!!* You cannot fail, for a host are battling for you.   LUCY JANE PACKARD HASTINGS."

This dear sister of Mr. Packard's had at this date been dead about three years. In her earth life she had been one of my choicest friends—one of the few who seemed to understand and appreciate me while others would misapprehend and therefore misrepresent me.

These manuscripts were laid by among my choicest papers, and although seldom spoken of in conversation with others, yet, I " pondered these sayings in my heart," waiting for the light of the future in which to interpret this prophecy of the past.

As the reader already has my subsequent experience to the present time, in which to trace a likeness to the original, I shall leave each one free to apply its fulfillment as their own reason dictates.

Another incident which struck me very forcibly as a new and strange phenomena in the realm of Spiritualism took place in the year 1866, while in Chicago. I had arrived that day in the city, whither I had come to prepare the way for the passage of the " Personal Liberty Bill." I took board and lodging with Mrs. Lull, a widow, living on the West side, hitherto an entire stranger to me. Her house being crowded with boarders, I was admitted on condition that I room with her. I retired early and had dropped into a sound sleep before she came to rest. After laying perfectly quiet a few moments she spoke and said:

" Mrs. Packard, are you awake ? "

" Yes, I am. What is your request ? "

" I wish to tell you, that your father is here! and he says he wishes to speak to you."

"Very well, I am most happy to welcome him, and will most gladly listen to all he has to say."

Mrs. Lull then said, he sends you the following message :

" I want to ask her forgiveness for not coming to her help when in the Insane Asylum. I can now see how blinded I then was. I was led by that dark spirit, Theophilus, to do this great wrong. Oh! How dark he looks ! He is in outer darkness. There is not one ray of light about him. All I can see of him is the faintest glimmer of light in a far distant region —'tis not equal to a spark—'tis a mere glimmer !

"And only think, my daughter, how I have been led by such a dark spirit to neglect you, and let you suffer so much when I ought to have gone to your rescue. I see now how I sinned in neglecting you.

"Oh ! can you forgive me, my daughter ?

" How you have suffered ! I suffer now correspondingly, because I did not help you when I might and ought to have done so. I see heaven before me, but I cannot enter there until I have sojourned on earth long enough to atone for the sin of neglecting you. I must now raise the fallen and help the oppressed, as I ought to have done by you. I can never be happy until this atonement is thus made.

"Oh, my Daughter! you are on the plane of true progression. How I wish I could exchange places with you! But vain wish! My Theology was my ruin. My life has been a failure in disseminating such false doctrines. Oh! how many souls have I thus led into darkness. The blind has led the blind.

"You are now on so different a plane from myself, I cannot assist you as I would wish, but I shall do all I can to help you. I shall go with you to Springfield and help you to influence the minds of the Legislature in favor of your Bill.

"I am glad I changed my will in your favor. I only wish I had given you more."

Saying this he left, when Mrs. Lull inquired:

"Who is Theophilus?"

"My husband. Did you never know his name?"

"No; or if I ever had known it, I have forgotten it."

We being entire strangers, and I knowing nothing of her being a medium, it seemed to be not only a novel event in my experience, but a remarkable one.

Now, with these facts before me, I cannot but feel that it would be wrong for me to deride Spiritualism as an acknowledged fact. Still, in its present undeveloped state, I do not think it safe or proper to depend upon it as a guide for human conduct. The only infallible rule or guide for us is God's word, as it is interpreted to us through our individual reason and conscience, and any spirit in the body or out of the body, who attempts to. *dictate* to the conscience of another, except through the reason of the one they wish to guide, ought to be looked upon as an enemy to their soul's highest interests.

CHAPTER XVIII.

Can you Forgive Mr. Packard?

Yes, I could, freely, promptly and fully forgive him on the gospel condition of practical repentance. This condition could secure it, and this alone.

As I understand Christ's teachings, he does not allow me to forgive him until he does repent, and in some sense make restitution. He directs me to forgive my brother if he repent —yea, if he sins and repents seventy times seven, I must forgive as many times.

But if he does not repent, I am not allowed to forgive him. And so long as he insists upon it, both by word and deed, that he has done only what was right, and that he shall do the same thing again, if he has a chance, I do not see any chance for me to bestow my forgiveness upon a penitent transgressor.

Dr. McFarland asked me one day·just after Mr. Packard had visited the Asylum and I had refused to speak to him:

"Mrs. Packard, do you think it would be considered as natural, for a true woman to meet one who had been a lover and a husband, after one year's separation, even if he had abused her, without one gush of affection?"

"Yes sir, I do say it is the dictates of the higher nature of a woman to do so in my case. He has by his own actions annihilated every particle of respect I have ever felt for his manhood, and thus my higher moral nature instinctively abhors him. In doing so I have obeyed the dictates of my conscience."

"Do you feel sure yours is a right conscience?"

"It is one I am willing to go to God's judgment bar with."

"Do you believe the Bible?"

"Indeed I do, every word of it! It is our sure word of prophecy."

" Does not the Bible require forgiveness ? "

" It does, sir, on the ground of repentance, even seventy times seven. But without it, we are not allowed to forgive, lest it harden the offender in his sins. Mr. Packard has never by word or deed intimated that he has done one unjust or wrong deed in treating me as he has done, much less that he is sorry for it, and now for me to treat him as my husband, would be saying to him :

" I think you are doing all right in treating me as you do!

" Thus I should be upholding him in his sins, by thus disregarding God's express directions."

He feels that I am the one to ask forgiveness, for not yielding my opinions to his dictation, instead of causing him so much trouble in trying to bring me under subjection to his will, in this particular.

He does not claim that I ever resisted his will in any other particular—and I have not felt it my duty to do so. I had rather yield than quarrel any time, where conscience is not concerned.

He knows I have done so, for twenty-one years of married life. But to tell a lie, and be false to my honest convictions, by saying I believed what I did not believe, I could not be made to do.

My truth-loving nature could never be subjected to falsify itself—I must and shall be honest and truthful. And although King David said in his haste, " all *men* are liars," I rejoice he did not say all *women* were, for then there would have been no chance for my vindication of myself as a truthful woman!

This one thing is certain, I have been imprisoned three years because I could not tell a lie, and now I think it would be bad business for me to commence at this late hour.

I cannot love oppression, wrong, or injustice under any circumstances. But on the contrary, I do hate it, while at the same time I can love the sinner who thus sins, for I find it in my heart to forgive to any extent the penitent transgressor.

I am not conscious of feeling one particle of revengeful feeling towards Mr. Packard, while at the same time I feel the deepest kind of indignation at his abuses of me.

And furthermore, I really feel that if any individual ever deserved penitentiary punishment, Mr. Packard does, for his treatment of me.

Still, I would not inflict any punishment upon him—for this business of punishing my enemies I am perfectly content to leave entirely with my Heavenly Father, as he requires me to do, as I understand his directions. And my heart daily thanks God that it is not my business to punish him. One sinner has no right to punish another sinner. God, our Common Father, is the only being who holds this right to punish any of his great family of human children. All that is required of me is, to do him good, and to protect myself from his abuse as best I can. And it is not doing him good to forgive him before he repents.

It is reversing God's order.

It is not to criminate him that I have laid the truth before the public. Duty demands it as an act of self-defense on my part, and a defense of the rights of that oppressed class of married women which my case represents. Neither do I ask punishment for him at any human tribunal; all I ask is protection for myself, and the class I represent.

God commands us to " do good to our enemies," and if I fully obey this direction, I must not only pray for him, but I must act and labor for his welfare. Judging from my own feelings, I do not see how I can really love an enemy and let him go unreproved and unwarned. But perhaps if I hated a human being I might answer the demands of my conscience by simply praying for him; but since I never knew what that feeling was by experience to hate any one, I may not be qualified to judge one who has.

My nature prompts me to hate the sin and love the sinner, and my love for the sinner is so genuine and so real, that I can leave no means untried to bring him to see his sins and repent, since I know pardon from his Judge can be bestowed on no other condition.

The greatest sin of my life as I now view it, lies in the fact that I have been too ready to forgive the wrong doer, and in my impatience to extend my pardon I have sometimes forgiven before I ought to have done so—that is, I have forgiven the *im*penitent instead of the penitent, and thus encouraged the transgressor in his sins:

But through the discipline of my heavenly Father I now see my sins in this respect, so that henceforth I shall aim to extend to the impenitent the love message of warning and rebuke, and to the truly penitent, the love message of forgiveness and encouragement in well doing.

To extend forgiveness to the impenitent, degrades ourselves also as guilty accomplices in their iniquities.

As I understand Christ's directions the next step following unheeded warning and reproof is to withdraw fellowship while the sinner still persists in his incorrigible condition. This too I have also done. I have withdrawn all fellowship from Mr. Packard in his present attitude towards me. I do not so much as speak or write to him, and this I do from the principle of self-defense, and not from a spirit of revenge. I know all my words and actions are looked upon through a very distorted medium, and whatever I say or do, he weaves into capital with which to carry on his persecution. And I think I have Christ's example too as my defense of this course ; for when he was convinced his persecutors questioned him only for the purpose of catching him in his words, " he was speechless."

I have said all I have to say to Mr. Packard in his present character. But when he repents, I will forgive him.

CHAPTER XIX.

Mr. Packard Condemned by the Popular Verdict.

Where the truth is known, and as the revelations of the court-room developed the facts exactly as they were found to exist, the popular verdict is decidedly against Mr. Packard. Indeed, the tide of popular indignation rises very high among that class, who defend religious liberty and equal rights, free thought, free speech, free press.

I state this as a fact which my own personal observation demonstrates. In canvassing for my book in many of the largest cities in the State of Illinois, I had ample opportunity to test this truth, and were I to transcribe a tithe of the expressions of this indignant feeling which I alone have heard, it would swell this book to a mammoth size. A few specimen expressions must therefore be taken as a fair representation of this popular indignation.

"Mr. Packard cannot enter our State without being in danger of being lynched," is an expression I have often heard made from the common people.

From the soldiers I have often heard these, and similar expressions :

"Mrs. Packard, if you need protection again, just let us know it and we will protect you with the bullet, if there is no other defense."

"If he ever gets you into another Asylum, our cannon shall open its walls for your deliverance."

The Bar in Illinois may be represented by the following expressions, made to me by the Judges of the Supreme Court, in Ottawa Court-House.

" Mrs. Packard, this is the foulest outrage we ever heard of in real life ; we have heard of such deep laid plots in romances, but we never knew one acted out in real life before. We did not suppose such a plot could be enacted under the laws of our State. But this we will say, if ever you are molested again in our State, let us know it, and we will put Mr. Packard and his Conspiracy where they ought to be put ! "

The pulpit of Illinois almost universally condemns the outrage, as a crime against humanity and human rights. But the truth requires me to say that there are some exceptions.

The only open defenders I ever heard for Mr. Packard, came from the church influence, and the pulpit. Yet, among all the ministers I have conversed with on this subject, I have found only two who uphold his course.

One Presbyterian minister told me, he thought Mr. Packard had done right in treating me as he had :

" You have no right," said he, " to cherish opinions which he does not approve, and he did right in putting you in an asylum for it. I would treat my wife just so, if she did so ! "

The name and residence of this minister I could give if I chose, but I forbear to do so, lest I expose him unnecessarily.

The other clergyman was a Baptist minister.

Said he, " I uphold Mr. Packard in what he has done, and I would help him in putting you in again should he attempt it ! "

The name and place of this minister I shall withhold unless self-defense requires the exposure.

When I have added one or two more church members to those two just named, it includes the whole number I ever heard defend, in my presence, Mr. Packard's course.

Still, I have no doubt but that these four represent a minority in Illinois, who are governed by the same popish principles of bigotry and intolerance as Mr. Packard is.

And I think it may be said of this class, as a Chicago paper did of Mr. Packard, after giving an account of the case, viz. :

" The days of bigotry and oppression are not yet past.   If three-fourths of the people of the world were of the belief of Rev. Packard and his witnesses, the other fourth would be burned at the stake."

And here I will add, that this same transmutation of public sentiment took place in New England after the facts became known, as expressed by a lawyer in Worcester, Mass., who had at first identified himself as Mr. Packard's defender, said he :

" Mrs. Packard, there is not a man in Massachussetts, neither do I think there is one in the United States who would dare openly to defend Mr. Packard's course, when the facts are known as they exist."

The opinion of his own church and community in Manteno, where he preached at the time I was kidnapped, is another class whose verdict the public desire to know also.

When he put me off, his church and people were well united in him, and as a whole, the church not only sustained him in his course, but were active Co-conspirators.

When I returned, he preached nowhere. He was closeted in his own domicile on the Sabbath, cooking the family dinner, while his children were at church and sabbath school. His society was almost entirely broken up. I was told he preached until none would come to hear him ; and his deacons gave as their reason for not sustaining him, that the trouble in his family had destroyed his influence in that community.

Multitudes of his people who attended my trial, who I know defended him at the time he kidnapped me, came to me with these voluntary confessions :

" Mrs. Packard, I always knew you were not insane."

" I never believed Mr. Packard's stories."

" I always felt that you were an abused woman," etc., etc.

These facts indicated some change even in the opinion of his own allies during my absence. I leave the public to draw their own inferences from the facts above stated.

CHAPTER XX.

Mr. Packard's Monomania.

The question is sometimes asked, " Mrs. Packard, is your husband's real reason for treating you as he has, merely a difference in your religious belief, or is there not something back of all this? It seems unaccountable to us, that mere bigotry should so annihilate all human feeling."

This is a question I have never been able hitherto to answer, satisfactorily, either to myself or others; but now I am fully prepared to answer it with satisfaction to myself, at least; that is, facts, stubborn facts, which never before came to my knowledge until my visit home, compel me to feel that my solution of this perplexing question is now based on the unchangeable truth of facts."

For I have read with my own eyes, the secret correspondence which he has kept up with my father, for about eight years past, wherein this question is answered by himself, by his own confessions, and in his own words.

And as a very natural prelude to this answer, it seems to me not inappropriate to answer one other question often put to me first, namely :

" Has he not some other woman in view? "

I can give my opinion now, not only with my usual promptness, but with more than my usual confidence that I am correct in my opinion. I say confidently, he has not any other woman in view, nor never had.

And it was only because I could not fathom to the cause of this " Great Drama," that this was ever presented to my own mind, as a question.

I believe that if ever there was a man who practically

believed in the monogamy principle of marriage, he is the man. Yes, I believe, with only one degree of faith less than that of knowledge, that the only Bible reason for a divorce never had an existence in our case.

And here, as the subject is now opened, I will take occasion to say, that as I profess to be a Bible woman both in spirit and practice, I cannot conscientiously claim a Bible right to be divorced. I never have had the first cause to doubt his fidelity to me in this respect, and he never has had the first cause to doubt my own to him.

But fidelity to the truth of God's providential events compel me to give it as my candid opinion, that the only key to the solution of this mysterious problem will yet be found to be concealed in the fact, that Mr. Packard is a monomaniac on the subject of woman's rights.

It was the triumph of bigotry over his manliness, which occasioned this public manifestation of this peculiar mental phenomenon.

Some of the reasons for this opinion, added to the facts of this dark drama which are already before the public, lie in the following statement:

In looking over the correspondence above referred to, I find the " confidential " part all refers to dates and occasions wherein I can distinctly recollect we had had a warm discussion on the subject of woman's rights; that is, I had taken occasion from the application of his insane dogma, namely, that " a woman has no rights that a man is bound to respect," to defend the opposite position of equal rights.

I used sometimes to put my argument into a written form, hoping thus to secure for it a more calm and quiet consideration. I never used any other weapons in self-defense, except those paper pellets of the brain. And is not that man a coward who cannot stand before such artillery ?

But not to accuse Mr. Packard of cowardice, I will say, that instead of boldly meeting me as his antagonist on the arena of argument and discussion, and there openly defending himself against my knock-down arguments, with his Cudgel of Insanity, I find he closed off such discussions with his secret " confidential" letters to my relatives and dear friends, saying:

" That I have sad reason to fear my wife's mind is getting out of order ; she is becoming insane on the subject of woman's rights ; but be sure to keep this fact a profound secret —especially, never let Elizabeth hear that I ever intimated such a thing."

I presume this is not the first time an opponent in argument has called his conqueror insane, or lost to reason, simply because his logic was too sound for him to grapple with, and the will of the accuser was too obstinate to yield, when conscientiously convinced.

But it certainly is more honorable and manly, to accuse him of insanity to his face, than it is to thus secretly plot against him an imprisonable offence, without giving him the least chance for self-defense.

Again, I visited Hon. Gerrit Smith, of Peterborough, New York, about three years before this secret plot culminated, to get light on this subject of woman's rights, as I had great confidence in the deductions of his noble, capacious mind ; and here I found my positions were each, and all, indorsed most fully by him. Said he :

" Mrs. Packard, it is high time that you assert your rights, there is no other way for you to live a Christian life with such a man."

And as I left, while he held my hand in his, he remarked :

" You may give my love to Mr. Packard, and say to him, if he is as developed a man as I consider his wife to be a woman, I should esteem it an honor to form his acquaintance."

So it appears that Mr. Smith did not consider my views on this subject as in conflict either with reason or common sense.

Again, his physician. Dr. Fordice Rice. of Cazenovia, New York, to whom I opened my whole mind on this subject, said to me in conclusion:

"I can unravel the whole secret of your family trouble. Mr. Packard is a monomaniac on the treatment of woman. I don't see how you have ever lived with so unreasonable a man."

I replied, "Doctor, I can live with any man—for I will never quarrel with any one, especially a man, and much less with my husband. I can respect Mr. Packard enough, notwithstanding, to do him good all the days of my life, and no evil do I desire to do him; and moreover, I would not exchange him for any man I know of, even if I could do so, simply by turning over my hand; for I believe he is just the man God appointed from all eternity to be my husband. Therefore, I am content with my appointed portion and lot of conjugal happiness."

Again. It was only about four years before I was kidnapped, that Mr. O. S. Fowler, the great Phrenologist, examined his head, and expressed his opinion of his mental condition in nearly these words:

"Mr. Packard, you are losing your mind—your faculties are all dwindling—your mind is fast running out—in a few years you will not even know your own name, unless your tread-mill habits are broken up. Your mind now is only working like an old worn out horse in a tread-mill."

Thus our differences of opinion can be accounted for on scientific principles. Here we see his sluggish, conservative temperament, rejecting light, which costs any effort to obtain or use—clinging, serf-like to the old paths, as with a death grasp—while my active, radical temperament, calls for light to bear me onward and upward, never satisfied until all available means are faithfully used to reach a more progressive state.

Now comes the question. Is activity and progression in

knowledge and intelligence, an indication of a sane, natural condition, or is it an unnatural, insane indication ?

And is a stagnant, torpid, and retrogressive state of mentality, a natural or an unnatural condition—a sane, or an insane state ?

In our mental states we simply grew apart, instead of together. He was dwindling, dying—I was living, growing, expanding.

And this natural development of intellectual power in me, seemed to arouse this morbid feeling of jealousy towards me, lest I outshine him. That is, it stimulated his monomania into exercise, by determining to annihilate or crush the victim in whose mental and moral magnetism he felt so uneasy and dissatisfied with himself.

I have every reason to believe he ever regarded me as a model wife, and model mother and housekeeper. He often made this remark to me :

"I never knew a woman who I think could equal you in womanly virtues."

While on this recruiting tour, I made it my home for several weeks at Mr. David Fields's, who married my adopted sister, then living in Lyons, New York. I made his wife my confidant of my family trials, to a fuller degree than I ever had to any other human being, little dreaming or suspecting that she was noting my every word and act, to detect if possible, some insane manifestations.

But to her surprise, eleven weeks observation failed to develop the first indication of insanity.

The reason she was thus on the alert, was, that my arrival was preceded by a letter from Mr. Packard, saying his wife was insane, and urged her to regard all my representations of family matters as insane statements. Then he added:

"Now, Mrs. Field, I must require of you one thing, and that is, that you burn this letter as soon as you have read it; don't

even let your husband see it at all, or know that you have had
a letter from me, and by all means, keep this whole subject a
profound secret from Elizabeth."

My sister, true to Mr. Packard's wishes, burned this letter,
and buried the subject entirely in oblivion.

But when she heard that I was incarcerated in an Asylum,
then in view of all she did know, and in view of what she did
not know, she deeply suspected there was foul play in the
transaction, and felt it to be her duty to tell her husband all
she knew.

He fully indorsed her suspicions, and they both undertook
to defend me, when she received a most insulting and abusive
letter from Mr. Packard, wherein he, in the most despotic
manner, tried to brow-beat her into silence.

Many tears did this devoted sister shed in secret over this
letter and my sad fate—as this letter revealed Mr. Packard's
true character to her in an unmasked state.

"Oh, how could that dear, kind woman live with such a
man!" was her constant thought.

Nerved and strengthened by her husband's advice, she determined to visit me in the Asylum, and, if possible, obtain
a personal interview.

She did so. She was admitted to my room. There she
gave me the first tidings I ever heard of that letter. While
at the Asylum, my attendants, amongst others, asked her
this question:

"Mrs. Field, can you tell us why such a lady as Mrs. Packard, is shut up in this Asylum? We have never seen the least
exhibition of insanity in her." And one in particular said,
"I saw her the first day she was entered, and she was then
just the same quiet, perfect lady, you see her to be to-day—
now do tell us why she is here?"

"It is because her husband is a villain! and if ever there
was a man who deserved to be hung it is Mr. Packard! I

am not a defender of capital punishment, yet I do say Mr. Packard ought to be hung, if any one ever ought to be!"

In my opinion, sister would have come nearer the truth, had she said he ought to be treated just as he is treating his wife —as a Monomaniac.

And I hope I shall be pardoned, if I give utterance to brother's indignant feelings, in his own words, for the language, although strong, does not conflict with Christ's teaching or example.

Among the pile of letters above alluded to, which Mr. Packard left accidentally in my room, was one from this Mr. Field, which seemed to be an answer to one Mr. Packard wrote to him, wherein it seemed he had been calling Mr. Field to account for having heard that he had called him a "devil," and demanded of him satisfaction, if he had done so; for Mr. Field makes reply:

"I do believe men are possessed with devils now-a-days, as much as they were in Christ's days, and I believe too that some are not only possessed with one devil, but even seven devils, and I believe *you are the man!*"

I never heard of his denying the charge as due Mr. Field afterwards!

From my own observations in an Insane Asylum, I am fully satisfied that Mr. Field is correct in his premises, and I must also allow that he has a right of opinion in its application.

Looking from these various stand-points, it seems to me self-evident, that this Great Drama is a woman's-right struggle. From the commencement to its present stage of development, this one insane idea seems to be the backbone of the rebellion.

A married woman has no rights which her husband is bound to respect!

While he simply defended his insane dogma as an opinion only, no one had the least right to call him a monomaniac;

8

but when this insane idea became a practical one, then, and only till then, had we any right to call him an insane person.

Now, if the course he has taken with me is not insanity—that is, an unreasonable course, I ask, what is insanity?

Now let this great practical truth be for one moment considered, namely, all that renders an earth-life desirable—all the inalienable rights and privileges of one developed, moral, and accountable, sensitive being, lie wholly suspended on the arbitrary will of this intolerant man, or monomaniac.

No law, no friend, no logic can defend me in the least, legally, from this despotic, cruel power; for the heart which controls this will has become, as it respects his treatment of me, "without understanding, a covenant breaker, without natural affection, implacable, unmerciful."

And let another truth also be borne in mind, namely, that this one man stands now as a fit representative of all that class in society, and God grant it may be found to be a very small class! who claim that the subjection of the wife, instead of the protection of the wife, is the true law of marriage.

This marriage law of subjection has now culminated, so that it has become a demonstrated fact, that its track lies wholly in the direction of usurpation.

And therefore this track, upon which so many devoted, true women, have taken a through or life ticket, is one which the American Government ought to guard and protect by legal enactments; so that such a drama as mine cannot be again legally tolerated under the flag of our protective Government.

God grant! that this one mute appeal of stubborn fact, may be sufficient to nerve up the woman protectors of our manly Government to guard us, in some manner against woman's greatest foe—the women subjectors of society.

It may be proper here to add the result of this recruiting tour. After being absent eleven weeks from my home, and this being the first time I had left my husband during all my

married life, longer than one week's time, I returned to my
home, to receive as cordial and as loving a welcome as any wife
could desire.

Indeed, it seemed to me, that the home of my husband's
heart had become " empty, swept and garnished," during my
absence, and that the foul spirits of usurpation had left this
citadel, as I fondly hoped, forever.

Indeed, I felt that I had good reason to hope that my logic
had been calmly and impassionately digested and indorsed,
during my absence, so that now this merely practical recognition of my womanly rights, almost instantly moved my forgiving heart, not only to extend to him unasked, my full and free
forgiveness for the past, but all this abuse seemed to be seek
ing to find its proper place in the grave of forgetful oblivion.

This radical transformation in the bearing of my husband
towards me, allowing me not only the rights and privileges of
a junior partner in the family firm, but also such a liberal
portion of manly expressed love and sympathy, as caused my
susceptible heart of affection fairly to leap for joy.

Indeed, I could now say, what I could never say in truth
before, I am happy in my husband's love—happy in simply
being treated as a true woman deserves to be treated—with
love and confidence.

All the noblest, purest sensibilities of woman's sympathetic
nature find in this, her native element, room for full expan-
sion and growth, by stimulating them into a natural, healthful exercise.

It is one of the truths of God's providential events, that the
three last years of married life were by far the happiest I ever
spent with Mr. Packard. So open and bold was I in this
avowal, during these three happy years, that my correspondence of those days is radiant with this truth.

And it was not three months, and perhaps not even two
months previous to my being kidnapped, that I made a verbal

declaration of this fact, in Mr. Packards' presence, to Deacon Dole, his sister's husband, in these words:

The interests of the Bible-class had been our topic of con versation, when I had occasion to make this remark:

" Brother, don't you think Mr. Packard is remarkably tolerant to me these days, in allowing me to bring my radical views before your class? And don't you think he is changing as fast as we can expect, considering his conservative organization? We cannot, of course, expect him to keep up with my radical temperament. I think we shall make a man of him yet!"

Mr. Packard laughed outright, and replied:

" Well, wife, I am glad you have so good an opinion of me. I hope I shall not disappoint your expectations!"

But, alas! where is he now? Oh, the dreadful demon of bigotry was allowed to enter and take possession of this once garnished house, through the entreaties, and persuasions, and threats, of his Deacon Smith, and his perverted sister, Mrs. Sybil Dole.

These two spirits united, were stronger than his own, and they overcame him, and took from him all his manly armor so that the demon he let in " brought with him seven other spirits more wicked than himself, and they enter in and dwell there " still; so that I sadly fear " the last state of that man will be worse than the first."

I saw and felt the danger of the vortex into which his sister and deacon were dragging him, and I tried to save him, with all the logic of love and pure devotion to his highest and best interests; but all in vain.

Never shall I forget this fatal crisis. When just three weeks before he kidnapped me, I sat alone with him in his study, and while upon his lap, with my arms encircling his neck, and my briny cheek pressed against his own, I begged of him to be my protector, as delineated in the first volume.

From this fatal evening all appeals to his reason and

humanity have been worse than fruitless. They have only served to aggravate his maddened feelings, and goad him on to greater deeds of desperation.

Like Nebuchadnezzar, his reason is taken from him on this one subject; and unrestrained, maddened resentment fills his depraved soul—his manliness is dead! Is he not a Monomaniac?

CHAPTER XXI.

Strong Language an Appropriate Drapery for Reformers.

I acknowledge that truth is stranger than fiction ; and also that strong language is the only appropriate drapery in which some truths can be clothed.

For example, the only appropriate drapery to clothe a lie in, is the strong language of lie or liar; not misrepresentation, a mistake, a slip of the tongue, a deception, an unintentional error, and so forth.

And for unreasonable, and inhuman, and criminal acts, the appropriate drapery is, Insane acts ; and an usurpation of human rights and an abuse of power over the defenseless, is appropriately clothed by the term, Despotism.

One who defends his creed or party by improper and abusive means, is a Bigot.

One who is impatient and unwilling to endure, and will not hear the utterance of opinions in conflict with his own, without persecution of his opponent, is Intolerant; and this is an appropriate word to use in describing such manifestations.

A person under extreme physical torture gives utterance to strong expressions, indicating extreme anguish. Have we, on this account, any reason or right to call him insane? So a person in extreme spiritual or mental agony, has a right to express his feelings in language corresponding to his condition, and we have no right to call him insane for doing so.

Upon a calm and candid review of these scenes, from my present stand-point, I maintain that the indignant feelings which I still cherish towards Mr. Packard, and towards Dr.

McFarland, for their treatment of me, are not only natural, sane feelings, but also Christian feelings. For Christ taught us, both by his teachings and example, that we ought to be angry with sin, and even hate it, with as marked a feeling as we loved good. "I, the Lord, hate evil." And so should we.

But at the same time we should not sin, by carrying this feeling so far as to desire to revenge the wrong-doer, or punish him ourselves, for then we go too far to exercise the feeling of forgiveness towards him, even if he should repent. We are not then following Christ's directions, "Be ye angry and sin not."

Now I am not conscious of ever cherishing one revengeful feeling towards my persecutors; while, at the same time, I have prayed to God, most fervently, that he would inflict a just punishment upon them for their sins against me, if they could not be brought to repent without. For my heart has ever yearned to forgive them, from the first to the last, on this gospel condition.

I think our Government has been called to exercise the same kind of indignation towards those conspirators who have done all they can do to overthrow it; and yet, they stand ready to forgive them, and restore them to their confidence, on the condition of practical repentance.

And I say further, that it would have been wrong and sinful for our Government to have withheld this expression of their resentment towards them, and let them crush it out of existence, without trying to defend itself. I say it did right in defending itself with a resistance corresponding to the attack.

So I, in trying to defend myself against this conspiracy against my personal liberty, have only acted on the self-defensive principle. Neither have I ever aggressed on the rights of others in my self-defense. I have simply defended my own rights.

In my opinion, it would be no more unreasonable to accuse the inmates of " Libby Prison " with insanity, because they expressed their resentment of the wrongs they were enduring in " strong language," than it is to accuse me of insanity for doing the same thing while in my prison.

For prison life is terrible under any circumstances. But to be confined amongst raving maniacs, for years in succession, is horrible in the extreme.

For myself, I should not hesitate one moment which to choose, between a confinement in an insane asylum as I was, or being burned at the stake. Death, under the most aggravated forms of torture, would now be instantly chosen by me, rather than life in an insane asylum.

And whoever is disposed to call this " strong language," I say, let them try it for themselves as I did, and then let them say whether the expressisn is any stronger than the case justifies. For until they have tried it, they can never imagine the horrors of the maniac's ward in Jacksonville Insane Asylum.

And here I will add, I do not write books merely to tickle the fancy, and lull the guilty conscience into a treacherous sleep, whose waking is death. Nor do I write to secure notoriety or popularity.

But I do write to defend the cause of human rights ; and these rights can never be vindicated, unless these usurpations be exposed to public view, so that an appeal can be made to the public conscience, on the firm basis of unchangeable truth— the truth of facts as they do actually exist.

I know there is a class, but I fondly hope they are the minority, who will resist even this solid basis—who would not believe the truth should Christ himself be its medium of utterance and defense.

But shall I on this account withhold the truth, lest such cavilers reject it, and trample it under foot, and then turn and rend me with the stigma of "Insanity," because I told them the simple truth?

By no means? For truth is not insanity; and though it may for a time be crushed to the earth, it will rise again with renovated strength and power.

Neither is strong and appropriate language insanity. But on the contrary, I maintain that strong language is the only suitable and "appropriate drapery for a reformer" to clothe his thoughts in, notwithstanding the very unsuitable and inappropriate stigma of "Insanity," which has always been the reformer's lot to bear for so doing in all past ages, as well as the present age.

Even Christ himself bore this badge of a Reformer, simply because he uttered truths which conflicted with the established religion of the church of his day. And shall I repine because I am called insane for the same reason?

It was the spirit of bigotry which led the intolerant Jews to stigmatize Christ as a madman, because he expressed opinions differing from their own. And it is this same spirit of bigotry which has been thus intolerant towards me.

In my opinion bigotry is the most implacable, unreasonable, unmerciful feeling that can possess the human soul.

And it is my fervent prayer that the eyes of this Government may be opened to see wherein the laws do not now protect or shield married woman from this same extreme manifestation of it, such as it has been my sad lot to endure, as the result of this legalized Persecution.

CHAPTER XXII.

Testimonials.

That principle of self-defense, which depends wholly on certificates and testimonials, instead of the principle of right, truth and justice, is not able to survive the shock which the revelation of truth brings against it.

A lie, however strongly fortified by testimonials and certificates, can never be transformed into a truth. Neither can the truth, however single and isolated, and alone, be its condition, ever be transformed into a lie, nor crushed out of existence.

No, the truth will stand alone and unsupported. Its own weight, simply, gives it firmness to resist all shocks brought against it, to produce its overthrow. Like the house built upon a rock, it needs no props, no certificates to sustain it. Storms of the bitterest persecution may beat piteously upon it, but they cannot overthrow it, for its foundation is the rock of eternal truth.

But a lie is like the house built upon the sand. While it does stand, it needs props or certificates on all sides to sustain it. And it cannot even resist the effect of a ventilating breeze upon it, for it must and will fall, with all its accumulated props, before one searching investigation; and the more props it has so much the more devastation is caused by its overthrow.

In view of the facts and principles upon which this narrative is based, I feel sure that the array of sophisms which this conspiracy may attempt to marshal against it, will only be like arguing the sun out of the heavens at noonday.

And although my cause, being based in eternal truth, does not depend upon certificates and testimonials to sustain it, and stands therefore in no need of them; yet, as they are sometimes called for, as a confirmation of my statements, I have asked for just such testimonials as the following gentlemen felt self-moved to give me.

I needed no testimonials while prosecuting my business in Illinois, for the facts of the case were so well known there by the papers reporting my trial so generally. I needed no other passport to the confidence of the public.

But when I came to Boston to commence my business in Massachusetts, being an entire stranger there, I found the need of some credentials or testimonials in confirmation of my strange and novel statements. And it was right and proper, under such circumstances, that I should have them.

I therefore wrote to Judge Boardman and Hon. S. S. Jones, my personal friends, in Illinois, and told them the difficulty I found in getting my story believed, and asked them to send me anything in the form of a certificate, that they in their judgment felt disposed to send me, that might help me in surmounting this obstacle.

Very promptly did these gentlemen respond to my request, and sent me the following testimonials, which were soon printed in several of the Boston papers, with such editorials accompanying them, as gave them additional weight and influence by securing for me the confidence of the public, in the revelations I had to make in this dark conspiracy.

Judge Boardman is an old and distinguished Judge in Illinois, receiving, as he justly merits, the highest esteem and confidence of his cotemporaries, as a distinguished scholar, an eminent Judge, and a practical Christian.

Mr. Jones is a middle aged man, of the same stamp as the Judge, receiving proof of the esteem in which he is held by his cotemporaries, by having been for successive years a member of the Legislature of that State. He was in that position when he sent me his certificate.

Judge Boardman's Testimonial.

To all persons who would desire to give sympathy and encouragement to a most worthy but persecuted woman!

The undersigned, formerly from the State of Vermont, now an old resident of the State of Illinois, would most respectfully and fraternally certify and represent:

That he has been formerly and for many years, associated with the legal profession in Illinois, and is well known in the north-eastern part of said State. That in the duties of his profession and in the offices he has filled, he has frequently investigated, judicially, and otherwise, cases of insanity. That he has given considerable attention to medical jurisprudence, and studied some of the best authors on the subject of insanity; has paid great attention to the principles and philosophy of mind, and therefore would say, with all due modesty, that he verily believes himself qualified to give an opinion entitled to respectful consideration, on the question of the sanity or insanity of any person with whom he may be acquainted.

That he is acquainted with Mrs. E. P. W. Packard, and verily believes her not only sane, but that she is a person of very superior endowments of mind and understanding, naturally possessing an exceedingly well-balanced organization, which, no doubt, prevented her from becoming insane, under the persecution, incarceration, and treatment she has received.

That Mrs. Packard has been the victim of religious bigotry, purely so, without a single circumstance to alleviate the darkness of the transaction! A case worthy of the palmiest days of the inquisition!!

The question may be asked, how this could happen, especially in Northern Illinois?

To which I answer that the common law prevails here, the same as in other States, where this law has not been modified or set aside by the statute laws, which gives the legal custody of the wife's person, into the hands of the husband, and therefore, a wife can only be released from oppression, or even from imprisonment by her husband, by the legal complaint of herself, or some one in her behalf, before the proper judicial authorities, and a hearing and decision in the case; as was finally had in Mrs. Packard's case, she having been in the first place, taken by force, by her husband, and sent to the Insane Hospital, without any opportunity to make complaint, or without any hearing or investigation.

But how could the Superintendent of the Insane Hospital be a party to so great a wrong?

Very easily answered, without necessarily impeaching his honesty, when we consider that her alleged insanity was on religious subjects; her husband a minister of good standing in his denomination, and the Superintendent sympathizing with him, in all probability, in religious doctrine and belief, supposed, of course, that she was insane. She was legally sent to him by the authority of her husband as insane; and Mrs. Packard had taught doctrines similar to the Unitarians and Universalists and many radical preachers; and which directly opposed the doctrine her husband taught, and the doctrine of the Church to which he and Mrs. Packard belonged; the argument was, that, of course, the woman must be crazy!!

And as she persisted in her liberal sentiments, the Superintendent persisted in considering that she was insane!

However, whether moral blame should attach to the Superintendent and Trustees of the Insane Hospital, or not, in this transaction, other than prejudice and learned ignorance; it may now be seen, from recent public inquiries and suggestions, that it is quite certain, that the laws, perhaps in all the States in relation to the insane, and their confinement and treatment, have been much abused by the artful and cunning, who have incarcerated their relatives for the purpose of getting hold of their property; or for difference of opinion as to our state and condition in the future state of existence, or religious belief.

The undersigned would further state : That the published account of Mrs. Packard's trial on the question of her sanity, is no doubt perfectly reliable and correct. That the judge before whom she was tried, is a man of learning and ability, and high standing in the judicial circuit in which he presides. That Mrs. Packard is a person of strict integrity and truthfulness, whose character is above reproach.

That a history of her case after the trial was published in the daily papers in Chicago, and in the newspapers generally, in the State ; arousing at the time a public feeling of indignation against the author of her Persecution, and sympathy for her ; that nothing has transpired since to overthrow or set aside the verdict of popular opinion ; that it is highly probable that the proceedings in this case, so far as the officers of the State Hospital for the insane are concerned, will undergo a rigid investigation by the Legislature of the State.

The undersigned understands that Mrs. Packard does not ask pecuniary charity, but that sympathy and paternal assistance which may aid her to obtain and make her own living, she having been left by her husband without any means or property whatever.

All of which is most fraternally and confidently submitted to your kind consideration.   WILLIAM A. BOARDMAN.

Waukegan, Ill., Dec. 3, 1864.

Hon. S. S. Jones' Testimonial.

To a Kind and Sympathizing Public :

"This is to certify, that I am personally acquainted with Mrs. E. P. W. Packard, late an inmate of the Insane Asylum of the State of Illinois. That Mrs. Packard was a victim of a foul and cruel conspiracy I have not a single doubt, and that she is and ever has been as sane as any other person, I verily believe. But I do not feel called upon to assign reasons for my opinion in the premises, as her case was fully investigated before an eminent Judge of our State, and after a full and careful examination she was pronounced sane, and restored to liberty.

Still I repeat, but for the cruel conspiracy against her, she could not have been incarcerated as a lunatic in an asylum.

Whoever reads her full and fair report of her case, will be convinced of the terrible conspiracy that was practiced towards a truly thoughtful and accomplished lady. A Conspiracy! worthy of a demoniac spirit of ages long since passed, and such as we should be loth to believe could be practiced in this enlightened age, did not the records of our court verify its truth.

To a kind and sympathizing public I commend her. The deep and cruel anguish she has had to suffer at the hands of those who should have been her protectors, will, I doubt not, endear her to you, and you will extend to her your kindest sympathy and protection.

Trusting through her much suffering the public will become more enlightened, and that our noble and benevolent institutions—the asylums for the insane—will never become perverted into institutions of cruelty and oppression, and that Mrs. Packard may be the last subject of such a Conspiracy as is revealed in her books, that will ever transpire in this our State of Illinois, or elsewhere.

Very Respectfully,

S. S. Jones."

St. Charles, Ill., Dec. 16, 1864.

Editorial Remarks.

"Assuming, as in view of all the facts it is our duty to do, the correctness of the statements made by Mrs. Packard, two matters of vital importance demand consideration:

1. What have 'the rulers in the church' done about the Persecution? They have not publicly denied the statements; virtually, on the principle that under such extraordinary circumstances silence gives consent, they concede their correctness.

Is the wrong covered up? the guilty party allowed to go unchallenged lest "the cause" suffer by exposure?

If they will explain the matter in a way to exculpate the accused, these columns shall be prompt to do the injured full and impartial justice. We are anxious to know what they have to say in the premises. If Mrs. Packard is insane because she rejects Calvinism, then we are insane, liable to arrest, and to be placed in an insane asylum! We have a personal interest in this matter.

2. Read carefully Judge Boardman's statement as to the bearing of "common law" on Mrs. Pakard's case. If a bad man, hating his wife and wishing to get rid of her, is base enough to fabricate a charge of insanity, and can find two physicians "in regular standing" foolish or wicked enough to give the legal certificate, the wife is helpless! The "common law" places her wholly at the mercy of her brutal lord. Certainly the statute should interfere.

Humanity, not to say Christianity, demands that special enactments shall make impossible such atrocities as are alleged in the case of Mrs. Packard—atrocities which, according to Judge Boardman, can be enacted in the name of "common law."

We trust the case now presented will have at least the effect to incite Legislative bodies to such enactments as will protect women from the possibility of outrages, which, we are led to fear, ecclesiastical bodies had rather cover up, than expose and rebuke to the prejudice of sectarian ends—the 'sacred cause.'"

As I have said, there was a successful effort made in the Massachusetts' Legislature to change the laws in reference to the mode of commitment into Insane Asylums the winter of 1865, and as Hon. S. E. Sewall was my "friend and fellow laborer," as he styles himself, in that movement, I made application to him the next winter, for such a recommend as I might use to aid me in bringing this subject before the Illinois Legislature that winter, for the purpose of getting a change in their laws also. But finding that the Illinois Legislature did not meet that year, I have had no occasion to use it, as I intended. Having it thus on hand, I will add this to the fore going.

Hon. S. E. Sewall's Testimonial.

"I have been acquainted with Mrs. E. P. W. Packard for about a year, I believe. She is a person of great religious feeling, high moral principle, and warm philanthropy. She is a logical thinker, a persuasive speaker, and such an agitator, that she sometimes succeeds where a man would fail. I think she will be very useful in the cause to which she has devoted herself, I mean procuring new laws to protect married women.

I give Mrs. Packard these lines of recommendation, because she has asked for them. I do not think them at all necessary, for she can recommend herself, far better than I can.

S. E. SEWALL."

Boston, November 27, 1865.

Said an honorable gentleman, an eminent lawyer, who thought he understood the character of my books :

"Mrs. Packard, I believe your books will yet be read in our Legislative Halls and in Congress, as a specimen of the highest form of law ever sent to our world, and coming millions will read your history, and bless you as one who was afflicted for humanity's sake."

It must be acknowledged that this intelligent gentleman had some solid basis on which he could defend this extravagant opinion, namely : that God does sometimes employ "the weak things of the world to confound the mighty."

CHAPTER XXIII.

Dangerous to be a Married Woman in Illinois!

One day while in the asylum, after seating himself in my room, Dr. McFarland commenced a conversation by asking this question:

" Mrs. Packard, would it not be natural for me, in order to ascertain what had been your conduct before coming here, to inquire, first of husband, then of parents, then of brothers and sisters, and on their testimony form some opinion of your state ? "

" Yes, naturally you would ; but in my case, these relatives have not seen me for seven years, except brother Samuel, of Batavia, who has visited me only once during that time. And besides, opinions will not convict a criminal. Facts are needed as proof. A murderer is not convicted on opinions, but on facts."

" But insanity is not a crime, but a misfortune, and different kind of evidence is required to prove it. It is a disease, and as physicians detect disease by the irregularities of the physical organization, so they must judge of insanity by the ' views ' they take of things."

" But, Doctor, is not the conduct the index of the mind, and if ' these views ' are not accompanied with irregularities of conduct, ought ' these views ' alone to be treated as evidences of insanity ? "

" Yes, a person may be insane without irregularities of conduct."

" But have we any right to restrain the personal liberty of any one whose conduct shows no irregularities. For instance, should you like to be imprisoned in one of these wards on the simple opinion of some one that you had an insane idea in your head, while at the same time all your duties were being faithfully performed ? ''

He made no reply.

After a silence of a few moments, I added :

" Now, if you, Doctor, or any other individual, will bring forward one act of my own, showing lack of reason in it, I will own you have a right to call me insane.''

After waiting a long time, he said :

" Was it not an insane act for you to fall down stairs, and then to be carried back to your ward ? ''

" That was not *my* act in being carried back to my ward. It was your own act, and my falling down stairs was an accident, caused too, by *your* ungentlemanly interference ; and the object I had in view by asserting my rights, was a rational one, for I had good reasons for doing so.''

" Oh, no, no, the *reasons* are nothing.''

" Yes, they are ; for unless you know the reasons which influence the actions of others, many acts would appear insane, that would not, if we knew the reasons which prompted the act. I asserted my right to my liberty from principle, not from impulse, in compliance with the advice of Gerrit Smith, viz. :

" When you have done all that forbearance, kindness and intelligence can do to right your wrongs, all that is left for you to do is, to ' assert your rights,' kindly, but firmly, and then leave the issue to God.''

After another pause he said :

" What motive, Mrs. Packard, could I have for making you out insane, if I considered you were not ? Would money prompt me to do it ? ''

" No, Doctor, I don't think money has influenced your mind in my case ; but you have so long been in the habit of receiving women on the simple verdict of the opinion of the husband, without proof, that you seem to think there is no necessity of using your own judgment at all in the case. And you do not seem to apprehend the glaring truth of the present day, that woman's most subtle foe is a tyrant husband.

"It is might, not right, that decides the destiny of the married woman.

"You know I am not by any means, the only one you have thus taken in here, to please a cruel husband. You have received many since I have been here, such as Mrs. Wood, Mrs. Miller, Mrs. Kenny, and many others. Indeed Doctor, this fact has become so notorious here, that our attendants echo the remark made by Elizabeth Bonne, the other day, viz. :

'I did once think I would get married; but since I have been here, and seen so many wives brought here by their husbands, when nothing ails them, I am firmly resolved never to venture to marry in Illinois! I can take better care of myself, alone.

"And Doctor, I agree with her in this conclusion :

"It is fatally dangerous to live in Illinois, under such laws, as thus expose the personal liberty of married women."

This kind of married slavery is worse than negro slavery, and it must be abolished before the reign of righteousness prevails.

Resolution is pacific; and I am resolved to secure peace on no principle but justice, freedom and right. With resolution, firm and determined, I am resolved to fight my way through all obstacles to victory—to the *Emancipation of married women!*

I assume that my personal identity is my God-given right, and I claim that this right shall be recognized in the settlement of this great woman question.

None to my knowledge sustain me in my path of self-denying obedience to the cause of "married woman's emancipation." But when the victory is achieved, there will be no lack of voices to chant this triumph. If, while in the hottest of this battle, some of these plaudits could be heard, it would be a help far more needed and welcome than when we have laid off our armor.

But he whom God guards is well guarded. It is the fate of many who seek to do good, to have to resist their friends, and face their foes.

To be God's chosen instrument to raise woman to her proper position is a glorious office, and those who win this crown, must be willing to bear this cross. The public conscience is in motion, and the great moral force my enemies are struggling against is the gospel enforced by conscience, and every energetic act in us adds potency in the moral element by which it is to be moved to action.

Every act of a moral agent influences the entire moral universe.

Each upright act adds to the strength of goodness or righteousness, and every evil act gives additional power to the principle of evil. It is like throwing a stone into a lake, the utmost bounds of which feels the influence of the ripple occasioned by its fall.

As the ocean is made up of drops, so the moral universe is composed of individual moral acts. Good and evil seem now to commingle in this great ocean life promiscuously, and the current of both seem now to alternate with almost equal force.

What is needed is a condensation of the good influences of the universe into one vast gulf stream, sweeping irresistibly through the great ocean of moral life, bearing down all obstacles which evil interposes to its progress. When this gulf stream is once formed and set in motion, its progress will be irresistible throughout the moral universe. God is now at work separating these elements, and the good is to accumulate and condense into one great engine of power for the world's benefit.

CHAPTER XXIV.

Passage of the Personal Liberty Bill in the Illinois Legislature.

Feeling confident that public sentiment was prepared for the passage of a bill for the protection of the Personal Liberty of married women, I left Massachusetts in the winter of 1866, and came to Chicago to organize an effort for this purpose.

With the aid of Judge Bradwell and other legal advisers, I drew up a petition for this object, and spent one week in circulating it among the most prominent and influential men in this city, who kindly allowed me a patient hearing, while demonstrating the absolute necessity of some legislation that would effectually shield the married women of this State against the liability of their suffering from the injustice of the present law as I had done.

And strange as it may seem, I found but one man, among the thirty-six men who signed the petition, who knew that we had so infamous a law on their statute book to be repealed.

The petition was headed by I. N. Arnold, a Congressman, and followed by the Mayor, Aldermen, Judges, Lawyers, Editors, and some members of the Board of Trade, and the Chamber of Commerce, and some of the heaviest merchants and business men of Chicago. These names represented the intelligent, popular element of this city, and were so regarded by the Legislature.

Thanks are here due both to the *Tribune* and the *Times*, for a voluntary editorial which each gave in favor of the object of the petition.

The petitioners expressed the kindest wishes in behalf of the cause, and some advised me to go with it to Governor Ogelsby and get his advice as to the best mode of bringing it before the Legislature, adding with emphasis:

" Governor Ogelsby will aid you in this matter ; if he don't, he isn't the man we think he is."

In accordance with this advice, on arriving in Springfield, I sought the Governor at his residence, and met him in the hall, on his way to his dining-room with his invited guests. Of course, under these circumstances, I could not detain him, and therefore, merely inquired when it would be convenient to give me one half hour for conversation and advice.

He inquired: " What is your business ? "

" In relation to bringing a certain bill before the Legislature."

" What is the object of the bill ? "

" Governor Ogelsby, I cannot explain my business in less time than half an hour : can I be allowed that time or not ? "

" But I wish to know what your bill is about."

" ' Tis about the Asylum at Jacksonville, but I cannot explain without taking you too long from your party."

" Oh, I think that is doing well enough, I am acquainted with Dr. McFarland, and esteem him very highly as my personal friend."

" But, Governor, all I wish now to know is, can I have an interview of half an hour at any future time you may appoint ? "

And while repeating this inquiry the third time, I drew from my pocket my petition, and asked him to please just look at the names appended, and added :

" These men approve of the bill, and desire its passage, and moreover, advised me to lay the subject before the Governor, adding : ' Governor Oglesby will approve of the bill, and aid you in getting it passed, or he isn't the man we think he is.' "

As he glanced over the names and found among them the

leaders of his political party, on whose influence and vote depended, perhaps, his seat in Congress, his tone and manner changed at once, and in a most civil and manly style he unhesitatingly offered to give me the whole hour, between eleven and twelve o'clock the next day, at his office, in the State-House.

Accordingly I met him there, and in the most patient and courteous manner he listened, and not only indorsed my argument in defense of the bill, but also volunteered his advice and assistance to help me in every possible way.

He ordered his Secretary what to write, and gave it to his porter to take with me to the door of the Representatives Hall where I remained, while he delivered the message to Mr. Baldwin, who soon appeared at the door, saying, as he looked at me :

"I have a message from the Governor to meet Mrs. Packard at his office, at once."

He accompanied me back to the Governor's office, where the Governor explained why he had summoned him, and then referred him to me to explain the object as I had to him, and suggested at the same time the propriety of having several others to meet in his office at three o'clock in the afternoon, and there consult upon what would be considered the best course to be pursued to bring about the desired result.

When we met at the hour appointed, the Governor ordered all present to leave the office until we had arranged matters to our mutual satisfaction.

This delegation invited me to bring the subject before the members in the library room, at seven o'clock, the following Friday evening.

Printed posters were put up around the State-House, independent of any knowledge or agency of my own, notifying the Legislature of this appointment and inviting their attendance.

The Governor kindly offered me his office as a place where I could meet the members at any future time.

I wrote out my argument and read it to a very respectable number of members at the time appointed.

After expressing their views of the importance of the subject, they advised, that I meet the Judiciary Committee and confer with them.

This Committee approved of the object and advised that I draft a bill to meet the case, and meet them again to test its merits.

Senator Ward, of Chicago, very kindly drafted the bill for me, which he said was incomplete, but might serve as a basis for action. After hearing it read, the Committee asked if it suited me. I told them:

" Gentlemen, it does not—it is incomplete."

" What change do you wish made ? "

" It needs a penalty attached, for as it now stands 'tis merely legislative advice."

They then added a penalty of fine and imprisonment for admitting a patient into the asylum without a jury trial.

" Is there anything now wanting ? "

" There is no time appointed for the trial of the inmates of the asylum."

They specified sixty days from the passage of the bill.

" Is there anything more ? "

" There is no tribunal before whom they shall be tried."

" The State's Attorney should fill this place."

" Is there anything more ? "

" No, Gentlemen, the bill suits me now."

" Then we will recommend its passage as it is."

This was the courteous manner in which this cause of woman was treated by this honorable body.

And here it is due the cause of " Woman's Rights " that I should just express the sentiment into which this gentlemanly

9

conduct educated me—viz.: That it is the honest intention of
the Legislation of the present day to protect the rights of
woman as well as their own rights. And it is not the fault
of these law-makers that they find so many relics of barbarism to be repealed by legislation, in order to restore to married woman the legal identity which the old common law
denies her.

It does not seem that woman need become a legislator in
order that suitable and just laws be made for her protection ;
for man, being the natural protector of woman, furnishes a
principle in his nature to appeal to, in behalf of " Woman's
Rights," which is not found in woman.

And for this reason, if I had a good cause to defend in behalf of woman, I should feel more assurance of success in
presenting these claims to a man legislature than to a woman
legislature

Woman was made *to be* protected by man.

Therefore it would seem that the order society has already
established, in making man the legislator and executor of the
laws, harmonizes with nature, as God has made it.

All that seems to be needed, is an appeal to the intelligence
of our present law makers, by convincing arguments, showing
wherein her wrongs consist, and her rights are invaded, in
order to secure protection for her *in her sphere, as a woman,*
not as a man.

Again, the Government ought to be a power that can
defend itself and others also. But woman can do neither.
Therefore is she incapacitated by nature to be, herself, the
Government, while man is thus capacitated.

Again, at first view, it would seem, that women who hold
property ought to have a voice in relation to the taxes imposed
upon it. But here injustice is by no means the certain or
inevitable result, since, in most cases, woman being the
minority property holder, man votes upon her no taxes which

his own property is not bound for, so that he is no more unjust to her, than he is to himself in this respect.

If our present system is in harmony with nature, it is better to sustain and perpetuate it, rather than to try to supplant it by one in conflict with nature, for this attempt must, ere long, prove fruitless, as nature is destined to be the final conqueror in all cases.

And should this " Woman's Rights " movement prevail so far as to secure for women the ballot, together with its responsibilities, it is my opinion, that the practical workings of this system would prove to be a detriment not only to woman's own interests, but also that of society at large.

For there is a possibility that a class of women might be led to become so eager in their aspirations for political office, to which the ballot would render them eligible, as to lead them to regard the office of maternity as secondary in importance. Or in other words, such might be led to feel that it would be a greater honor to fill some office at Congress than it would be to fill the office of maternity.

Whereas in reality there is no higher office a woman can fill than that of maternity.

But with this temptation before them, this class might be induced to leave their children to the care of Bridgets while they go to Washington to make laws. And if our daughters should be induced thus to pervert these noble aspirations of womanhood, I fear future Congressmen might become even more corrupt than those of the present day, for want of a mother's judicious and effective training.

CHAPTER XXV.

Opposition to the Bill.

Nothing good can be accomplished without opposition, and sometimes, the more sensible, reasonable and consistent, the more virulent, unreasonable, fierce and determined this opposition.

Although so desirable and important as to secure the co-operation of every unbiased mind, yet, self-interest in Doctor McFarland, Superintendent of Jacksonville Asylum, prompted him to organize an opposition, whose determination it was to defeat the passage of this bill.

For this purpose he used to meet the members at the hotels and boarding-houses where they congregated, and, in these secret sessions, endeavor to convince his listeners that I was an insane person, and therefore it was unsafe and foolish for them to be influenced by my logic or statements in relation to the bill.

Some, whom he thus psychologized into his opinions, used their influence with others to treat my business not only with indifference, but also with open opposition in casting their votes.

This opposition made lobbying on my part an imperative necessity.

I therefore went round to these boarding-houses, and asked permission of the landlords to meet the members at his house, in his parlor, after tea, and also to introduce me to them.

This favor being cheerfully granted, I thus had the opportunity of a personal interview with many of them, which was faithfully improved, by calling their personal attention to the intrinsic merits of the bill.

At these interviews a two-fold object was secured, viz., conviction in their minds of my sanity, and also a secret determination to uphold and vote for the bill upon its own intrinsic merits.

Their manly sympathy was also enlisted in my cause by Dr. McFarland's very unjust attack upon my reputation; for it became known that Dr. McFarland had refused my request for admission into his " star chamber," for the purpose of answering personally to the charges he was there bringing against me.

Over the minds of these members with whom I had these interviews, I had no further fear of Dr. McFarland's influence. And such as I could not meet, I sometimes employed some outside influence to work upon by proxy, for me.

Besides this, the Chicago *Tribune* and the Springfield *Journal* and *State Register*, all helped me, by allowing their columns to be used in setting forth the necessity of such legislation, by my anonymous articles on this subject.

These articles called the opposition party into this field, which was fearlessly met by a still plainer array of facts, as challenged contradiction. Their sophistry and misrepresentation were so entirely exposed by the strong argument of truth and facts, that even a distinguished Judge, who undertook to defend Dr. McFarland's interests, retired ingloriously from the field, like a vanquished foe before the pursuer.

This public controversy between truth and falsehood, logic and sophistry, drew public attention towards the bill, which was constantly growing in favor with the enlightened public. This rallying force of public sentiment accelerated the progress of the bill, which was still on its slow, but sure passage.

In the House it passed its third reading by only six voting against it.

The Senate Judiciary took it through its second reading, without hesitation, and here it lodged, and I could do nothing effectual to bring it forward to its third reading.

I feared for its destiny, knowing that Dr. McFarland had several strong, firm friends in that body, and there seemed to be some occult influence at work against it, such as I could not ferret out.

Still I waited and watched, paying my board in Springfield during the entire term, for this sole purpose.

At length, on the Monday previous to the last Thursday of the session, I was told the bill had passed the third reading in the "omnibus" with other bills.

Rejoiced as I was at this announcement, for some unknown cause, I could not help feeling a little incredulous about this statement, and, acting upon this impression, I engaged one of the employees at the House to look and see if the bill was really passed.

Soon he returned with the sad intelligence that:

"The Personal Liberty Bill is missing! The number of the bill, 608, is scratched out, and the bill itself is nowhere to be found."

This was Tuesday evening, and only one day and a-half remained of the session, in which to hunt up the bill and secure its passage; or if lost, to draft a new one in its stead, and get it through both houses again, before Thursday noon. As the case demanded the most prompt and efficient action, I determined to go to work myself, directly in its behalf, and lose not one moment for my work to be done by proxy.

Early Wednesday morning, I called upon Mr. Bushnell, the chairman of the Judiciary of the Senate, at the "Leland House," and told him of the condition of the bill.

He replied he was too full of business to render me any assistance in this emergency, and he feared I should find this to be the case with all the other Senators; still, he sincerely hoped I might succeed in my efforts in finding the bill and in getting it passed.

I then called at the room of Lieutenant-Governor Bross, the

Speaker of the Senate, and laid the case before him, and although he expressed an interest in the subject, and a warm sympathy for me in my troubles, yet, said he:

" I can do nothing for your bill. You must go the Senators for help."

" Yes, you can, Governor Bross. You can be a little patient when it is up and not hurry it upon the table, as you sometimes seem to do with other bills in the rush of business. Now, you will favor my bill in this way, won't you ? "

He smiled at my earnest persistency, and I left, with his hearty good wish that I might succeed.

Finding by this time that the Senators had gone to the State-House, I accordingly followed them to the Senate chamber, which was soon crowded with Senators and lobbyists.

The Senators were generally strangers to me, as almost all I had interviews with were House members. I therefore sought the chairman, Mr. Bushnell, and asked him to please introduce me to the member nearest him, which he kindly did.

I then in as few words as possible, told him how the Married Woman's Bill was imperilled, and then appealed directly to his manliness in its behalf.

Then came the usual demonstration of a willingness to help, if the rush of business did not render it impossible.

But instead of leaving him, as I had the speaker, Governor Bross, with good wishes merely, I exacted a promise that he would not only vote for the bill if brought forward, but defend it also, if necessary.

I then asked him to please introduce me to his next neighbor, which he did, and I labored with him in like manner, until I had secured his promise of honor that he would both vote for and defend the bill, if necessary.

Then he introduced me to the next, and so on, until I had spoken to fifteen Senators, and secured a promise from each to vote for my bill, and defend it if necessary.

From five of these I obtained an additional promise that they each would " call up the bill," hoping that among the five, one might possibly find an opportunity and remember so to do.

But now my lobbying was abruptly terminated, by a call of order from the Speaker, to commence business.

In retiring to the gallery, I was compelled to elbow my way through the crowd of lobbyists on the outside, who I saw were watching my movements on the inside among the members, with such intense curiosity, that a single glance in that direction would almost confound me, when it was accompanied with the thought:

" They are wondering if that is a sane woman lobbying in this style among the Senators, doing what no lady was ever found doing before her ! "

The instantaneous response which I found myself mentally making, was:

" I will not quail before your suspicions. I am engaged in a good work, and it shall be done, in spite of this bugbear of insanity in my path ; for the Personal Liberty of all the Married Women in Illinois is in imminent danger, and they know it not ! "

The agitation my movements had aroused, caused, as it would seem, alarm in the breast of the thief, who had stolen my bill, lest his detection might be the result, for, when the bill was called up, with the inquiry as to where it was, it was found on hand, and produced by the clerk, without delay, or farther investigation.

Thus in the great rush of closing up the large amount of unfinished business on hand the culprit escaped detection for the present ; but his crime is chronicled upon the page of the recording angel's book to be revealed in God's appointed time to his shame and confusion.

Finding the bill safe, the motion was made and carried, that it be acted upon in its proper time when the house bills would come up for action.

Hundreds of bills being on hand to dispose of before noon of the following day, the principal business of that day seemed to be, to " kill these bills " as fast as possible, as the most summary way of disposing of them.

The gallery was crowded with anxious lobbyists, who, like myself, were watching with, perhaps, equal solicitude the fate of their own bills, and as this wholesale carnage seemed to thicken and deepen with every passing hour, disappointment seemed everywhere to prevail, as those whose bills were passed, were only the rare exceptions, while the murdered ones were the rule.

The agitation of my bill became so general that the afternoon session found the front gallery full of ladies, who were in sympathy with me, for the fate of the bill for the protection of the personal liberty of their own sex.

As the evening approached, and the " house bills " were not called for, we began to feel that if they were, we could expect nothing more than to see it share the now almost universal fate of being " killed," like the others.

As its fate became momentarily more and more doubtful, in an impatient and despairing spirit, all the ladies left, one after another, leaving me alone, with only a few gentlemen lobbyists, as their dinner hour had arrived, and the evening lamps were being lighted.

At this juncture, amid the roar and confusion of battle, as it seemed to me, the " House Bills ! " were called for.

Now the hungry tired Senators, more impatient than ever for despatch, pursued their murderous business upon these bills faster than ever before. Even before finishing the reading of the titles of some bills, the motion to " Lay it on the table ! " was made and carried.

My anxiety had already become so intense that, when the

"Personal Liberty Bill!" was called out, amid the din of this confused battle, my heart almost stopped its pulsations, so keenly did I realize the importance of the present moment.

The confused tumult slightly abated, and instead of the monotonous response, "Lay it on the table!" was heard :

"Read the bill!"

This the clerk commenced doing, when he hesitated—and remarked :

"There is no 'Enacting Clause' to this bill!"

Hon. Murry McConnell, of Jacksonville, Dr. McFarland's strongest ally, cried out :

"Lay the bill on the table!—We have no time to attend to bills presented to us in that condition—and it is of no more use than so much white paper if it is passed as it is."

There was silence in the Senate!

No one spoke—and the bill was passed to Mr. Bushnell, the chairman of the Judiciary, who, with extended hand, asked to look at it, doubtless feeling chagrined that the bill had passed through his hands, and been recommended, while in that defective condition.

While he stood, looking in silent amazement at the bill, this strange, solemn silence was at last broken by Governor Bross, the Speaker, remarking :

"Perhaps the bill could be returned to the House, from whence it originated, and the 'Enacting Clause' be inserted, and we yet pass the bill."

The motion was at once made and seconded that, the bill be returned to the House from whence it had originated, and get the "Enacting Clause" inserted. This motion quickly passed, and the bill was put into the hands of the proper officer to be carried to the House, and the Senate in the mean time, resumed their old business—"Killing Bills."

The message reached the House just as the motion to adjourn was being made.

But when this message from the Senate was read, Mr. Conkling, the chairman of the Judiciary in the House, who, like Mr. Bushnell, seemed to feel reproved by passing on so incomplete a document, at once suggested that they suspend the motion to adjourn until this business was attended to.

This being carried, he motioned that the clerk be instructed to insert the " Enacting Clause," and we pass the bill.

And here perhaps it is proper to state that in order that no means be left unemployed to secure the passage of the bill, I had spent the entire recess at noon in explaining to this chairman, and as many other members of the House as I could meet, how our bill had been stolen or lost. Mr. Conkling had remarked, very sympathetically :

" I will do all I can for you, but I fear 'tis too late to save it now."

And now lest the defeat of the Bill might be attributed to his carelessness or oversight, he became earnest and valiant in its defense.

The bill again passed its first, second and third reading, and the vote was again taken by yeas and nays. This time all voted for it, including the six who before voted against it.

The messenger at once returned to the Senate with the message that:

" The House have inserted the 'Enacting Clause,' and passed the bill, and recommended its passage in the Senate."

The reading of the bill was called for, and it was read entire.

Now came the tug of war! Many had never heard it read before, except by its title. And now to find what a radical bill it was—what an inevitable upheaving of the Institution must be the result of a jury trial of all its inmates—and what expense and trouble must attend the enforcement of the law a jury trial in every case of subsequent committal, &c.—they were tempted to demur, in spite of their promise to stand by the bill.

Various questions were asked and answered satisfactorily; while, to my astonishment, I saw Senator Mac, of Kankakee, one of the fifteen who had pledged me his promise of honor to defend the bill if necessary, act. as if he meant to defeat the bill if he could, and yet, shrink from assuming this responsibility himself, when he was brought out by the question :

" Mac, are you in favor of the bill, or not ? " Mac hesitated.

Turning his eye upward to the gallery, and meeting my own looking down directly upon him, he quickly replied :

" I am in favor of the bill, and shall vote for it ! "

The wave of sympathy for the bill now seemed universal, as under its influence, even Murry McConnell arose and said :

" I shall not oppose the bill, but shall vote for it ! "

All opposition being thus overcome, the Bill was ordered into the omnibus to be passed with others that were sustained without opposition.

Here a motion for adjournment was introduced, and was quickly laid aside by the motion to pass the omnibus before they adjourned, which was carried.

The omnibus was then passed, including my bill, by a vote of yeas and nays, and every one voted for it.

Thus the bill finally passed by a unanimous vote of both houses.

Until this point was attained, I was in a state of almost breathless suspense, and when a gentleman sitting by me exclaimed :

" Mrs. Packard, your bill is safe ! "

I felt such a relief, accompanied with an indescribable emotion of joy and thankfulness, even surpassing as it seemed, to me, the feeling of grateful joy experienced when the verdict of the jury at Kankakee proclaimed my own personal liberty ; for in that decision, only the interests of one individual were involved, while on this decision, the personal liberty of hundreds was suspended.

Senate Scene in Springfield, Illinois.
"Mrs. Packard, your Bill is safe!" See page 204.

As we dispersed I met them at the door, and grasped the hand of as many as was convenient, and thanked them for standing so nobly by the bill.

But there was one, and one only, of those whose hand I grasped, who evidently did not reciprocate my joyful emotion; and this was Senator Mac, of Kankakee. I could not help noticing an evident misgiving in the manner he responded to my thankful congratulations, which impressed this sentiment upon my heart, viz. :

" No thanks are due me, Mrs. Packard, for the triumph of your bill, for it was my intention to prove traitor to my promise, and defeat the bill ; but dared not risk such an attempt, under the circumstances ! "

And when I thanked Governor Bross for his patience, and timely interference just at the crisis between its life and death, he replied :

" Yes, Mrs. Packard, your bill had a very narrow escape— it was but just saved."

But saved it was ! in spite of all the evil machinations formed against it, to be a blessing to the interests of humanity, not only in this State but throughout the country, since Illinois is now regarded as having the best law on committals into Insane Asylums of any state in the Union.

Here I would pause for a moment and note the overruling Providence of God in this transaction.

It is as yet an unsolved mystery how this Enacting Clause happened to be omitted. If any of the Engrossing Clerks had been hired to omit it, in transcribing the bill, with the intention of thus defeating it, this " counsel of Ahithopel was brought to naught," by a second attempt to defeat it, by withdrawing it from the omnibus, for thereby this omission was detected and rectified.

I have been told that quite a large sum of money was paid to a certain clerk to induce him to steal the bill from the omnibus, trusting to the shortness of the time, and the pressure of business, as his means of escape from detection until it was too late, at least, to repair the injury.

But as it proved this attempt to defeat the bill was the very means of saving it from defeat. For had it been allowed to remain in the omnibus it would not have been known that this defect existed, until it would have been too late to have remedied it, and thus the bill would have been lost.

So this attempt to defeat the bill was the very means of saving the bill from defeat.

And if Dr. McFarland did pay this clerk for stealing the bill, to Dr. McFarland must be ascribed the credit of getting the bill through! His money was well appropriated to save *such* a bill from annihilation.

Thus the " wise are taken in their own craftiness," and the Lord overrules their own evil purposes to promote His good ones.

CHAPTER XXVI.

Signing of the Bill by the Governor.

Having been so long too familiar with the subtle devices of this arch enemy of the bill, I dared not leave Springfield until the bill had been signed by the Governor.

But as it would take two weeks more for my bill to come before the Governor in its natural order, being among the very last that had been passed, I ventured to make an effort to get it signed, as a special favor, forthwith.

I therefore sought the Secretary of State, Mr. Tyndal, as my helper in this matter, and asked him if he would be so kind as to ask the Governor to sign it at once. Said he :

"I will do this as a favor for you, although I never did such a thing before for any one, for I know how exceedingly vigilant and watchful you have been during all this long session. I feel disposed to help you through, if I can!"

He went to the Senate engrossing clerks to get the bill, and they told him it had been sent to the Governor's office.

He went there for it, and was told it had never been sent in, and returned with the most unwelcome intelligence that he could not find the bill!

I then followed in his tracks in search of the bill, but no traces of it could be found anywhere!

I began to be suspicious that the enemy was again on my track, and had stolen the bill. But upon pursuing my investigations, I found that the engrossing clerks of the House Bills were in a hall across the street. Thither I went in search of the lost bill, where to my great relief and joy, I found that one of these clerks had copied Bill 608, as his record showed, and it had been sent over to the State-House the previous day, to a Committee in the Representatives room.

Thither I went at once, not satisfied until I had actually seen the bill.

Here I found it—but was informed it could not be sent to the Governor until the Speaker of both Houses had first signed it.

The House Speaker, Mr. Corwin, then and there signed it; but Speaker Bross, of the Senate, had gone to Chicago and was not expected to return until the next week.

I waited until his return, and went for my bill, and was informed it had been sent in to the Governor, and taking my informant's advice, to go with it, myself, to the Governor for his signature, instead of getting Secretary Tyndal to go for me, I went into the Governor's ante-office, and here Mr. Harlan informed me, the bill was in his possession.

He looked for it, but could not find it!

He looked again and again and could not find it!

During this three-quarters of an hour he spent looking in vain for it, I had another mental conflict with doubt, suspense and suspicion. But relief came at last, as Mr. Harlan exclaimed:

"I have found the Personal Liberty Bill! and if you wish it, I will take it in and ask the Governor to sign it."

Most gratefully did I accept this kind offer; and after about one hour more of solicitude, lest he should not sign it, I at last heard his private secretary reading aloud my bill. Then I heard him exclaim, with emphasis:

"That is a good bill!"

"Yes, it is first-rate!" responded the Governor.

Hope revived, and in a few minutes Governor Oglesby came into the room, with the bill in his hand, which he handed me, saying:

"Mrs. Packard, your bill is signed!"

I then took his hand and said:

"In the name of the married women of Illinois, I thank you

for this act. Please now, Governor Oglesby, accept one of my books."

" Thank you, Mrs. Packard, I and my wife will be glad to read it."

" The bill is now complete as it is, I conclude."

" No, the Secretary of State must also sign it."

I started for the door with my bill to take to the Secretary, when I was told:

" None but the appointed messenger can be the bearer of the bill."

I handed it to the messenger, and followed him into the office of the Secretary, and saw Mr. Tyndal sign his name and affix the seal of the State, by which it was made a law, to take effect in sixty days from date.

Mr. Tyndal very kindly gave me a certified copy of the bill in his own hand-writing, free of charge. This was only one of the many favors I received at the hands of this, one of the best of nature's noblemen.

This copy I still retain as a memento of this noble philanthropist, and also as a record of my first attempt to serve the State of Illinois, as a member of the " Third House."

My only apology for giving so full and detailed an account of this winter's campaign is, that other novices in this work may learn something of the complicated machinery of legislation, before entering, ignorantly, as I did, upon the work of reforming the laws under which we live.

And if any other victim of bad laws is goaded on to undertake to remove this liability from others, as was the experience of the writer, they may hope that as their day is so shall their strength be.

CHAPTER XXVII.

The Personal Liberty Bill and its Application.

The following Act for the protection of Personal Liberty, was passed by the Illinois Legislature of 1867, and approved by the Governor, March 5, 1867.

Section 1.—*Be it enacted by the People of the State of Illinois, represented in the General Asssmbly:*

That no superintendent, medical director, agent or other person, having the management, supervision or control of the Insane Hospital at Jacksonville, or of any hospital or asylum for insane and distracted persons in this State, shall receive, detain or keep in custody at such asylum or hospital any person who has not been declared insane or distracted by a verdict of a jury and the order of a court, as provided by an act of the General Assembly of this State, approved Feb. 16, 1865.

Section 2.—Any person having charge of, or the management or control of any hospital for the insane, or of any asylum for the insane in this State, who shall receive, keep or detain any person in such asylum or hospital, against the wishes of such person, without the record or proper certificate of the trial required by the said act of 1865, shall be deemed guilty of a high misdemeanor, and liable to indictment, and on conviction be fined not more than one thousand dollars, nor less than five hundred dollars, or imprisoned not exceeding one year, nor less than three months, or both, in the discretion of the court before which such conviction is had; *provided,* that one-half of such fine shall be paid to the informant, and the balance shall go to the benefit of the hospital or asylum in which said person was detained.

SECTION 3.—Any person now confined in any insane hospital or asylum, and all persons now confined in the hospital for the insane at Jacksonville, who have not been tried and found insane or distracted by the verdict of a jury, as provided in and contemplated by said act of the General Assembly of 1865, shall be permitted to have such trial. All such persons shall be informed by the trustees of said hospital or asylum, in their discretion, of the provisions of this act and of the said act of 1865, and on their request, such person shall be entitled to such trial within a reasonable time thereafter; *provided*, that such trial may be had in the county where such person is confined or detained, unless such person, his or her friends, shall, within thirty days after any such person may demand a trial under the provisions of said act of 1865, provide for the transportation of such person to, and demand a trial in the county where such insane person resided previous to said detention, in which case such trial shall take place in said last mentioned county.

SECTION 4.—All persons confined as aforesaid, if not found insane or distracted by a trial and the verdict of a jury as above, and in the said act of 1865 provided, within two months after the passage of this act, shall be set at liberty and discharged.

SECTION 5.—It shall be the duty of the State's attorneys for the several counties to prosecute any suit arising under the provisions of this act.

SECTION 6.—This act shall be deemed a public act, and take effect and be in force from and after its passage.

Approved March 5th, 1867.

Thus the public may see that under the humane provisions of this act, all the inmates of every insane asylum in the State of Illinois, whether public or private, who have been incarcerated without the verdict of a jury that they are insane, are now entitled to a jury trial, and unless this trial is granted them within sixty days from the 5th of March, 1867, they are discharged, and can never be incarcerated again without the verdict of a jury that they are insane.

No person can be detained there after sixty days, who has not been declared insane by a jury.

Thus it was that the barbarities of the law of 1851 were wiped out by this act of legislative justice. Now all married women and infants who had been imprisoned " without evidence of insanity," as this unjust law allowed, and who were still living victims of this cruel law, would now be liberated from their false imprisonment. And the great question, who shall be retained as fit subjects for the insane asylum, must hereafter depend in all cases, upon the decision of the jury.

The Law of 1865 Providing a Jury Trial.

SECTION 1.—*Be it enacted by the People of the State of Illinois, represented in the General Assembly*: That the circuit judges of this State are hereby vested with power to act under and execute the provisions of the act passed on the 12th of February, 1853, entitled "An act to amend an act entitled ' an act to establish the Illinois State Hospital for the Insane,'" in force March 1st, 1847, in so far as those provisions confer power upon judges of county courts ; and no trial shall be had of the question of sanity or insanity before any judge or court, without the presence or in the absence of the person alleged to be insane. And jurors shall be freeholders and heads of families.

SEC. 2. Whenever application is made to a circuit or county judge, under the provisions of this act and the act to which this is an amendment, for proceedings to inquire into and ascertain the insanity or sanity of any person alleged to be insane, the judge shall order the clerk of the court of which he is judge to issue a writ, requiring the person alleged to be insane to be brought before him, at the time and place appointed for the hearing of the matter, which writ may be directed to the sheriff or any constable of the county, or the person having the custody or charge of the person alleged to be insane, and shall be executed and returned, and the person alleged to be insane brought before the said judge before any jury is sworn to inquire into the truth of the matters alleged in the petition on which said writ was issued.

SEC. 3. Persons with reference to whom proceedings may be instituted for the purpose of deciding the question of sanity or insanity, shall have the right to process for witnesses, and to have witnesses examined before the jury; they shall also have the right to employ counsel or any friend to appear in their behalf, so that a fair trial may be had in the premises; and no resident of the State shall hereafter be admitted into the hospital for the insane, except upon the order of a court or judge, or of the production of a warrant issued according to the provisions of the act to which this is an amendment.

SEC. 4. The accounts of said institution shall be so kept and reported to the general assembly, as to show the kind, quantity and cost of any articles purchased for use; and upon quarterly settlements with the auditor, a list of the accounts paid shall be filed, and also the original vouchers, as now required.

SEC. 5. All former laws conflicting with the provisions of this act are hereby repealed, and this act shall take effect on its passage.

Approved February 16, 1865.

Two years practice under this law developed its inability to remove the evils it was designed to remedy. This law, having no penalty to enforce it, was found to be violated in many instances, as it was ascertained to be a fact that Dr. McFarland was constantly receiving patients under the old law of 1851, which this law had nominally repealed. For this reason, therefore, the petition was sent to the Legislature of 1867, that "The Personal Liberty Bill" be passed, in order to enforce the wise provisions of this law of 1865.

But knowing the determined hostility of Dr. McFarland to the enforcement of this law, and seeing the arrogant spirit exhibited toward the Legislature who passed this bill, in his biennial report of 1866, I felt it my duty to present him in his own drapery to the scrutiny of the Legislature of 1867, by laying upon the desk of each member my review of this part of his report, which was published in the Chicago *Tribune*.

Dr. McFarland's Report Opposed to Jury Trials.

In Dr. McFarland's tenth biennial report of 1866, he utters severe criticisms on an act passed by the Legislature of 1865, and complains of the injustice of such legislation as allows persons accused of insanity to have a fair trial before imprisonment.

The act which he thus ignores, provides, as Dr. McFarland says :

" Any person whose condition requires his or her being sent to the hospital, shall be personally present in the court while the examination goes on, being served with notice, stimulated by counsel, invited to cross-examine witnesses, and placed, in all instances, and in every respect as the active defendant in the case. This act is so cruel in its effect upon those for whose interest it must be presumed to have been introduced, that silence is impossible, until attention is called to it. And his voice would be for the summary repeal of the act in question, to protest against the existence of which is the plain duty of this report. What antagonisms of the most painful kind are wantonly engendered ; what violations of delicacy, and often of decency, what outrages upon mental and physical suffering must be the result while this enactment exists. And these are only slight specimens of the wrongs of which this act will be the prolific stock."

We wish to ask any candid person a few simple, commonplace questions in reference to the above extract:

Which course would be the most likely to engender antagonisms—the consignment of a relative to an indefinite term of imprisonment, without allowing them any hearing or any chance at self-defense—or, by allowing them a fair trial and opportunity of self-defense before imprisonment ?

Which would be the most probable " prolific stock " of wrongs to humanity—the imprisonment of an individual on the decision of twelve impartial men, after a fair hearing of both parties—or, on the decision of one interested man, on the simple testimony of others, without proof?

Is it not more probable that *one* man may possibly be corrupted by motives of interest and policy to make an unjust decision, than that *twelve* men could be thus corrupted ?

Dr. McFarland asserts that " a wrong under the old law, under which nine-tenths of all the patients have been received, is as nearly a moral impossibility as can well exist."

Is it a moral impossibility to get a sane person into that institution, while a statute exists, which expressly permits a certain class of persons to be there imprisoned without evidence of insanity, and without any trial—which statute suspends the personal liberty of this class of citizens wholly upon the decision of one fallible man ?

And " is it as nearly a moral impossibility as can well exist," that this one man may possibly err in judgment ?

It is our candid opinion that there have been some awful mistakes in the lawful exercise of this one-man power within the last ten years of its existence ; and the public sentiment of Illinois now demands of their Legislature of 1867 to repair the injury done to its citizens by this unjust law, by allowing those now in the asylum who have never had a jury trial, either to be discharged from their place of involuntary confinement, or be allowed to have a jury trial, before perpetuating their imprisonment any longer.

Again, Dr. McFarland says:

" From what supposed necessity such an act originated, it is not easy to conceive, for in nearly three thousand admissions here, a question was never seriously raised in a single instance!"

Has the Doctor forgotten that the question has been once, at least, seriously raised by the court at Kankakee City, in the case of one whom that court decided had been falsely imprisoned for three years at that Hospital? For, after a full and fair examination of all the evidence in the case, it was decided that Mrs. Packard was sane.

We are of the opinion that Mrs. Packard's case is a type of many other cases of false imprisonment, now there; and the simplest claims of justice and humanity demand that this Legislature extend to such, a fair trial.

A LOVER OF JUSTICE.

Springfield, Jan. 21, 1867.

The Barbarous Law of 1851.

Under which so many had lost their personal liberty, during the sixteen years of its existence, reads thus:

" Married women and infants who, in the judgment of the medical superintendent (meaning the Superintendent of the Illinois State Hospital for the Insane,) are evidently insane or distracted, may be entered or detained in the hospital on the request of the husband of the woman, or the guardian of the infant, *without* the evidence of insanity required in other cases."

The sixty days of grace which Dr. McFarland was allowed by this law to prepare for these trials, were faithfully improved by him. He sent off hosts of sane patients, who had been unjustly confined there, under the specious plea that they were suddenly cured!

Indeed, the "Personal Liberty Bill" became a universal panacea for the sudden cure of these, his sane patients!

For this knowing Superintendent understood full well that in case he retained these sane patients until the verdict of a jury liberated them, it might not only reflect upon his intelligence and veracity as a Superintendent, but also give this host of witnesses a passport to the confidence of the public in their testimony against him.

The verdict of one jury at Kankakee, on Mrs. Packard's case, was all he chose to grapple with in the present state of public sentiment towards him!

Therefore, these oppressed ones were sent into the world, without being allowed even the privilege of having his brand of insanity first obliterated from them, by the much coveted verdict of sanity from an intelligent jury of their country.

And again, if this host of injured ones were found by the jury to be sane, while their personal liberty was suspended on the single testimony of this one man, the public would at once conclude either that Dr. McFarland did not know a sane from an insane person, or had been criminally indifferent on this momentous point, or he had been perversely wicked in allowing sane persons to be imprisoned for sinister purposes, while he was growing rich with the money the oppressors of these victims were lavishly bestowing upon him to induce him to conceal their crimes under his lying testimony that they were insane persons when he knew they were not insane.

And when it is once known that a public officer can be hired to tell a lie, under such circumstances, his ruin must be inevitable, by the verdict of the people.

Such quick destruction Dr. McFarland knew must be his unavoidable doom, if he allowed the investigation these, his

10

victims, desired, and being so used to treating his patients
with injustice he could add this act to this long list without
scruple, mentally pleading self-defense as his justification.

But to procure his own self-defense at the expense of his
injured victims' right to this same privilege, must be recorded
as a crime in that book whose records recognize no respect
of persons in judgment.

This politic plan of this artful sinner proved a success so far
as to suspend, for the time being, the verdict of the people
against him; for when it was found by the verdict of the jury
that no sane patients were found in the institution sixty days
from the passage of the bill, the natural conclusion would be
that no sane persons were allowed in the asylum as patients.

But the subsequent report of the Investigating Committee
unravelled this mystery, by showing that there had been
double the number of discharged patients on the plea of
recovered during this period than other previous periods.

And another most striking fact was developed by the report
of this Investigating Committee, showing that this " Personal
Liberty Bill " was an imperative necessity, as an protection
against false commitments, which fact is expressed in their
own report as follows :

" From a careful examination of the papers on file, it did
appear that since 1865 there had been one hundred and forty-
eight admitted without the proper *legal evidence* of insanity,
and the security required by law! That there should be so
large a proportion of the admissions in violation of law, shows
a carelessness without excuse and deserving of censure.

Now if one hundred and forty-eight were found on record
as admitted during these two years alone, and this too in violation of the law, how many must then have been admitted
during the fourteen previous years, when the law for the admission of married women and infants expressly stated, that
such might be admitted *without* evidence of insanity!

Who, who is to be held responsible at God's bar, for the false imprisonment of this host of innocent victims of this barbarous law ?

Who does not see that the law for admission should have a penalty attached to enforce it, since the law of 1865 required a trial, but as there was no penalty to enforce it until the " Personal Liberty Bill " was passed, it was merely a dead letter in practice.

The judges of the State decided that it was a good law and ought to be enforced.

Rumors of false committals can now be tested, and the penalty of fine and imprisonment can be enforced if the Superintendent is found guilty of receiving any patient in defiance of this wholesome law.

CHAPTER XVIII.

Appointment of the Investigating Committee.

Among the agencies employed for the enlightenment of the legislature of 1867, in order to ensure a thorough ventilation of Jacksonville Insane Asylum, the *State Register* very kindly allowed me the use of their columns to portray facts of the most startling character for the perusal of the members, and among others of a similar character, the following article was published, and every member was furnished with a copy of the paper containing it, viz.:

Insanity a Crime!

It is a fact too little known and appreciated by the public, that insanity is treated as a crime, instead of a misfortune, at the State Institution of Jacksonville, Illinois. The inmates now there are being treated as criminals rather than unfortunates. This being the case, the Legislature who hold the control of that institution, ought to know of it, so as to interpose to prevent this perversion of the intent of its founders.

Facts in abundance are already within the reach of this Legislature, now in session. But, lest this truth be concealed under the favorable reports of committees appointed to visit that institution, we would solicit this honorable body to read the following fragment of a letter, and then consider whether their duty is done towards the inmates of that institution. Let them consider while reading it, that possibly they or some of their family may, ere another meeting of this body, be inmates there, and thus learn by bitter experience the sad truths this letter delineates.

The writer of this letter, Mrs. S. A. Kain, now at Taylorville,

Christian County, Illinois, holds herself in readiness to substantiate the truth of the statements she makes, and is ready to give under oath, any amount of similar testimony, if desired. She wrote this letter, intending it for the Governor, with the promise from the employees in that institution that they would sign it also. She was an attendant there at the time it was written, but left soon after, because she could not carry out the inhuman rule of the house.

JACKSONVILLE, January, 1866.

To his Excellency, the Governor of Illinois :

SIR—It is with profound respect and a deep feeling of reverence for its laws that permits the weakest of its subjects to appeal direct to the ear of the Executive, without passing through a barrier of nobility or the parade of parliamentary rules, when simply asking for justice for an imprisoned and suffering community.

I speak of the Insane Asylum at Jacksonville. I have had an opportunity of witnessing scenes in this institution so brutal and heart-rending that I shrink with horror from it. Here are females incarcerated in this disgusting prison, subject to every indignity, whose finer feelings are outraged every day, addressed with abusive language, insulted, debased like the negro ; and the majority fully sensible of it, insane though many of them may be.

A great many of them are no more insane than the writer, and I believe the imputation has never been cast upon me, but placed there by friends. By friends did I say ? No, by those who have the power, some for pecuniary motives, some that they may marry again, or carry on a life of licentiousness, and some to hide their own shame.

And there is one whom I have every reason to believe stands at the head of that institution, ready to take any one who is

presented, provided sufficient bribe is paid, but which is received so secretly that it cannot be proved against him.   But
who can go through that institution, and see its *secret* workings as I have done, without its becoming a self-evident fact,
that there are cases there which nothing but heavy bribes
would induce him to receive or retain, as the law would not
recognize the right.

Perhaps you may ask, where are the trustees ? And what are
they about ?   What do the trustees or any other stranger know
to come in once in three months, and stay in some wards two
or three minutes, the best wards perhaps fifteen minutes, when
every jacket is taken off, every strap hid, and the patient compelled by fair or foul means, generally the latter, to keep their
seats, or by threats of the screen-room or cold bath to act as
decorous as their poor crazy brains will allow.

Word is always sent to the attendants from fifteen to thirty
minutes ahead of the Trustees that they have arrived and are
coming, and all things must be in order when they come.   I
know not as they have any knowledge of the institution, except
by what they see, and this is nothing, and through the Superintendent, and he tells them what he pleases, and no more.
He keeps only his tools about him, who do his bidding without any question, and should he get any by chance that he
cannot make tools of, he soon discharges them.

He keeps everything as secret as he can.   It reminds one
of the old inquisitorial prisons.   Even a letter cannot pass
through the office to or from a patient without inspection by
himself or his satellite, the assistant physician, and it is immediately destroyed if it unfortunately contains anything
which he disapproves of.

I have referred to the screen-rooms and cold baths.   I will
describe them.   A screen-room is where there is a close iron
screen covering the window to keep fractious patients from
breaking the window, and is a very good place to secure them

until their excitement or "spell," as it is usually called, passes over. But it is often perverted to a different use. The patient is usually jacketed, that is, a strong, closely fitting waist, with sleeves coming below the hand and sewed up, with a loop-hole through which can be passed a strong cord. Their arms are then crossed in front with their hands drawn tightly behind them, and when thus tightly and firmly secured, they are thrown upon the floor of the screen-room, their faces downward, their clothing removed or turned back, and then beaten until their flesh is often but a jelly, while their screams might be heard at a great distance, but for thick walls and closely fitting doors.

The cold bath, O, my God! it makes me shudder to think of it. The patient, often for a small offense, perhaps, for striking in excitement an attendant, or another patient, is taken to the bath-room and made to strip; the water is then let into the bath-tub, sometimes hot, but usually very cold, and after being tied hand and foot, plunged into it, and held there under it until almost dead, and then drawn out only long enough to catch their breath and then plunged in again, and so on.

S. A. KAIN.

So notorious had the evils of the asylum now become, that the legislature of 1867 were driven to the conclusion that the honor of the State demanded a thorough investigation into the charges and current evil reports to ascertain whether they were true or false.

They therefore appointed a committee of five—three from the House and two from the Senate to visit the hospital for the insane, after the adjournment of the legislature, with power to send for persons and papers, and to examine witnesses on oath. They were to ascertain whether any of the inmates were improperly detained in the hospitals, or unjustly placed there, and whether the inmates are humanely and kindly treated, and to confer with the Trustees of said hospital in regard to the speedy correction of any abuses found to exist and to report to the Governor from time to time at their discretion.

The names of this committee were:

Hon. E. BALDWIN, Farm Ridge, La Salle County.
Hon. T. B. WAKEMAN, Howard, McHenry County.
Hon. J. B. RICKS, Taylorville, Christian County.
      On the part of the House of Representatives.
Hon. C. A. FULLER, Belvidere, Boone County.
Hon. A. J. HUNTER, Paris, Edgar County.
      On the part of the Senate.

The committee first met at the Dunlap House, in Jacksonville, on the 14th of May, and after taking the testimony of a few witnesses found the need of a thorough investigation more and more important.

They therefore advertised in the Chicago papers asking all who had any testimony they desired to present to the committee, to meet them in Jacksonville on the 4th of June. This meeting lasted till the 10th; July 10 and 11 they met at Chicago. On the 17th they met again at Jacksonville, and continued in session until the 26th of July. On the 20th, 21st and 22d of August, they met again at Chicago. On the 26th and 27th of September they met at Springfield. On the 12th of November they met at Bloomington. And on the 29th of November met at Jacksonville again, where they adjourned on the 3d of December, *sine die.*

At these meetings testimony concerning the mal-treatment of the patients increased to such a volume, and the conclusions arrived at were so unanimous, as left no doubt in the minds of the committee of the existence of crimes—heinous crimes on the part of the Superintendent, as well as outrages and abuses of the most cruel kind on the part of the attend-ants. The committee say:

" It plainly appears in the evidence they had presented them, that sixty patients had been abused by the attendants, and about twenty-five attendants had been guilty of these abuses."

It is the honest opinion of the writer that if this number were quadrupled it would not then cover the number of actually abused patients, since the abused patients was the rule at that hospital, while those justly and kindly treated were the exceptions.

So overwhelming was the testimony of mal-treatment and mismanagement that the senior man on that Committee, Mr. Baldwin, most forcibly and frankly remarked:

" I have come to the conclusion that our Insane Asylums are grand failures! That their entire destruction, on their present basis, would be a blessing to the world! "

This Committee very justly remarked:

" Dr. McFarland's government of his patients is believed too severe, and his discipline of attendants too mild."

He was found also to be very neglectful of his sick patients. They found also that he had not only admitted sane patients and kept them for years, but he often kept the patients there after they had fully recovered, so long, that they had been made incurably insane by allowing them no hope of ever being liberated. This class were compelled to work constantly for his benefit.

But the records of the house were so artfully kept that it was almost impossible to detect this mode of purloining public treasure, talent and labor.

The women worked in the sewing and dining-rooms, the wash-rooms and ironing-rooms and kitchen, and the men on the Doctor's great farm, which was entirely carried on by this slave labor—slave labor in the sense that the laborers were never allowed to be paid one dime for all this toil for the Superintendent's pecuniary benefit.

But as an atonement for this sin of extortion from his own

patients, Doctor McFarland would often have it lauded to his generosity that he had donated, from his own farm, potatoes for the poor in Jacksonville!

Yes, 'tis true. This noted Dr. McFarland was, indeed, the most benevolent man, in his way, I think, that ever lived.

He never abused patients but it was for " their good ! " He never kept the sane at work for him years after they were fit to go home but for " their good ! " He never robbed his patients of their better clothing and exchanged it for very inferior clothing unless it was for " their good ! " He never wrote to their friends the intelligence that these his sane patients were not fit to be with sane people, and therefore should not be removed, but for " their good ! " He never denied them the right of corresponding with their friends except for " their good ! " He never sent his sick or convalescent patients to the washroom to do the day's work of a well one, but for " their good ! " He would refuse the request of friends to see their relatives in his wards for " their good ! " He would brand as incurable his sane patients who dared to tell him they should expose him when liberated for " their good ! " He would not allow his sick or tired patients to lie upon their beds in the day time for "their good ! " He would deny their request for papers and books to read for " their good ! " He would turn a deaf ear to his patients' complaints for "their good ! " He would not credit the testimony of his patients for " their good ! "

In short, this benevolent man never did anything from a selfish motive—but always for " the good " of some one besides himself !

Indeed, Benevolence was one of his largest phrenological developments; but the truth must be told, his benevolence was *perverted* to mere selfish ends and selfish purposes. That is— he would carry on his selfish and nefarious schemes under the ostensible plea of " the good of his patients," while, in reality, no injustice to them was too great for him to perpetrate if he saw his selfish interests required it, or could be promoted thereby.

The above seems a sad picture of the character and actions of a public servant, whose character had so long been regarded as above suspicion, and this ostensible plea of benevolence, or regard for others, had been the bait with which their confidence had been secured.

But for the truth of this picture, I would refer my readers to that massive volume of testimony now in the archives of the Library Room in the State-House at Springfield, collected by this Committee, as a standing monument of the corruption and guilt of that public servant who is held responsible for the revolting details it contains of perverted public trusts and public confidence.

The writer, who has been allowed the unrestricted privilege, as is the right of all citizens of Illinois, of examining these manuscripts to her entire satisfaction, is prepared to state that all the charges I have ever brought against Dr. McFarland are there fully corroborated by the most reliable testimony; such testimony as left no doubt in the minds of these faithful and patient investigators of the truth of all the charges I had brought against him.

CHAPTER XXIX.

Dr. McFarland's Punishment of Mr. Wyant.

Since the public are so very unwilling to believe that insanity is treated as a crime rather than a misfortune, in our public hospitals, and as the writer knows this to be a fact, she has therefore introduced one fact, found in these records, demonstrating her position. And this is by no means an isolated case, but is only one of many, which might be mentioned, showing that punishment is the chief and almost the only treatment patients receive in Jacksonville, as a cure for their insanity.

The case mentioned is that of a Mr. Wyant, a gay, sprightly, sensitive young man, who had placed his ardent affections upon a beautiful young lady, who unfortunately was beloved by another young man of like passions with himself. These rival lovers agreed to settle the question, as to who should win this contested prize, by a duel, which was fought as agreed.

Mr. Wyant's shot proved fatal to his antagonist, and his antagonist shot off Wyant's arm above the elbow.

This duel occurring in the Northern States instead of the Southern States, Wyant was tried for murder, and Dr. McFarland was called to testify to the charge of insanity, instituted in his defense.

This expert, of course, found him insane, as is his uniform practice in all such cases.

Thus Wyant's sentence of death was commuted to imprisonment in an Insane Asylum, as an incurable! A doom far worse than death. Yes, could I have my choice between death on the gallows, or life in an Insane Asylum, I would choose death without a moment's hesitation, now that I know, by experience, what life is in an Insane Asylum!

But poor Wyant! was allowed no such choice; for by the verdict of Dr. McFarland, he was made his helpless prisoner; and although as sane as any duelist, he was compelled to be treated as a lunatic.

But in being put upon that plane practically, his aspiring, sensitive, manly nature rebelled. He claimed his right to be treated as a human being, not as a brute.

But this right was denied him.

And when his attendant, a young man of about his own age, would insist upon bestowing upon him this contemptible abuse, and would make no distinction between his treatment and that which he bestowed upon the maniacs in his ward, he could not suppress his indignant feelings as they would instinctively rebel against it.

But for poor, defenseless, one-armed Wyant there was no redress for grievances—no tribunal of justice to appeal to—no opportunity for self-defense, and no hope of there ever being a termination of his woes.

One day while he was walking out with his attendant and other patients he found the handle of a hatchet, which he slyly concealed in the armless sleeve of his coat, and took it to his ward, without the knowledge of his attendant.

One day, soon after, his attendant provoked him, as usual, beyond his power of endurance, when his long pent up indignation found vent in the energetic use of his hatchet handle upon the head of Dr. Bell, who so often had thus insulted him beyond his power of endurance. A single blow cut a gash into the forehead of Dr. Bell; when he was instantly disarmed, and the power was again all on the side of his attendant, and the weakness and dependence all on Mr. Wyant's side.

For, as a matter of course, if a patient hurts an attendant, 'tis a crime in Jacksonville Asylum, deserving the severest tortures the institution can inflict: but if an attendant hurts, maims for life, or even kills a helpless patient, 'tis no crime at all, not even a misdemeanor, so long as it can be concealed from outside knowledge, under the covert of lies and misrepresentation!

Mr. Wyant was, of course, reported to headquarters for punishment, where he was sure of getting it; for in the government of Jacksonville Asylum there is no such thing as mercy or pardon, however penitent the culprit, or however aggravated was the temptation to resist tyranny by the instinct of self-defense.

The mode in which Mr. Wyant was punished for this act I give in the words of the witness, as found in the report of the Investigating Committee.

The witness, Mrs. Graff, formerly Mrs. P. L. Hosmer, was a directress in the sewing-room for four years and a half, and she testified that she had frequently known of cruel punishments inflicted upon patients; that the cases were so numerous she did not pretend to remember them all.   Mrs. Graff says:

" That in the spring before she left the institution, the spring of 1861, the Doctor inflicted a terrible punishment upon a one-armed patient, who had been sent to the hospital after a trial for murder ; that the punishment was for striking an attendant, Dr. Bell—that the attendant was struck in the morning, and as she was going at night for water she met the engineer and porter going up stairs with chains and buckets of water—that soon after she heard the voice of the patient, away up in the upper part of the wing, in the further corner, crying:

' Oh, Doctor! Oh, Doctor! Oh, Doctor!' "

She says she knows he was chained and punished with a shower bath, because she saw the engineer going up with chains, and that the patient afterwards had the chains upon him while she remained there—and though she did not follow

Dr. McFarland punishing One-Armed Wyant.
" O Doctor! O Doctor! O Doctor!" See page 230.

the porter and others, who had pails of water when they went up, she is well satisfied he was put into a shower bath.

And she knows the Doctor directed it, because she went to the Doctor that night and asked him to pay her and let her go.

He replied, " perhaps you do not understand the case. I have saved that man from the gallows; and I witnessed the punishment myself."

Dr. Bell, the attendant who was struck, testifies to the same thing, being an eye-witness, and that he begged the Doctor to desist from such severity.

The Committee remark, " that the water and chains were applied there cannot be a doubt. The whole circumstances of the case appear revolting. And the justification interposed, that he might be thus punished because his life had been saved by the Doctor's testimony, is almost too shocking to be believed, and shows that the will which directed the punishment must belong to a man of iron, and the mind which could entertain such claims of gratitude must be fatally bent on mischief."

CHAPTER XXX.

Dr. McFarland's Infamous Proposal to Miss Julia A. Wilson.

In the Report of this Investigating Committee is found, and corroborated by most responsible testimony, the following infamous proposal of Dr. McFarland to Miss Wilson.

Miss Wilson, from Buffalo, N. Y., visited the institution at the time the Investigating Committee were there in session taking testimony, for the purpose of visiting her sister, Mrs. Brown, who had been a patient there since 1861, and if possible procure her discharge.

From the acquaintance she had made with the Doctor during this time, she had formed the most exalted opinion of his character as a gentleman and as a superintendent. And during her interview with the Doctor on this occasion, she frankly avowed this esteem for, and confidence in, his judgment and integrity, in response to his expression of solicitude as to the termination of this investigation. She told him she was confident there was no ground for his solicitude, fully believing, as she and the public generally did, that his unblemished character could stand the test of the closest scrutiny.

These kind words of womanly sympathy seemed to be most highly appreciated by this afflicted Doctor, and being fascinated by her good looks and attractive manners, as it would seem, he invited her to become their guest at the asylum for a week, at least, until arrangements could be satisfactorily made for the removal of her sister. But, said he:

" I am compelled to ask you to defer this visit until this Committee leaves, as we cannot give you so comfortable accommodations as we would like until then."

He urged as a reason for this visit that it would afford her an opportunity to see how to manage her sister in case she should remove her, as he did not consider her as a restored patient.

This plausible argument induced her to accept his invitation, and as she had some purchases to make for her sister's wardrobe, she said she would stop with her friend, Mrs. Dr. Grant, of Jacksonville, until their guests had left.

The Committee left Friday noon, and Miss Wilson returned to the Asylum Saturday afternoon, at about five o'clock. She met the Doctor in the reception-room, when he immediately showed her up to the guest-chamber which she was to occupy, and talked with her about the condition of her sister. He said she was not in a condition to be removed, that she was not fit to live among sane people, but that she had better remain awhile and she could see for herself.

This unexpected intelligence affected her to tears, and she asked the Doctor to let her see her sister immediately, and said she had hoped she could occupy the same room with her, as she had clothes to fit and make for her before her removal.

Examining the windows he said: "They are not safe!"

This alarmed her, and she decided not to have her sister remain with her over night.

The Doctor left her and soon returned, and after a short time her sister was ushered into the room by an attendant.

He then left again, but soon returned and took a seat, and after talking a few moments, handed her an envelope, saying, as he did so:

"I wish you to examine this—the key of Mrs. Brown's ward is there."

And went out.

But as Miss Wilson supposed it contained some directions respecting her sister's room or treatment, she did not open the envelope for sometime but sat and talked with her sister.

Her tears seemed to annoy her sister, and she asked what she was crying for.

She told her because the Doctor had convinced her of the impracticability of taking her home with her.

She took her sister to the door of her ward and gave her to an attendant, and returned to her room and opened the envelope, which contained an infamous proposal, which was expressed in these words:

"An appreciative friend, who deeply sympathizes with you in your troubles, wishes to know if his company will be agreeable after retiring hours."

Signed "A. M. F." as she thinks, but is not positive, for under the impulse of instantaneous indignation she tore the infamous note to pieces, and scattered it upon the floor.

But the contents were so indelibly impressed upon her heart and memory that she does not hesitate to take her oath upon it that these were the exact words of the note.

This astounding revelation of the Doctor's character, which before she regarded as above suspicion, so rebounded upon her feelings and judgment as led her to the firm determination that she should take her sister away, and stay with her until she could do so. Her unshaken confidence in the integrity of the Doctor being thus summarily overthrown, her mind was left open to see his faults, to which she was before entirely blind.

Upon further acquaintance with her sister she found he had entirely misrepresented her condition; that instead of being wild, furious, or unsafe, she was calm, quiet and perfectly safe for her companion, both night and day, as she was ever after her room-mate during her stay at the Asylum.

She also found to her astonishment that her sister's statements of physical abuse she had received from the Doctor were all true—that she had been the victim of cruel, unreasonable and inhuman treatment, and now that the bandage had been removed from her own eyes, she could see the artful policy and cruel deception and misrepresentation which had been palmed off upon herself and the public, instead of the truth.

The scenes she this week witnessed behind the curtain, demonstrated to her mind the necessity of a most thorough investigation, and also that the charges of neglect of his patients and his cruelty towards them were all true.

So satisfied did she become from what she saw, independent of testimony, during this week, that when I met her just about as she was leaving Jacksonville, she gave me her hand as her pledge before God, that she would carry out the vow she had made to expose Dr. McFarland's true character to the world.

While witnessing this solemn consecration to be the defender of the truth, I could not but believe God had in his Providence raised up a witness to co-operate with me in my own determination to fulfill this same vow which I had many times before made.

Miss Wilson wrote an indignant reply to this note, as she felt that she could not look at him, accusing him of cruelty to her, informing him he had misjudged her, and saying, if she was compelled to remain on her sister's account she demanded a situation while she did remain. She felt it unsafe for her to express the full extent of her indignation, lest the Doctor might thwart her purpose in regard to her sister's removal.

But the next day after the insult she wrote to her brother-in-law in Chicago, concerning it, and also informed Mrs. Dr. Grant, of Jacksonville, and others, including the writer, and advised with them concerning her duty.

Mrs. Grant invited her to stay with them until her sister was ready to leave; but she feared if she left without her sister she could never get her again, and as her sister stayed in the same room with her, she had no fear of being again insulted by the Doctor.

She adhered to her purpose, and as her reward for her persistent determination she succeeded in seeing her sister safely reach home and enjoy comparative health and happiness.

When the Doctor returned after she had torn up the note, he noticed the pieces and said:

" What is this ? "

" It is that infamous note ! "

She asked him what it was in her appearance that induced him so to offend her, when he said :

" Oh, nothing—I merely took it at a venture ! "

But, alas ! What a " venture ! " Just at this important crisis of his reputation !

The Investigating Committee had only left the hospital the day before, while he, whose character was being thus suspended before the public upon his own actions, could " venture" to present to a visitor at this public hospital, such a request, in his own handwriting and over his own initials ! "

Such a verbal request would have been hazardous even, but to put it in writing was doubly dangerous as a witness against him.

Now the natural inference seems to be, if a man under such circumstances, should dare to run such a risk or " venture," we might infer he was no novice in this kind of business; for even common prudence would have deterred any but the most hardened, callous sinner, from committing such a suicidal act.

This being true, what husband or father could trust his helpless wife or daughter to the care of such a public servant, and then too, cut off from all communication with their natural protectors, except through the censorship of this man.

If the victims of his lust and power could only write to their relatives and friends without these letters being read by the Superintendent, from whom they need protection, and of whose insults they make complaint, their exposure would be far less, and their appeal for protection would be more likely to be sent to the post-office than into the fire, as is the case at present.

The writer has often sent bills to our legislatures allowing an unrestricted correspondence by the removal of this censorship, as she knows the need of her defenseless sex there, for want of these means of protecting them from insult and outrage.

But the Superintendent and his party are sure, if possible, to defeat such bills.

On the 16th and 17th of October, 1867, Dr. McFarland and Mr. Dummer, his attorney, and the chairman of the Committee, took the depositions of Miss Wilson, and her mother, Mrs. Julia A. Wilson, and J. D. H. Chamberlain, Esq., before James S. Gills, Esq., in the City of Buffalo.

The testimony shows that the character of Miss Wilson was irreproachable at home, and she has challenged investigation of it in Jacksonville.

In closing up their report of Miss Wilson's case the Committee say:

" This testimony the Committee fully believe. And in the opinion of the Committee, testimony of the moral character of Dr. McFarland cannot prevail against such unquestionable proof of facts; and however painful and humiliating it may be to us, as citizens, to believe a man who occupies such a position should be guilty of such grave improprieties, it is nevertheless our plain duty to express the opinion of his guilt, which the evidence clearly shows."

CHAPTER XXXI.

Testimony Presented to the Committee by Mrs. Tirzah F. Shedd, of Aurora, Illinois.

It is for the benefit of those now in Jacksonville Insane Asylum that I give the following testimony to the public, hoping it may stimulate the people to provide some remedy for existing evils.

This is to certify, that I, Mrs. T. F. Shedd, was incarcerated in this Asylum on the 7th of July, 1865. I was imprisoned there fourteen weeks. My baby was five months and a half old, when I was taken from her, and my two other little girls, and *forced* entirely against my will and protest, into this prison-house, for an indefinite length of time, on the charge of mono-mania on spiritualism, brought against me by my husband.

True I had a mock jury trial at Geneva court-house, as the statute law of 1865 requires, still I felt that justice could not be done me before such a tribunal of prejudice as existed against me on the ground of my spiritualism. And so it proved. My case was not fairly tried before an impartial tribunal, and therefore, I was condemned as insane on the subject of spiritualism.

This decision therefore placed my personal liberty entirely in the hands of my husband who was fully determined to use this legal power to subject my views to his will and wishes. I, of course, resisted this claim, and assured him I should never yield my right to my personal liberty to him or any other power ; for so long as he could bring nothing against me but what I regarded as my religion, I claimed the protection of my personal liberty under the flag of religious toleration.

Notwithsanding all my arguments, my entreaties, my prayers, my protests and my vigorous resistance, by fighting single-handed and alone my six strong men captors, for forty-five minutes, I was finally taken from my sick bed, bruised and sore from this brutal assault, and carried in my undress to the cars, with the handcuffs dangling at my side, leaving my little girls screaming in agony at this unnatural bereavement of their tender, loving mother. And yet this is a land of religious freedom! It may be a land of freedom for the men, but I am sure it is not for the married women!

And although entirely sane, the heartless Dr. McFarland did receive me, when my last hope of liberty died within me, and I found myself entirely in the power of a man, whom I had sad reasons to fear was not worthy of the unbounded trust and confidence he was then receiving from the people of Illinois. After I was discharged, I expressed this same opinion to him in a letter as follows:

"Dr. McFarland, I gathered facts from every department of the Asylum—and your private conduct towards me which I well understood at the time—enough to ruin you!"

I have no confidence in that man's honesty. His policy is stronger than his principles; and I told him this opinion too, in my letter to him in these words:

"You took my husband by the hand and when alone said to him, 'Mr. Shedd, this woman, meaning me, is not crazy, nor ever has been. Excited she may have been from various causes, but temporary derangement is not possible with such an organization, although I shall pronounce her hopelessly insane, because she will not say she has changed her mind!'"

Is not this decision that I am insane, the dictation of his selfish policy, instead of his honest conviction? It seems to me that he is willing to belie his own judgment to shield himself and my persecutors from harm. And the written advice he gave my husband, strengthens this conviction, viz.

" Mr. Shedd, you must not tyrannize over her, but flatter her with presents, and let her have her own way as much as you can."

Why is this? Is he not afraid I shall become exasperated toward this party including himself, and expose them in consequence ? It seems so to me, for he says it is impossible for me to become insane, and this advice did not seem to be needed for my protection or good.

I think Dr. McFarland is not fit for his place, and as I view it, the safest course for him to pursue now is to resign ; and I advised him to do so in my letter, viz. :

" All that I now ask is that you give up that position which you confessed to me you were sick of five years ago, and re-lease those women you hold there as prisoners, under the will of cruel husbands, and others who call themselves friends."

This letter from which these extracts are made, was sent back to my husband with this single sentence added to it :

" Is Mrs. Shedd becoming more insane? A. M."

There were a great many spiritualists there, whom he called insane like myself, for this reason alone, seeming to fear them as witnesses against him, unless they carried his diploma of " hopeless insanity " upon them. He has been obliged to liberate many such of late, by the enforcement of the law for the " Protection of Personal Liberty," and he was very careful too to send this class of " hopelessly insane " (?) prisoners before the time appointed by the Legislature for their jury trial, so that by this policy they were denied the opportunity of a jury trial, in vindication of their sanity. And had the jury's decision contradicted the Doctor's opinion, as it did in Mrs. Packard's case, he might have had more reason to fear their influence.

One day after I had cut and made me a neat and becoming white dress, the Doctor seeing me in it remarked :

" I don't see how a man could put a lady like you from her home."

At another time, he remarked :

" If you were my wife, I should want you at home." Would he want an *insane* wife at the head of his family ?

I enjoyed many privileges there which others did not, and I might have used these liberties to escape ; but I chose rather to remain until all my prison keepers had had a fair opportunity to see that I was not insane. I also wished to look into the secret workings of this prison, but in order to do this I knew I must first secure their entire confidence, and any attempt to escape I knew would at once circumscribe my limits of observation. By the course I have pursued the Doctor has had a fair opportunity for arriving at the candid conviction he expressed to my husband of my sanity, viz :

" Mrs. Shedd is not crazy nor can she be with her organization."

The confidence my keepers had in my sanity was expressed in various ways. One was by their allowing me to have my own pen-knife and scissors during all my incarceration, which act is strictly forbidden by the by-laws ; and, of course, it would be necessary to keep these articles from insane people.

Another fact I found out through them was, that this house is used as the headquarters for the Masons to get their bountiful feasts in ; and yet the prisoners have heard the Doctor deny that he was a Mason, himself !

But feasting the Masons is not the only feast the Doctor is in the habit of bestowing at the State's expense, and at the sacrifice too of the much needed table comforts of the invalid prisoners, such as fruits, berries, melons, butter, cream, milk, wines, vegetables and such like.

I know the State has a heavy wine bill to pay yearly, charged for the " good of the patients ; " but judging from both of the Doctors' appearance at times, I should think they made free use of it themselves, and I am sure they and their guests use far more of it than the patients do.

11

The prisoners are kept uniformly on the plainest and coarsest kind of fare, far better suited to a class of working men, than sick women. Even butter is not always furnished, and when it is, it is often so very poor that it is not fit to eat, and I have known meat sent to the wards so very foul that the attendants would not put it upon the table, and the boarders would have nothing left them to eat but molasses and bread.

Only once a week are we allowed any kind of sauce or relish of any kind to eat with our butterless bread. It is true the prisoners have the privilege of looking through the iron grates of their prison windows at the twenty-five nice fat cows, "headed by the buffalo," on their way to and from their rich pasture; but it would afford us far more solid satisfaction to have been allowed to use some of their new milk and sweet butter, for our health and comfort.

It does seem that with all the money the State expends on this Institution that its boarders ought to be decently fed. But they are not.

Great injustice is done the prisoners in respect to their clothing, by losing much of it, which the Doctor accounts for on the false plea, oftentimes, that "the patients tear their own clothes." Some of the prisoners do tear their own clothes, but most of their losses in clothing, are the result of wrong conduct on the part of the employees.

I once saw Miss Conkling held under the water, until almost dead, and I feared she would never get her breath again.

I saw Mrs. Comb held by the hair of her head under a streaming faucet, and handfuls of hair were pulled from her head, by their rough handling, simply because she would not eat when she was not hungry.

I have seen the attendants strike the hands of the patients with their keys, so as to leave black and blue spots for days.

I have seen them pinch their ears and arms and shoulders,

and shake them, when they felt that they could not eat; and were thus forced to eat when their stomachs were so rejecting it as to be retching at the time.

There is one married woman there who has been imprisoned seven times by her husband, and yet she is intelligent and entirely sane?

When will married woman be safe from her husband's power?

And yet, she must assert her own rights, for the government does not protect her rights, as it does her husband's, and then run the risk of being called insane for so doing! I do not think the men who make the laws for us, would be willing to exchange places with us.

This house seems to me to be more a place of punishment, than a place of cure. I have often heard the patients say:

"This is a wholesale slaughter-house!"

And there is more truth than the people ought to allow in this remark. They bury the dead in the night, and with no more religious ceremony than the brute has. We can hear the dead cart go round the house in the night to bury those prisoners who have been killed by abuse; and their next door room-mates would not know, sometimes for months, what had become of them, because they were told they had gone home, when they had gone to their silent graves!

I have heard of one case where the patient had been dead one year, before the Doctor informed the friends of the death of their relative!

The prisoners are not allowed to write to their friends what kind of treatment they are receiving, and an attempt to do so clandestinely, is punished as an offense. The punishment for this offense is, they must have their term of imprisonment lengthened for it. I once knew the Doctor to threaten to keep one prisoner longer even for aiding another in getting a letter to her friends.

The indefinite time for which they are imprisoned renders this prison all the more dismal. If the prisoner could but know for how long a time he must suffer this incarceration, it would be a wonderful relief. Then the Superintendent could not perpetuate it at his own option, as he now can and does.

These prisoners are much more at the mercy of their keepers than the penitentiary convicts. As it is now conducted I should choose the place of the convict in the penitentiary, rather than the place of a patient in Jacksonville Insane Asylum. And yet there is not one in a hundred probably, of the patients who is treated as well as I was during the fourteen weeks I was imprisoned there.

The above statement, I stand responsible for as the *truth* as it was when I was there; and I now challenge the people of Illinois to bring forward proof, if it can be found to refute it. Indeed I court and invite the most rigid investigation, knowing that the result will only be a confirmation of this statement.

TIRZAH F. SHEDD.

Aurora, May, 1867.

CHAPTER XXXII.

Testimony of Eight Employees Taken by the Committee Under Oath.

The following is only a specimen of what the Investigating Committee received in great abundance from a large number of reliable witnesses, the whole of which is found in detail in the archives of the Library Room at the State-House, Springfield, Illinois, the mere abstract of which would make a ponderous volume. Within the limits of this book therefore I can only give a mere sample of what those faithful investigators collected for the perusal of future ages, showing that the present age had imperative reason for agitating the subject of Asylum Reform.

Testimony of Miss Kain, an Attendant.

Miss Kain testified, that she was forty-four years old, resided in Christian County, and was an attendant in hospital from about the middle of August, 1865, until the latter part of December, of the same year.

When she went there Dr. McFarland told her he wanted her to assist in taking charge of a ward, then in charge of an attendant who, although not officially reported to him, yet he knew to be cruel to patients. He told her she would hear a great many hard stories about the institution, but she must not believe a word of them.

A Mrs. Dorcas Ritter was the co-attendant of witness, in the new Eighth Ward; and the first thing witness noticed was the cruelty of this Mrs. Ritter to the patients. Mrs. Ritter would not let them sit down, and if she found them so sitting, she would take them by the hair of the head and lift them on the seat, and if they resisted she would often shove them back against the wall and choke them, or compel them in some harsh way to comply.

The benches in the ward were straight backed and hard to sit upon ; and Mrs. Ritter told witness, that if she allowed the patients to sit upon the floor and rest them, that Dr. McFarland would be mad, and which witness subsequently found to be true.

This Mrs. Ritter, for a slight offense upon the part of the patients, would give them what was called a cold bath, which punishment consisted in putting the patients in a bath-tub, half or two-thirds filled with cold water, their hands and feet tied, and if they resisted, a straight jacket was placed upon them, their heads plunged under the water as long as it was safe to leave them, then lifted out for a few moments to allow them to breathe and cast the water from their stomach, and the same process continued as long as the patient was thought able to bear it.

Witness further swore, that this Mrs. Ritter told her she came near killing a patient named Miss D. Haven, and that Dr. Dutton, who chanced to be passing shortly after, observed that the patient looked sick, and on being informed that Mrs. Ritter had been giving her a bath, the Doctor told her how long it was safe to keep them under water, and if they kept them in until they vomited, there was danger of their dying. Witness further stated that in giving patients these baths they were generally plunged three or four times, until quite prostrate and unable to resist.

Miss Kain stated that this Mrs. Ritter remained in the institution about three or four weeks after Miss Kain went there, but that before Mrs. Ritter left, she administered these baths three or four times to different patients ; and that Mrs. Ritter told her that the attendants were not allowed to administer these baths, without instructions from the Doctor, but that they sometimes did do it without such instructions, and the Doctor knew it; and that the Doctor and Miss Belle Bailey and Mrs. Haskett set them the example of giving the patients these baths, and " breaking them in," as they called it. Miss Kain swears that the patients were sick for several days, and sometimes two weeks, after receiving these baths.

Witness also swore that her ward was the new Fifth, and was made up of some of the hardest and most obstinate cases from the other wards; that she saw this Mrs. Ritter frequently jacket and beat patients; that at one time, during witness' stay in the institution, eleven patients were sick with flux in her ward, and that they were not furnished with medicines, nor she with any extra help or nurses, and that four of them died; that she, witness, made no complaints to Dr. McFarland of these abuses, because it was understood in the institution that such complaints would receive no attention.

Witness also mentioned another case of a Mrs. Magin, who was indecently treated by Mrs. Haskett. Soon after she entered the institution, Mrs. McFarland, who from the evidence, appears to have been a most kind and sympathetic lady, told witness that the patients were not being kindly treated, and that there must be a change, as the matter was getting out and would damage the institution.

Testimony of Mrs. Graff, Directress of the Sewing Room.

Mrs. Graff, formerly Mrs. P. L. Hosmer, testified that she resided near Jacksonville; was fifty-two years old; had been directress in the sewing-room about four and a-half years.

Mrs. Graff swears to the punishment of a Miss Jane Barackman, by shower-bath, for improper conduct to an attendant. The patient had been taken out of the water, and was just able to speak. At another time this same patient was strapped with her hands behind her back, in the morning, and the straps kept on until the next morning, and her groans during the night kept the witness from sleeping; and the witness further states, that she had known instances where the straps had been drawn so tightly as to cut through the skin, and into the flesh.

Another instance named was a new patient, on the night after arrival, whom the witness thought, from the sound of the voice, was being choked by two attendants. She told Mrs. McFarland of it, who informed the Doctor. The Doctor went into the room where the patient was, and after staying some time, came out but did not speak to witness. The next morning she asked the Doctor if what she said about choking the patient was a lie, and he said " no," but it was best to say nothing about it, as one of the attendants was going away, and it would hurt the institution to have it go out.

Another case was that of Mrs. Boyce. This was a very emaciated patient, " and her stomach all crushed in as it were." She was a wild patient, and would tear up and take off her clothes, but witness could always manage her better than others. Witness had seen her sitting day after day with her feet tied ; and on one occasion she and Mrs. McFarland found her in the screen-room, laying on her back on a hard pallet of straw, with her feet tied, and her hands tied behind her back with a large bed-cord, and just alive. She had a straight-jacket on, and the jacket was laced up with ropes as large as a bed-cord. The witness held the light, and Mrs. McFarland manifesting her grief in groans, untied the patient. Witness afterwards showed the jacket to Miss Dix, when she was there, and the pattern of the jackets was afterwards changed, and softer cords used in lacing the jackets.

Testimony of Miss Jenny Kee, an Attendant.

Miss Jenny Kee, who is twenty-four years old, resides in Jacksonville, and was an attendant from the spring of 1861 to 1862, about fourteen months.

Swears to a case of cruelty about one month after she went there to a patient named Anna Myers, by an attendant named Elizabeth Bonner. The attendant took the patient, who was a very insane and idiotic patient, by the hair of the head and pounded the floor with it. She saw this punishment inflicted several times. Also knew of same attendant punishing a Mrs. Thompson, by taking her by the hand and twisting her arm; and a Miss Kate Daly, by striking her hands with keys, leaving marks. Also a Mrs. Loop, by same attendant, by pulling her and putting her wrist out of joint. The Committee says: "This Elizabeth Bonner, who appears from the testimony of several witnesses, to have been a merciless and brutal wretch, was in the Institution as an attendant when this witness went there and when she left."

Testimony of Mrs. Sarah Bland, an Attendant.

Mrs. Sarah Bland, aged 39 years, and a resident of Jacksonville, was attendant from March, 1863, to October, 1865, a part of the time was in sewing-room, and had opportunities of knowing the general treatment of patients.

This witness mentions the abuse of Miss Eames, who was a very stupid, quiet and delicate looking patient. In the spring of 1865, the witness heard screams in the bath-room. A Miss Kate Snow came out of the room and inquired for the Doctor, and said that Miss Lawrence, the attendant, had Miss Eames in the bath-room and was beating her brutally. Witness went into the wash-room, and, on coming out, heard the blows, and then went into the ward, when Miss Lawrence came out of the bath-room and locked the door, and said witness could not have any patients out of that ward. In the evening witness saw Miss Eames in bed, and told witness, her eyes filling with tears at the time, that Miss Lawrence had almost killed her, and asked to look at her back, which witness was prevented from doing by Miss Lawrence, who came in and told witness to go out of the ward—that she should not come in and excite the patients. Witness had three patients to go out of the ward into the sewing-room; and Miss Lawrence took them by the back and pushed them violently into the ward. The patient died one week after the morning she was pounded.

The next was in the spring of 1865. A Mrs. Sutton, who was not a violent patient and seemed to be in good health, was punished very badly by two attendants—Mrs. Lydia Riggs and Miss Bell Bailey—and was confined to her room for two weeks after her punishment; at the expiration of which time the witness saw her, when the patient's face was a dark green color, without any natural flesh except around the mouth. This Miss Bailey is still retained, and is supervisoress in the hospital, and denies that punishments are ever inflicted in the hospital, or that she ever, intentionally, injured a patient!

The next case mentioned by this witness was that of Maggie Rowland, in the summer of 1865. The witness heard a strugle in the bath-room and attempted to go in, but was prevented by Miss Bailey who was in the room, and put her foot against the door and shut it. The witness stayed near by for some time, and heard brutal blows administered to patient. The patient was kept in the bath-room for some time after. In the evening witness saw her, and her face was badly beaten up; and on being spoken to by witness, the patient cried and looked as though she had no friends. This patient, who was lame, was a talkative, noisy person, who did not appear to be violent. The witness says that the reason she did not tell the Doctor was, that she was afraid of getting into a scrape if she told, for the Doctor had, before this, told her he did not wish to have her make any mischief by getting up excitement among the patients she was with. She says she afterwards, however, did report a case to the Doctor, and he told her to mind her own business, and she after this did not report other cases to the Doctor because of this conversation.

The last case which this witness mentions was that of a Mrs. Clark, who had been sick sometime in bed, and as the attendants were dragging her to the bath-room, she asked them not to take her there, but to let her die where she was. As they raised the patient to put her in the bath-tub, she dropped down dead. The names of these attendants are Miss Mary Rice and Miss Mary Smith.

Testimony of Mrs. Mary Cassell, Assistant Matron.

Mrs. Mary Cassell is twenty-four years of age, and has lived in Jacksonville eight years; was employed in the hospital from April, 1860, to May, 1861, as assistant matron, and filled the place now called supervisoress.

Does not personally know of any case of abuse which she saw administered. Remembers the case of Mrs. Farenside, a patient who appeared one morning at the breakfast table in fifth ward, the worst, after having been removed from the seventh, the best, with a black eye. Inquired the cause, and patient and Elizabeth Bonner said that Dr. McFarland struck her. One eye was black, and one side of her face was very much bruised and blackened for several days. After these bruises were inflicted, the patient was taken from the best ward, the seventh, to the new fifth, which was unoccupied, and confined in a room by herself. Never knew the patient to be boisterous, and think if she had been unmanageable she would not have been in the best ward. Patient and Elizabeth Bonner both told witness that Dr. McFarland kicked her.

Witness then testified that she thought the patients ought to be more kindly treated generally; that many times, when they were sick and feeble, they were prevented from taking proper rest during the day on their beds—it was the practice of the house not to allow them to lie down during the day-time, and the idea advanced was that the patients did not know when they needed rest—that they were inclined to lie down more than was good for them; and it was a most universal complaint in the female wards, on the part of those who were too feeble and weak to sit up, that they were not allowed to lie down in the day-time—remembered one particular case where the patient was ill and wanted to lie down, and her attendant, Miss Eagle, said no, the Doctor did not allow it, and the face of the patient, witness well remembered.

Testimony of J. C. Edmundson, Assistant Engineer.

John C. Edmundson, aged thirty-five years, was assistant engineer in hospital from April, 1861, to October 2d, 1865.

Testified that before he had been there a week he saw a patient knocked down by Joseph Tinker, an attendant, with a stick, because he absent-mindedly picked a thread out of his coat.

Witness proposed to report the case to Dr. McFarland, but Eastman, the principal engineer, who had been there three years, told witness he had better not report it if he wanted to stay in the institution.

The patient on being knocked down seemed perfectly dead; was not able to get up; had no government over himself, and was taken away and put in the screen-room.

The next case mentioned by this witness was George Richards, a patient of Jacksonville, who was kept in the screen-room entirely naked, in the cold winter; and when witness came to work in the morning, to raise steam, at one, two or three o'clock, patient would beg for warmth.

It was about fifty feet from screen-room to bath-tub, and the attendants would take the patient by the heels and drag him over the floor.

One day, as they were about to bathe this patient, witness says, they had drawn the tub full of hot water and had him up in their arms ready to plunge him in the tub, when another patient, by the name of Cooper, jumped in and saved him.

Witness says this patient was kept in the screen-room the most of the winter of 1863–4; that the room had nothing in it, except sometimes a little straw, a straw tick or blanket, which he would tear up and wrap around him for warmth. This patient died the summer or fall after this confinement.

Mr. Haitt, of Chicago, was also kept in a screen-room almost constantly, and beat and bruised until his limbs were swollen. He was jerked and jammed until his legs were almost a perfect jelly. He went home and came back. Witness heard him speak very kindly of Mrs. McFarland for doctoring his limbs after they were bruised.

The two attendants in the ward who abused this patient were Germans. Patient complained that these attendants would not give him anything; and if he asked for anything they would beat and kick him; and witness has given him water, put through the window.

When patient left the institution the second time, he said, it he ever came across the attendant who abused him so, he would kill him, if they hung him for it. The witness gave the names of the German attendants who abused the patients, as Pepenbring and Smultz, and said they both resided in Jacksonville. This witness said that he did not believe Dr. McFarland approved of these abuses, and that the reason he did not report them was that he was afraid if he did he would lose his place.

When he talked with the Doctor about business, he got a very short answer, or a nod of the head; and he came to the conclusion there was not much satisfaction.   He left the institution because he got tired of it—requested to be relieved several months before he left, but the Doctor requested him to stay.

Testimony of George Merrick, Attendant.

George Merrick, aged forty-five years, and residing in Jacksonville, was an attendant in hospital from February to June, 1866.

He testifies to the abuse of Jacob Myers, a young patient, by the supervisor, Mr. Doane, who, without provocation, caught him by the ankles when he was undressing and threw him on the floor and injured him severely.

Also David Ayres, a very docile man, and consumptive and sick and feeble, who, the witness states, was neglected by Dr. Dutton and refused medical treatment, and soon after died.

Also, David Smith, about twenty-six years of age, a patient who was very bad and crazy.   One day witness heard a loud noise in the ward where Smith was, and looking into the ward he saw the attendant, William Roy, jamming his head against the ceiling.   Smith made no resistance, but his nose bled and his eye was black.

Also a patient by the name of Creighton, who was a small Irishman about twenty-five years old.   Witness one day saw him on a bench, and he was wholly speechless—could not move his head; was swollen and was badly bruised.   Akers, the attendant, told witness that the patient was a bad man, and they had a hell of a time with him.   That night witness helped the patient to bed on the floor, and the next night he died.

Witness says that he did not know of any medical attendance or medicines furnished him, and he should have probably known it if they had.

Witness assisted in laying out the patient, whose head and face were very much swollen; was black under the eyes and on the cheek bones; there were bruises about his arms and shoulders and other parts of his body, and had a wound on the face.

The patients informed witness that a few days before this, James Akers, Thomas Kearney, John Doan, supervisor, John Roy and William Roy, employees of the institution, had beat the patient.

Another case was a wild young patient by the name of Veach, who escaped. Was retaken, and on arriving at the hospital, knocked Mr. Supervisor Doan down with a brick in again making his escape. On being taken he was handcuffed; his feet shackled; put in a crib and put up in one of the bedrooms of the third ward, where he was kept about three months.

The crib was made of strips of plank about three and a half inches wide and two and a half inches apart, and was about two feet high, five and a half feet long, and two and a half feet wide.

The witness says the patient could not be in any other position in the crib but on his back; and there was some bedding in the crib, and he thinks, a pillow under his head.

This witness says he had difficulty with Akers and Doan about their abusing the patients cruelly, and he supposes he was discharged on that account.

When inquired of by Dr. McFarland if he had not been taking liquor the evening of the difficulty with Doan and Akers, he said he had not; that he was not in the habit of drinking liquor, and resented any such imputation; that he was sometimes, by permission, absent Saturday evenings at the choir meetings, and on Sunday and Wednesday evenings at the prayer meetings; and that his character was established and well known in the community.

Testimony of John Henry, Steward of the Asylum.

Witness John Henry, who has resided in Jacksonville about forty years, and was a member of the State Senate when the act of incorporation was passed, in 1847, and afterwards steward of the hospital, about one year, from 1848 to 1849.

His situation made him acquainted with the general treatment of patients; and knew of cases of cruelty and inhuman treatment to them.

One case was an Englishman, whose name he does not remember. Said he had, on one occasion, returned from down town, and was standing outside of the building, and heard a distressing voice in the second ward, and went into the building and found the patient in the hands of two men holding him on his back, and the third man standing on the bathing tub and pouring water in his face and nose from a pail. The patient was struggling and strangling for breath.

The witness rescued the patient, and drove the attendants from the room, and reported the case to Dr. McFarland.

He subsequently called the Doctor's attention to the case, with the view of having it investigated, and had a Mr. Crandley do the same.

Being satisfied that the case was not investigated, he reported it to Mr. Stephenson, the President of the Board, and told him if such things occurred again he would make complaint to the grand jury.

He says he frequently heard of other cases of cruelty, from persons employed about the building.

Witness thinks Dr. McFarland is destitute of common sympathy to the patients, and did not listen to their complaints with kindness; nor give that personal attention to the conduct of the attendants which was necessary to a personal knowledge of their treatment; and appeared indifferent when complaints of cruelty were made to him.

The Committee say :—" These eight witnesses, in their testimony specially above referred to, have described particular and atrocious abuses, by attendants, to over twenty different patients, whose names are given ; and the most of the cases are mentioned by them with circumstantial minuteness. The names of eighteen different attendants are mentioned by them as being engaged in these cruelties. The most of them are of comparatively recent date ; and they are within the recollection of witnesses now living and accessible."

CHAPTER XXXIII.

Dr. McFarland's Self-Accusation.

Guilt is its own accuser—So with Dr. McFarland. When he found the "Personal Liberty Bill" had actually passed into a law, and the "Investigating Committee" were also appointed, it seemed to him as if his day of judgment had come, such fear and terror possessed him.

I have been told by a relative of his sister, who lives in Zanesville, Ohio, and she received this information from his sister's own lips that when her brother found the investigation was decided upon by the legislature, and the Committee appointed for this purpose, that he left his family without their knowledge, and without even knowing himself where he should go, with only a small satchel of clothing with him.

He arrived at her house in the evening and, meeting him at her door, in response to his knock, was accosted with this strange inquiry:

" Can you lodge a poor fellow here to-night?"

" Why, Brother Andrew, how do you do? To be sure we can. What do you mean? Come in."

He entered, and in reply to her inquiry said:

" Sister, I am ruined! I am a ruined man!"

" Brother, what ails you? What is the matter?" asked his astonished sister.

" That woman has ruined me! She has got a Committee of the legislature appointed to investigate the asylum. And I am ruined!"

" What lady has ruined you?"

" Mrs. Packard—I kept her in the asylum at her husband's request, and now she has exposed me, and I am ruined."

Dr. McFarland's Self-accusation.

"I am ruined! I am ruined! Mrs. Packard has ruined me!" See page 259.

" Brother, no woman can ruin you. You need not fear her influence. Your character is too well established to be ruined by slander."

" But, Sister, the Committee are appointed—and they are to investigate. And I am ruined! I do not know what to do. I left my family in Jacksonville, without telling them where I was going—I did not know myself."

This panic-stricken sinner's fears could not be allayed by all the reason and argument and entreaties his friends could urge in his behalf. His monotonous response would invariably be :

" I am ruined! Mrs. Packard has ruined me ! "

His friends thought he was insane, that trouble had dethroned his reason and driven him mad, as insanity was hereditary in his family.

They accordingly telegraphed to his wife that they so regarded him—that they would detain him until he became more calm, and would not let him wander farther, unattended. She need not fear, as they should not let him leave their house until he had got over his intense excitement.

At night they visited his room, and instead of finding him in bed, he was walking his room ringing his hands in agony, exclaiming :

" I am ruined! I am ruined! Mrs. Packard has ruined me ! "

Now, is it not true, as the Committee express it :

" That a fair and impartial investigation never injures the *innocent,* but is frequently the means of their vindication, and a restoration of public confidence, where that confidence has been causelessly impaired."

Why, therefore, did Dr. McFarland so dread this investigation if he was innocent, and had conscious rectitude to stand upon ?

In such a case he would have nothing to fear, but everything to hope for, from an impartial investigation.

But did he fear his evil deeds would be exposed, and he be brought to justice by an incensed public ?

So it seems, from his fleeing when no one was pursuing him.

No pursuer !—did I say ?

Yes. He was pursued by a guilty conscience, from which he found it impossible to escape.

It is the wicked or guilty " who flee when no man pursueth;" but the righteous or innocent are " bold as a lion," because they have no reason to fear evil results from conscious rectitude.

CHAPTER XXXIV.

Result of the Investigation.

As seen in the foregoing pages, the Committee found Dr. McFarland a guilty man—guilty of all the charges brought against him—and therefore unworthy the confidence the public had been reposing in him, and these conscientious, faithful investigators had the moral courage to place this public servant just where his own actions placed him.

They had no power delegated to them to depose him. Their instruction from the Legislature was:

" To confer with the trustees for the correction of abuses, and to report to the Governor at their discretion."

This they did ; but they found the trustees determined to defend the Doctor in spite of all this overwhelming testimony of his guilt.

' Therefore to confer with them was useless, so far as correction of abuses was concerned, since they were so blind they would not even see that these abuses did exist.

All that remained now for them to do, was, " to report to the Governor," which they did, Dec. 1st, 1867.

This report was published in the *Tribune* and *Times,* and the verdict of the people plainly coincided with that of the Committee, viz.:

That the present incumbent, Dr. McFarland ought to be removed at once.

But the laws governing the institution admit that no other method of removing the incumbent, except through the trustees who appointed him.

The Committee were powerless to act in that direction, while the trustees sustained the Superintendent. All they had power to do to get him removed they did do, by reporting to the Governor, and if he did not call a special meeting of the Legislature to attend to this business, they must wait until a year from that time, as the Legislature met only once in two years.

But when they did meet in 1869 they reported to that body and their report was accepted and adopted. The following is copied from this report.

The Committee say that in entering upon their duties:

" They had well hoped that, although there might be mistakes or even neglect on the part of the Superintendent nothing involving his character as a humane man and gentleman, would be shown to exist.

" In this, however, the Committee have been grievously disappointed. Familiarity with suffering and sorrow has apparently to some extent, deadened his sensibilities and sympathies; and long accustomed to govern, he has become about the hospital a kind of supreme law, and the rule of force has too often usurped the law of love.

" And the classification of patients in their wards does seem, in many cases, fundamentally wrong. The refined and cultivated are found many times placed where they are annoyed by the vulgar and profane, and often perfectly quiet patients are placed with the noisy, excited, violent and dangerous ones.

" As to ' restraints,' it appears that those in use in the hospital, are the screen-room, the straight-jacket or camisole, the wristers, the crib-bedsteads and the bath-tub, all of which, when properly used, as means of restraining or controlling patients in their paroxysms, seem proper and necessary; but when used as instruments of torture by inhuman angry attendants, as the testimony shows they have been, is reprehensible. The ordinary bath-tub has also been so used in this hospital by the attendants, as a means of punishment, that the threat of a bath has more terrors attached to it than a straight-jacket.

"Again, his police regulations are bad, and fatal to his government. He assumes that insane patients are never to be believed, and therefore does not listen with favor to their complaints.

"He substantially denies the right of petition and investigation, and like all public officers who do this, he finds himself, too late, surrounded with difficulties, and imposed upon.

"He does not require or encourage attendants to report to him each other's delinquencies, and for this reason he is ignorant of a large portion of the abuses. His government of patients is believed too severe, and his discipline of attendants too mild.

"The Committee, throughout the investigation, have endeavored to jealously guard the true interests of the institution— to neither shield the guilty nor magnify their faults—but to carefully ascertain as far as possible, the truth, and when ascertained, to fearlessly declare it.

"They have believed, and still believe, that in view of a late public distrust in its management, justice to all persons officially connected with it, as well as the patients, demanded a thorough investigation, to the end that if complaints so commonly made were without foundation, the officers might be vindicated, and if true, they might be dismissed.

"And the Committee do not at all sympathize with the feelings, very naturally entertained by many persons residing in the vicinity of our State institutions, that they who listen to complaints or promptly investigate them, are enemies to the institution. Such are its true friends.

"The testimony was finally closed on the 30th ultimo, and after hearing the argument of the counsel, and carefully reviewing and considering the evidence, the Committee unanimously resolved that it seemed their imperative duty to recommend:

"*An immediate change in the office of Superintendent*, and the correction of abuses shown to exist."

Signed by the Committee :   ALLEN C. FULLER,
                                   ANDREW J. HUNTER,
                                   ELMER BALDWIN,
                                   T. B. WAKEMAN,
December 2d, 1867.   JOHN B. RICKS.

Action of the Legislature.

REPORT OF JOINT COMMITTEE.

The foregoing reports and evidence and papers relating thereto, having been referred to the Committee on State Institutions of the House, said Committee would respectfully report that the *evidence* relates solely to the management of the Hospital for the insane, and that the report of the Committee of Investigation contains a fair and substantial abstract of so much of said evidence as appears necessary to an understanding of the subject of the Investigation.

From an examination of said reports and evidence, we are satisfied that the investigation was thorough and impartial, and *adopt the conclusions arrived at by the Investigating Committee.*

February 20, 1869.   H. C. CHILDS, *Chairman.*
                                   SAMUEL WILEY,
                                   GEO. GAYLORD,
                                   CHARLES G. READE,
                                   E. H. TALBOT,
                                   C. W. MARSH,
                                   GEO. W. PARKER,
                                   A. KINYON,
                                   N. R. CASEY,
                                   JOHN W. ROSS,
                                   S. R. SALTONSTALL,
                                   JOS. COOPER.
Committee on State Institutions of the House.

The undersigned, Committee on State Institutions of the Senate, in compliance with a joint resolution of this General Assembly, directing them to report an abstract of the testimony taken by the Committee, appointed by the General Assembly, to investigate the affairs of the insane, and other Institutions, respectfully report:

That they have adopted the abstract of the evidence as found in the report of said Investigating Committee, to his Excellency, the Governor, and have caused the said report to be printed in full ; and herewith submit the same for the consideration of the Senate.

JOHN McNULTA, *Chairman.*
JOHN H. ADDAMS,
WILLIAM PATTON,
J. D. WARD,
T. A. BOYD,
J. L. TINCHER,
S. R. CHRITTENDEN,
JAS. M. EPLER,
J. J. R. TURNEY,
Committee on State Institutions of Senate.

12

CHAPTER XXXV.

Dr. McFarland's Exit from the Asylum.

The Investigating Committee finding Dr. McFarland guilty of all the charges brought against him, recommended his immediate removal from the Asylum.

The Legislature endorsed the conclusions arrived at by their Committee.

Governor Palmer fully coincided with the decision of the Legislature, that he be removed, and acted in accordance with his convictions in the course he took to accomplish his immediate exit from the Asylum, as the writer heard from the Governor's own lips. Said he:

" Since the Legislature have recommended the removal of Dr. McFarland, and feeling disposed to act in harmony with them, I therefore made this point a specialty in .the appointment of the Trustees, for by the laws governing this matter, the trustees are the only power that can remove the Superintendent; and determined to appoint no one on this board who would not pledge himself to remove Dr. McFarland at once."

" Did you carry out this purpose, Governor Palmer ? "

" I did, in this manner. Mr. Morrison, one of the trustees, came to me and said he had been appointed by the board to confer with me as to their re-appointment. He said it was self-evident the action of the Legislature required the removal of the Doctor ; that if they were displaced at the same time the verdict of public condemnation would rest upon themselves also. Therefore, to avoid this identification with the Superintendent's fall, they respectfully asked the Governor to re-elect them, saying :

' In the name of the Trustees we give you our pledge that we will remove Dr. McFarland at the earliest possible date.'

Mr. Morrison's Interview with Governor Palmer.

'In the name of the Trustees, we give you our pledge that we will remov'
Dr. McFarland at the earliest possible date!"   See page 266.

" Believing them to be honorable men whose veracity could be trusted in the fulfillment of this, their voluntary pledge of honor, I re-appointed them for another term, fully expecting that at their next meeting, in about two weeks from date, they would do as they had promised to do, viz.: Remove the Superintendent and appoint another in his place.

" But lo! instead of redeeming their promise, by accepting Dr. McFarland's resignation, they reinstated the Doctor and resigned themselves! "

Thus by a resort to deceit, and artfully wicked chicanery, these trustees—men whom the Governor and the people had trusted as the guardians of their institution—dared to set at naught their honor and honesty and recklessly disregard the known wishes of the Governor—the Committee—the Legislature—and the people of Illinois—who had every reason to believe they would do their duty, and carry out the wishes of their constituents by removing this, their unprincipled public servant, in the manner prescribed by law.

This persistent determination on the part of the Trustees to sustain the Doctor in defiance of public sentiment, of truth, honor or justice, demonstrated the fact that policy not principle influenced their action in this matter ; thus proving without a question, that they *deserve* the same condemnation the Superintendent receives from the verdict of the people.

The names of these Trustees are:

> E. G. MINER, *President.*
> FERNANDO JONES,
> JOSEPH T. ECCLES,
> FRANCIS A. HOFFMAN,
> RICHARD C. DUNN,
> ISAAC L. MORRISON.

It had been only about two weeks since this board had been re-appointed, and now, after breaking their solemn promise to the Governor to do the special work for which he had re-clected them, they resigned, leaving it incumbent on Governor Palmer to appoint a new board, which he did.

This board did not deem it their duty to undo the work of their predecessors, but only to take the institution as they found it, and discharge its appropriate duties.

Thus was Dr. McFarland's exit deferred.

As the Legislature would not meet again for two years, he would have, in the mean time, an opportunity to show to the world that he was not discharged as the result of the investigation, but as he remained in his office the natural inference would be that his character was vindicated!

But it was not.

The unmistakable voice of the people uttered its condemnation too distinctly to venture another expression of its wishes through the coming Legislature.

To avoid this, he therefore resigned before the meeting of the next Legislature, and his resignation was accepted and another appointed and installed in his place.

Dr. McFarland still resides in Jacksonville, in a house which he has built upon his large farm, which he has so long culti-vated by the unpaid labor of Illinois State prisoners, who have been falsely represented as Dr. McFarland's patients, when in reality they were his slaves.

From the avails of this labor, thus purloined, he has re-ceived a remunerative income, by which, added to the other robberies he has made upon the State's appropriated funds for their Asylum, he has become quite wealthy.

One of this Investigating Committee remarked to me in view of the deceit and chicanery developed by the investigation:

"I never saw such an exhibition of artifice, deceit and double dealing and robbery and purloining of public treasure in any department of society as was developed by the prac-tices of this corrupt Superintendent."

Rumor says, that Dr. McFarland is intending to convert his house into a private asylum, hoping the public will still patronize him as an expert in the cure of insanity!

But if the number he has cured by his treatment were balanced by the number he has killed and made hopelessly insane, it is my opinion the scales would indicate a decided balance in favor of those he has murdered and made insane maniacs, over the number he has cured.

And besides those he claims as his cured patients, are in a majority of cases those who were cured in spite of his treatment rather than in consequence of it. Like the infants thrown into the Ganges, those who are devoured and drowned are the rule, while those who escape this fate are the exceptions.

As far as *treatment* is concerned, the most indifferent nurse could do more towards curing an insane person than I ever knew Dr. McFarland to do, either directly or indirectly. For what one physician said of his treatment at Utica Asylum, New York, might with truth be said of many of the patients in Jacksonville Asylum while I was there, namely :

He said in consequence of loss of property and failure in business he became melancholy and partially insane and his friends advised that he go to the asylum at Utica, N. Y., for treatment. He went, and while riding over the country which intervened between his home and the asylum, a distance of several days' ride in a private vehicle, his mind became so diverted by the scenery of the country through which he passed, and the varied and new surroundings of asylum life, that before he had been in the asylum twenty-four hours he became entirely sane.

Now comes in the " *treatment* " he received. For three years after his reception for " treatment," the doctor never even so much as spoke to him, much less treated him medically !

He was kept a close prisoner five years, when he succeeded

in making his escape, and has since been a successful practitioner of medicine. He asserts that he was just as sane all these five years as he is at present, and would have been there still had he been dependent upon the Superintendent for his discharge.

Now we would inquire, what medical knowledge does a Superintendent or medical physician need in an Insane Asylum?

Judging of his application of his knowledge to the patients he needs none at all!

Any one who can turn a bolt with the key of the State is capacitated for a medical Superintendent of our present Insane Asylum system, conducted as that was by Dr. Andrew McFarland at Jacksonville.

The Investigating Committee reported that they found just, and abundant occasion for complaint of criminal indifference on the part of the Superintendent towards the interests of his patients.

I have been told, neither do I doubt the fact, that patients have been known to have been dead and buried one year in the asylum burial grounds before the Superintendent had even informed their friends of their death!

Such cases have doubtless been the victims of foul usage, whose corpses would have testified against him, had they been suffered to be examined by their friends, in a reasonable time after their decease. And the heathenish usage of insane asylums generally, of burying their patients secretly, and regardless of any Christian obsequies or ceremonies, affords these murderers a rare opportunity for escaping detection of their crimes, which, under other circumstances, would convict a man of a capital criminal offense.

At Jacksonville Asylum the patients are buried in the dead of night by lamp-light—without the least recognition of their humanity by any kind of burial service. But mournerless and palless the rough box containing the corpse is transported upon an ox-cart to the unenclosed and unadorned burial ground of the asylum, near by, where the hirelings bury them as they would a beast! and leave no monument to designate the spot where they lie, except a humble wooden slab at the head of the grave.

I will close this chapter, with an extract from "Mrs. Olsen's Prison Life," who has in her book given a graphic description of an asylum burial in these words, viz. :

" I wish here to mention that the deaths are kept as secret as possible. The body is carried away in the night, with no funeral, and either sent home or buried in the asylum cemetery.

" In one of my walks, I counted eighty-seven graves in that little enclosure, which, on inquiry, I found had been dug in less than four years—though I have reason to believe that the great majority of those who die are not buried there, but conveyed to their former homes in their coffins.

" How many go there to find their ' cure ' in death is more, I imagine, than is for the interest of Dr. McFarland to make public.

" Then hurry on some cheap shroud—hustle them into a cheap coffin—don't stop for a funeral—where are the mourners!—take them from their cells to the dead-room—step quickly, but carefully—make no noise—go out in twilight when no one sees—throw up the turf with hasty spade—and then by the trembling moon-beams aid, or " the lantern dimly burning, bury them darkly at dead of night!" No minister—no weeping—no matter—*they are insane!*"   •

> " Rattle their bones over the stones,
> They are lunatics! that no one but ' Jesus owns.' "

CHAPTER XXXVI

The Death Penalty to be Annihilated.

Dr. McFarland says he does not believe in annihilating the death penalty for murder—that he has not progressed so far as that—for he says :

" Did not God command life to be taken for life ?   Did He not command Agag to be hewn in pieces as his punishment ?"

I replied, " Yes, He did, but I do not therefore infer that we have a right so to do, for He himself was the law-maker and executive of the Jewish code.   Of course every law was just and right, being wisely adapted to the infant state in which the race of men then existed."

" Do you think the race is in any better condition now than it was then ? "

" I consider they are in a more developed state ; good and evil are both stronger and more vigorous, because their capacities have increased. In consequence of this growth or development, a different kind of training is required to adapt itself to man's higher nature.   For example, you would not feel justified in using the same kind of discipline over your developed son of twenty-one years, as with your son of three or five years. To attempt to compel him with penalties and restraints as you do your child, would be trifling with his manhood, insulting his manly feelings, and would justly bring you and your authority into derision.   So God having himself controlled the race in its childhood, and as their father until they were of age, when they must require a different kind of training, He then abrogated the Jewish code, and instituted in its place, the Christian dispensation, of which Christ was the expounder.   Now, instead of returning " an eye for an eye, and a tooth for a tooth," we must return good for evil, and leave judgment and vengeance for our wrongs, to Him who judgeth righteous judgment. For he says, " Vengeance is mine, I will repay."

I do not think it is right for one sinner to punish another sinner. None but a righteous person is capable of inflicting a righteous punishment. God knowing this, instructs us to leave this matter entirely to Himself. He may rise up and qualify a class of capacitated judges from the human race, to whom this power of judgment may be delegated.

But I think this will never be the case, so long as God's image in man is so defaced. The lost image of the godhead must be restored in man, before he can be fitted to be God's representative on the earth as judge of his fellow men.

I think the time is not far distant when righteousness shall be established on the earth ; when Christ-like men will rule supreme over fallen perverted humanity. Then the demon, Penalty, will give place to the law of love and kindness, by means of which the transgressor will be reformed and restored to virtue, instead of being crushed down and debased by pen-alties as he now is. His God-like nature is now trampled in the dust, and no effort to rise are encouraged, but rather smothered by attempts to degrade him to the level of a beast.

Punishments of a corporal kind are only adapted to man as an animal, in the earlier stages of his existence ; their influence can never be salutary after he has become a reasonable and accountable moral agent. He then sins through his reason and his intelligence, and he must be punished through his moral faculties as God has ordained. Shame and contrition must be awakened through the influence of respectful kindness to the wrong-doer ; not by trying to degrade the noble faculties of his nature to a state of insensibility to moral influences by punishments.

The more man becomes developed as a reasonable being, the

more sensitive he becomes to those penal enactments whose
legitimate tendencies are to obstruct, limit and destroy the
natural aspirations of a moral agent.

The age of penalties seems now to have culminated in this
horrible civil war, wherein the developed reason of man is
fiendishly employed in inventing means of destroying one another in the most barbarous manner.   This crisis once passed,
I believe the reign of peace will be inaugurated, wherein virtue
will be protected, and cultivated by the influence of love and
kindness, entirely independent of penalties and restraints.

Now I claim, that these principles of punishment are ap-
plicable to these asylum systems, and also of reforming Dr.
McFarland, and other great sinners.

Some of the moral forces of the universe have already ripened
into vigorous manhood, and through their combined influence,
evil is becoming timid, and seeks concealment, which is one
step towards its annihilation.

Like the concealing of the gallows from public observation
into the prison yard, within the prison walls, indicating that
the death penalty is to be destroyed, and is now on its way to
destruction—this may be what is meant by death and hell
being destroyed—that the death penalty and punishment both
are to be annihilated in that community where moral power
has acquired its manhood strength, and can stand alone, self-
reliant, independent of penalties for its existence, just as a
child naturally outgrows his educational influences, and with
them, the penalties of disobedience, which in his infancy and
childhood are necessary helps to his virtues.   But when these
have acquired manly strength, he no longer needs restraint and
penalties, but can be trusted to take care of himself independent of dictation or control from others.   In his own heart
he has the only monitor he needs for virtuous action, viz: the
dictates of an enlightened conscience.

I believe the time has come when this hard-hearted man

must be punished for his iniquities. For a long time he has sustained the responsibilities of his position with honors not deserved. He has for a long time been trying to cover up the barbarities of his treatment of the prisoners, and has succeeded in making it appear otherwise. He has so deluded the mind of the Trustees and Legislature, by his sophistry and deep, cunning artifice, as to secure such laws as protect him in doing his nefarious work thus long undetected and unmolested.

But the " searcher of hearts " can not be deceived or deluded. He cannot be controlled by misrepresentations and a covert of lies. Lo! God, himself, by his providence, is now bringing him to justice; for after his long forbearance towards him, by giving him opportunities and space for repentance, he persists in clinging to his sins, instead of repenting of them.

And now, Pharaoh like, he has sinned away his day of grace, so that repentance cannot now be accepted and pardon secured; but on the contrary, he must suffer the punishment due for his transgressions. The curse which his own conduct has secured, must come upon him, and no human power can prevent it.

I do believe Dr. McFarland is now, like Pharaoh, undergoing that hardening of heart process which God calls his work; that is, God will not let him repent until he has been punished. In other words, justice, stern justice, has taken the place which mercy before occupied. And when God hardens the heart no man can soften it. Inevitable destruction invariably follows God's hardening process.

This hardening process of the heart, such as God claims as his work, is only the developing of the real character, which character we have previously acquired by our own voluntary acts, while we have the liberty to choose for ourselves either the good or evil. But when we have reached a certain point, the ability to choose good is taken from us, so that we can then only choose evil. God is then in his way hardening the heart.

CHAPTER XXXVII.

The Imputation of Insanity a Barrier to Human Progress.

At one time I was made to feel exceedingly sad and sorrowful by a conversation I had with a lady who called upon me. I conversed freely and frankly with her, as usual, avowing my views and sentiments, and giving my reasons for the course I was pursuing.

In her undeveloped condition she failed to comprehend them fully, and therefore, since the brand of insanity was upon me, she concluded these points which she could not readily comprehend, were products of my insanity!

This, from her standpoint, being an inevitable conclusion, her mind would necessarily be barred against any convictions of truth which I might present to her reason or intelligence. These goggles of insanity through which she now looks, disturb all her mental vision, so that she can no more apprehend a new truth through me, as its medium, than the scales of bigotry will admit any light through those who war with its dogmas.

Now, supposing this position should be generally adopted, viz. : that what we cannot readily apprehend, is insanity ; what encouragement have we to make progress, or become the benefactors of our age, knowing that just as soon as we advance to any point of intelligence beyond another, we must be regarded and treated as insane, and thus expose ourselves to a life-long imprisonment unless we recant ?

Is not the imputation of insanity the devil's barrier to human progress ?

I feel that we ought to be very careful not to condemn what

we do not understand, for in Christ's case, his persecutors were condemned as guilty of "blasphemy," for doing this very thing.

The blinded Jews, who were wedded to their creed with as firm a tenacity as the Orthodox Church of the present day is to their own, could not therefore apprehend the principles of the new dispensation, which Christ came to introduce, because it conflicted with their church creed; therefore they accused this innovator with madness or insanity for promulgating such new and strange doctrines.

Like the same class at the present age, they did not wait to see evidence of his insanity in his evil actions, before they condemned him; but merely for his expression or utterance of opinions, he was condemned as a madman.

Now I think his accusers *acted* more like madmen than he did, when we come to take *actions* as evidence of insanity, instead of the expression of opinions. And even if we take their own basis of evidence, I think the Jewish dogmas which their church defended were as great an evidence of insanity in them, as the opinions which Christ taught in opposition to their standard of morals, were evidence of insanity in him.

But I do not think that the utterance of opinions in either case, is any evidence of insanity.

The Jews believed they had received their dispensation from God, and, of course, they were tenacious in its defense, and could not readily see that the time had come for the old to give place to the new.

So it is in all ages, some are slower than others to see that the time for the inauguration of any new truth has fully come, and therefore they oppose it with the same intolerant spirit which the Jewish ministers did.

But so far as the question of insanity goes, they show the greatest proof of being insane, who oppose this inauguration with vile slander, and ruinous scandal, and false imprisonment, and death, rather than those who calmly stand by the truth, and defend it with sound and invincible logic.

It was this very inoffensiveness in Christ which so exasperated them against him, plainly showing that it was they who had the devil of bigotry in them, not him. It was they, the Jewish ministers, who were the blasphemers, instead of him whom they accused of blasphemy.

The views and theories taught by Christ, were all humanitarian in their character; yet this did not shield him from the assaults of slander and the charge of insanity; neither will this armor prove a defense at the present age, even under the American flag of free religious toleration, so long as reformers are allowed to be publicly branded by these insane asylums.

Whoever has the diploma of this institution forced upon him, must submit henceforth to fight his way through fire and blood to carry out his benevolent purposes to humanity; for at every inch of progress, he is compelled to face the barbed arrow of insanity hurled at him by the intolerant and bigoted of his age. If by any possible means, the imputation of insanity can be removed from the track of the reformer, the wheel of human progress will be greatly accelerated.

Again my persecutors are guilty of the same act of uncharitableness in calling the natural developments of womanhood evil, or insanity, in me.

This undeveloped sister insists that it is impossible for me to be what I profess to be, a true woman, and not have overcome the evil in my husband; since goodness is omnipotent.

I acknowledge the potency of goodness, while I, at the same time add, that I do not believe that she or any other woman could have borne more patiently with a husband's faults, or have labored more kindly and indefatigably to overcome them than I have done. I regard such a man as a most subtle foe to conquer, and that ultimately, Christ may, through my instrumentality, conquer him. But the time has not yet come.

It is said of Christ, " Thou hast put all things in subjection under his feet," as I believe, for the purpose of raising them to a state of happiness and purity. Christ conquers not to punish, but to bless his foes.

I believe my twenty-one years of subjection to my husband's will, is not designed as a punishment to me, but as a blessed means of bringing me to lose all my natural loves in the love of God's will. Thus am I called to die to live again—to die naturally, to live spiritually. I hope this new life has begun in me. May it be developed into maturity !

Another point she could not understand in me is, that I call it a reproach to be called insane, when she says it is not a reproach to be insane.

I do not regard an insane person as an object of reproach or contempt, by any means. They are objects of pity and compassion ; for I regard insanity as the greatest misfortune which can befall a human being in this life. But to be regarded as an insane person, when I am not, is to me a reproach, which I find is a severe cross for me to bear ; such as for example, to be reported to be a bankrupt, when I am not, is a reproach, because it is a cruel slander.

But how much more malevolent and cruel is the slander, to be reported as lost to reason when we are not.

I think the sensitive feelings of Christ led him to feel it to be a reproach to have his age say of him :

" He hath a devil and is mad, why hear ye him ? " As much as to say, " Why will you listen to what this ' babbler ' says ? he is not worth noticing, for he is merely an insane person, who don't know what he is about."

Now, since he expressly says it is " blasphemy, in that they said he hath a devil ; " and since blasphemy is the blackest sin which can be committed against Christ. have we not reason to fear it is of the same type of magnitude when committed against his followers ?

But so far as I am concerned, I can forgive this injury which this sister has thus inflicted upon my sensitive feelings, although Christ says, blasphemy is a sin which cannot be forgiven, " either in this life, or the life to come." I do pray that she may never know from her own sad experience, how deeply she has wounded my feelings ; and never, until she is called to bear this same reproach, can she know how ponderous is the burden.

CHAPTER XXXVIII.

The Guilt of Folly.

There are some crimes, the charging of which, falsely, is worse than the crimes themselves.

So with my husband's false accusation of insanity in me, he commits a greater crime against me, than it would be in him to really become insane.

The false accusation is a crime, whereas the thing charged is no crime.

Neither is he guiltless in treating me as insane, when this delusion of his is only the result of misapprehension, for he is to blame for getting into this deluded state. He has resisted known light, and a persistence in his folly has so blinded him that now he cannot see correctly. At the same time, he is to blame, because he ought not to have got into this state. Like the drunkard, who unconsciously harms another, is guilty, for he ought not to have got into this unconscious state.

The good of society requires that folly, as well as rascality, should be responsible for their own actions.

Again, this state of folly can only be controlled by brute force or fear, since while in it, they are dead to all influences of a higher kind. And the just punishment of this folly is demanded as a warning to others to avoid such a state. These victims of folly must be held in check, by force, until consciousness so far returns as to lead them to see the wrong they have done ; and this time has not come, until they feel sorry for their trespass upon others' rights. My husband must see that there is no hope of help for him, until he can see that he has done wrong ; then he will be in a suitable state to receive his pardon from me. Until that time comes, he cannot appreciate forgiveness if it should be offered.　It is my duty to hold him there until he does.

Again, this accusation is a crime of great magnitude, because there is no chance of a termination of my imprisonment while on this basis.　Real insanity may possibly be cured, and thus hope lies for the insane in the future; but the case of the falsely accused is hopeless—for if unchanged, he is treated as insane, and if he becomes insane, his case is hopeless.

There were certainly some of the most reasonable persons in the world imprisoned there, apparently hopelessly, simply because some individual has chosen to represent them so, and they justify themselves in this accusation, on the plea that they have a right to their opinions.

So they have the same right to their opinion that a traitor has to justify himself, on the ground that it is his opinion that the government ought to be overthrown!　Traitors have a right to their opinions as traitors, and they also have a right to the penalty which the law attaches to such opinions when practically expressed.

The defamer pleads that he has a right to destroy the character of one whom he regards as an errorist, since he claims these errors injure society, and therefore a benevolent regard to community demands the slander.　Now we never have a right to do wrong, and no evil can be justified on the ground that good requires it.　Goodness is never dependent upon sin for its maintenance or support.　Right and justice are sometimes demanded by goodness, but never does it demand wrong or wickedness for its defense.

It is the highest treason to our Heavenly Father's government, to try to destroy the moral influence of a member of his family in order to promote their own selfish purposes. It is an attempt to overthrow God's government, in the individual, to represent him as insane when he is not, for it is his accountability he is thus trying to destroy.

That it is a crime to call a sane person an insane one appears too, in the mental torture this charge brings with it. It is very embarassing to a sensitive person to be looked upon in all they say or do, as an insane person. The least mistake, a slip of the tongue, a look, a gesture, are all liable to be interpreted as insanity, and the least difference of opinion, however reasonable or plausible, is liable to share the same reproach.

So that an advocate for any new truth, or any progressive science which must necessarily dethrone human dogmas, while under this charge, is under a paralyzing influence.

But let any other person who is not thus branded, advance the same ideas, they would be regarded as evidence of intelligence of a superior order. And although truth is not changed by the medium through which it passes, yet, as the world now is, in its undeveloped state, it more readily listens to a new truth coming through a medium of acknowledged sanity, than when it comes through one who has the diploma of insanity attached to his name. But still the medium is not the truth, neither is the truth enhanced or disminished by the medium who utters it.

Again, it is a crime because hundreds are kept there to whom an imprisonment is as much of an outrage as slavery is to the bondman. Because some insane persons are sometimes dangerous, it is thought right to keep all who are called insane, *prisoners!* Thus, the most sensible people on earth, are exposed to suffer a life-long imprisonment, from the folly of some undeveloped misguided person.

And the tendency of imprisonment itself, is sadly detrimental to a person who has intelligence enough to realize that he is held under lock and key.

To persist in treating them as though they were unable to take care of themselves, as to undermine self-reliance and self-respect. In short, it tends to destroy all that which is noble and aspiring in humanity, more directly, and more surely than any course the great enemy of the race has hitherto devised. To subject a human being to the legitimate influence of this insane asylum system, is like the Hindoos throwing their children into the Ganges, most of whom are drowned, of course, but the few who do escape are those who retain life with peculiar vigor and tenacity.

Yes, I am sure that any one who can go through there and come out unharmed may well be considered as insanity proof.

God's grace must work in them, to will and to do right in all things, or no security is granted them ; and these few cases of successful resistance are like the pure gold, the hotter the fire, the purer it becomes. The Christian graces which are there called into exercise, are thus strengthened, purified, concentrated, intensified, so that the minor temptations and onsets of the powers of darkness are now looked upon as mere skirmishes, compared with the fierce, deadly battles of this asylum life.

Is not the slander of insanity the most cruel kind of defamation that can be instigated against another ? From what right does it not exclude us, except that of eating and sleeping like animals ?

Nothing more or less.

And can this highest of all wrongs and insults to a human being, be looked upon with any degree of allowance, by him who bestowed these moral natures upon man ?—the very godhead thus crushed out of a human being, and he be made to believe that he is only a brute beast, with no claims upon his fellow creatures, higher than theirs—to put a high toned, sensitive, developed human soul upon this level, by base design, for base purposes, by the basest of malicious lies ?

Is it not a sin of the deepest dye ?

Can there be any greater blasphemy against God, or against the Holy Ghost ?

I know, by tasting this cup to its bitterest dregs, what it is to feel this deepest wrong—the kidnapping of the soul—depriving a human being of his God-bestowed accountability. To kidnap a human being, and treat him as a slave, is a terrible outrage upon human nature ; but this is not to be compared with the still blacker crime of kidnapping their accountability, and making them nothing but brutes.

Slaves are allowed to exert their abilities to work, and thus feel that somebody is benefited by them ; but the insane are considered below them. They are not allowed to feel that they are capable of being of any manner of service to the world, but degraded as useless burdens, which others must carry through life—as paupers, whose only satisfaction to themselves and others, is the fact that they can die, and thus rid the world of a useless animal !

This is the " treatment " for which Dr. McFarland endeavors to awaken gratitude in me, for having been permitted to enjoy here freely so long ! But I cannot manifest my gratitude for this great privilege, by thanking him for thus making me the recipient of so much misery.

Could I be guiltless in God's sight, and allow another to suffer what I have, for fear of any consequences attending myself ?

I could never meet my Judge in peace, unless I had given a truthful representation of this institution !

A few may have left here without realizing the nature and tendency of the Asylum System. Either they were too insane to detect and judge correctly of it, or too unsympathizing to feel for others.

Others there were, who saw and fully appreciated these things, but who were so overjoyed at their deliverance, that they seemed to forget their former impressions.

Others, remembering them with most vivid distinctness, were heard to avow their resolution, never to speak of these things, outside the institution, lest it revive these impressions.

They looked upon them as a kind of horrid nightmare, which they wished to banish, as soon as possible, from their recollection.

Again, the guilt attending this folly is great when we contemplate how very difficult it is to get out of this prison at all. I find this idea illustrated in my journal in the following manner :

" I have just been noticing the struggles of a fly, lying upon my window-sill. It vainly strives to regain its natural position, and every collateral influence only increases its fruitless struggles ; but when I placed my finger directly over so its feet could clasp it, immediately it assumed its upright position by a perfectly natural motion. All its previous efforts unaided, were not only fruitless, but exhausting to its energies, so that when help came, it was weak from this exertion.

" So I have been long striving to deliver myself, unaided, but all in vain. But when my efforts have attracted the attention of some competent influence directed by a power from above, I shall experience all needed help to rise to the position God has designed me to fill. Now, since my deliverance depends wholly upon the influence of a power above me, I must learn to trust it by faith, and like the fly, lie quietly prostrate, waiting patiently until help comes to my rescue."

Again, the guilt attending the folly of imprisoning sane people, or those who have never forfeited their right to their personal liberty by their own insane or criminal actions, is seen in the expense it incurs to keep them at Jacksonville Insane Asylum. It gives the tax payers a just cause to complain of enormously unjust taxes, while it costs the State of Illinois one thousand dollars a year to keep each of their prisoners at that institution. If the statement made before the Senate in the winter of 1867, by Senator Ward of Chicago, who was appointed by that body to investigate the management of that institution, is true—viz.: that as the institution is now conducted, it cost Cook County one thousand dollars a year for each occupant from that county; and he added:

" I will engage to take care of them at that price myself!"

Now, if the people would but exercise their own good common sense in this matter, they would find that their own afflicted friends could be far better cared for in their own homes, than they are now cared for at this institution, and that the expense attending it would be materially lessened, by a return to the simple principles of natural humanity and common sense in the treatment of this unfortunate class. Until this is the case, the guilt attending the folly of our present system must be needlessly enhanced by the enormous taxes demanded in support of these institutions on their present corrupt basis.

This principle was illustrated in my asylum life by the folly of my attendant, Mrs. De La Hay, leaving the gas at night so as to escape so freely as to endanger the lives of twenty helpless prisoners. I happened to hear complaints of an uncommon character in our dormitory, when I was so disturbed as to awake. Finding the cause, I succeeded, by persistent calling, in arousing our attendant to come to our rescue from death by suffocation. Had I failed to awaken her, we might all have been corpses before morning. Now her carelessness was criminal folly in thus exposing our lives, still I could not succeed in leading the Superintendent to see the criminality of this careless act, for she did not *intend* to harm us. Yet, had we all died from her foolish neglect, what would have been the difference to us whether she had intended it or not? Our lives would have paid the forfeit of her carelessness, and yet she was not criminal!

So our suffering false imprisonment for others' mistakes or follies is a crime, as was her careless act under the circumstances, and society ought so to be educated into this principle.

CHAPTER XXXIX.

Orthodox Heaven and Hell.

If Insane Asylums are not the Presbyterian heaven and hell combined, so long preached by Mr. Packard, I do not know what is! Endless torment, inflicted by a heartless despot, from whom it is impossible to escape, and whom it is as impossible to move to pity or compassionate his helpless victims, is but the symbol of this Pandemonium.

If hope once reaches here, it is in despite of him and his power and influence.

This is also their heaven; since we here have hard "seats" to sit upon, and nothing to do or amuse, except to sit and sing, in presence of the writhing of lost spirits! Rest and sing!

What *rest* can a benevolent sympathizing nature experience, while knowing another soul is in torment!

There is no rest for active benevolence. So long as one soul is unredeemed from Satan's power, I must work for *that* soul's deliverance before I can sing:

" Worthy is the Lamb that was slain to redeem mankind."

The confident assurance that it will be redeemed, is the only ground upon which I can rely for peace and quiet in the mean time. Attractive as are the hard seats of heaven for " rest" to the idler, to me they have no attraction. All my god-like powers thirst for action, and use.

Inert, stupid indifference to others' interests, is, to my social sympathetic nature, a moral impossibility; and I heartily pray God to deliver me from a mansion in such a heaven, in company with such spirits.

My experience of it here in this asylum, has been enough

for me. If this is the character of heaven, for which we have borne the discipline of our earth life, I wish my earth life never to terminate, for such a heaven of " rest" is hell to me.

Again, can hell be a worse institution than this, while it punishes the best citizens for the offenses of the worst?

There have been hundreds imprisoned in it whose only offense is being true to the promptings of the spirit of God within them.

They are more natural, more god-like than their cotemporaries, and the laws are so insane in their application, that they punish the best citizens for the offenses of the worst.

The dictatorial dogmatist contrives with the sagacity which the " old serpent" imparts to him, to so misrepresent and vilify the honest self-sacrificing Christian, who is striving to live out the dictates of an enlightened conscience, that he is either compelled to compromise with iniquity, or, if steadfast for the right, he is made to endure the false charge of insanity.

Henceforth he must be regarded as an incompetent being, incapable of self-government, and thus subject to all the abuses and insults which can be heaped upon him. Like his Master, he is now called to pass through Gethsemane's garden alone, with none to listen to his sorrows, or alleviate his anguish, with wakeful, generous sympathy. Even his own familiar friend, in whom he trusted, his bosom companion, has lifted his heel against him, and now no one dares to comfort or defend him against this accuser.

Thus forsaken. deserted, desolate, he finds no refuge left him, except the tower of faith, whose dome of love shelters his lonely heart. If that tower is so strongly fortified as to prove invulnerable, he is safe. If not, he is left refugeless, with no home or shelter on earth or in heaven. He is now the ready prey for the roaring lion, who delights in his ruin.

He then becomes insane, made so by the indefatigable efforts of his friends, aided by the evil influences of this Inquisition.

13

His high and noble nature is driven to desperation by these combined forces, and his reason becomes lost in frenzied impulse!

Why, Oh, why, is it that such institutions are permitted to get a foothold upon the free soil of our republicanism? Why cannot our natures, made in God's image here, be allowed free scope for a natural development? Why cannot the intellectual and spiritual nature of man here have free scope to run to perfection?

Is it because the spiritual nature of man can only become perfected by opposition, by restraint, by overcoming obstacles? Can its strength and power of self-reliance be only thus acquired?

Oh, if the blood of martyrs must be the seed of this Spiritual Church, as it has been of the Christian Church, cannot the long list of martyrs which this institution has furnished, be sufficient for this age of spiritual development? or, must every stage of spiritual progress be thus marked by the sable robes of martyrdom?

Is not the time at hand when man may be free to obey the impulses of his spiritual nature, without being called insane?

These holy influences I cannot, will not, resist, defenseless as I am. The inner law of my own mind shall never yield to human dictation, encouraged by the conviction that the end of this American Inquisition cannot be far distant.

CHAPTER XL.

My Effort in Connecticut Legislature.

After selling five hundred books in the city of New Haven, and conversing with twice that number of the most intelligent men of the city, the way, as they intimated, seemed prepared for the passage of a bill to remove some of the legal disabilities of married women.

Taking council, therefore, of some of the most prominent members of the bar in this city, and also Mr. Francis Fellowes, of Hartford, I drew up a Petition and circulated it among some of these patrons, asking the Legislature to ameliorate their condition, in the following terms, viz.:

To the Honorable Senate and House of Representatives in General Assembly convened:

"We, the undersigned citizens of Connecticut, respectfully represent that the Common law in relation to the social condition of married women, deprives her of any legal existence, and legal protection as a married woman, thus wholly excluding her while a married woman, from the protection in law of any of her natural rights, such as a right to herself, a right to her children, a right to her home—thus leaving the protection of all her natural rights, wholly at the will or mercy of her husband; that this unlimited power is liable to, and has become an oppressive power; that the law of divorce is one of the great evils which her present legal position necessarily entails upon society.

And further, while this licensed oppression reflects only the spirit of the common law of the dark ages, when the married woman was the mere slave of the husband; we now under the light of progressive civilization, assign her the place of companion of her husband and joint partner with him in his family interests.

Therefore, we, the undersigned, respectfully petition that your honorable body will take into consideration the present legal position of married women, and inquire, by committee or otherwise, whether this slavish principle of common law, viz.: *the legal nonentity of the wife*, cannot justly and profitably be either abolished, or so far modified, as to protect her against the abuse of this absolute power of her husband, by granting her legally the same protection in government, which the enlightened public sentiment of the present age grants her in her social position in society."

Two hundred and fifty men of the highest standing in New Haven signed the above petition, and it was presented to the Legislature, convened in New Haven, in May, 1866; was referred to the Judiciary Committee, and I was called upon to defend it.

But at the first interview, owing to the absence of some members, and limited time, it was agreed that I meet them one week from date, and that a notice be given to the Legislature that other members might be present.

In accordance with this arrangement, I went as appointed, and found to my surprise, that at Governor Hawley's suggestion, all the Committees had been advised to suspend their business at that hour for the purpose of listening to my defense.

As the result, a great crowd assembled in and about the room of the Judiciary Committee at the hour appointed. But as this room could not accommodate half this number it was suggested that we adjourn to the senate chamber.

A voice from outside cried out:

"The senate chamber can't accommodate half the number present!"

The chairman then inquired if I was willing to go to the legislative hall and make my defense.

I told him I was willing to go anywhere they thought best.

I accordingly followed this crowd to the legislative hall, and took my stand at the table below the speaker's stand, when a voice cried out:

"Go upon the speaker's stand! We can't see the lady."

Thither I went at the committee's request, and read my defense to a room full of attentive listeners.

Besides the members, there were many patrons present, including some clergymen, and Judge Dutton, the teacher of the law school, his pupils, and members of the bar and some ladies.

This was the first time I ever stood before an audience as a public speaker, and this position I did not seek or even anticipate when I prepared my address; however, as I had been a teacher and accustomed to speak from the platform of a large school-room, I found no difficulty in making my present audience understand my argument, as indicated by their silence while I spoke, and the burst of applause as I descended from the stand.

The chairman then inquired if there were any objections to this bill being passed.

No one spoke.

He repeated his question a second and third time.

Still no one ventured to bring forward the least kind of opposition.

The chairman smilingly remarked:

"There seems to be but one side to this question."

And after extending to me a very complimentary vote of thanks, with a request that the address be published, they adjourned.

It was printed in the *New Haven Journal*, and may be found in the appendix to this volume.

As an evidence that the true legal position of married woman was properly and truthfully delineated, I will venture to quote Judge Dutton's remark to me upon this subject:

"Mrs. Packard, you have given the true view of law throughout the whole civilized world. On the common law basis married woman is legally a slave."

And another eminent lawyer in that city also said to me:

" There is not a lawyer in Connecticut who could have given so correct an elucidation of the law as you have done."

But I regret to add, that the subsequent action of this committee demonstrated the fact that their silence did not indicate consent in this matter, for the petition was adversely reported upon.

Mr. Wait, the worthy chairman of the committee, stated that:

" They had listened to Mrs. Packard's eloquent appeal, and though they could not grant her petition, yet they deeply sympathized with her and her cause. They deemed it inexpedient to make such radical changes at the present time, but in the revision of the statutes soon to be made, this petition they hoped would be embraced in those laws. The petitioners were granted leave to withdraw."

I am happy to add that the subsequent action of the Connecticut Legislature has in part verified the wish expressed by the worthy chairman.

From a letter I have recently received from Mr. Francis Fellowes, of Hartford, in reply to my own, wherein I asked him for information upon this subject, I have reason to believe that Connecticut is not now an exception to her sister States in her modification of the common law for married woman's benefit.

The leaven of truth has at last penetrated the conservative element of Connecticut statesmen, and they also are verging towards that not far distant period, as we hope, when not only the married women of Connecticut but of all the States of this Union shall have legally granted to them the same protection in government which the enlightened public sentiment of the present age grants her in her social position in society

CHAPTER XLI.

The Opposition of the Conspiracy.

The history of my Connecticut campaign would be incomplete, did I fail to notice the opposition the conspiracy sent into the field as a terrible antagonist for me to encounter. Although it had been my constant aim to prosecute this work with as little notoriety as possible, yet, it seemed the enemy kept track of my movements, and in the most unexpected and unguarded moment made an attack upon me through the columns of the New Haven *Journal*, who sold them the right to publish a column of the most cruel and vile slanders against my moral character, which it would seem possible for the combined ability of Mr. Packard and Dr. McFarland to manufacture against me.

So notoriously cruel and false were the insinuations there cast upon my stainless character and reputation, that an eminent Judge, then acting as an attorney at law, seriously advised me to enter a prosecution, at once, against Dr. McFarland for defamation, and to bring in my damages at not less than one hundred thousand dollars, adding:

"And you will get it! and I should like to act as your attorney in this prosecution."

So far as I was concerned in this matter, as an individual, it mattered little to me, knowing that *false* accusation cannot in the end harm my character or reputation, still, for the cause I represented, I did feel deeply hurt to have this avalanche of scandal descend upon this community, whose entire confidence I seemed to have hitherto secured, just at that most important crisis, when the committee were about to take action upon this subject.

I know not what influence this scandalous article had upon their decision, yet, I do know, from their own confession, that some of my warmest friends were taken aback by it, and for a time held their favorable judgment of me and my work in abeyance. Yet in a short time the reaction came, and their confidence and sympathy became more than ever a souce of gratification and solace to my wounded feelings.

But before this point was attained the evil was done by the committee reporting adversely upon my petition.

One man very graphically and truthfully described the influence of this article to be like that experienced when the cry of " Gunpowder ! " is uttered to a crowd in a tone of warning to escape danger. The crowd would instinctively fall back and scatter under the influence of this panic even without stopping to inquire whether the alarm is a false or real one; and if it really was merely a fictitious alarm, it would necessarily take a little time to rally after such a panic, even when it was proved to be a false alarm.

So the legislature acting under the influence of this panic, perhaps, acted differently from what they might have acted, had they waited for an investigation, or had acted before this panic and independent of it.

Taking this view of the case, I felt it to be one of the severest strokes I had ever received from this cruel conspiracy, and I felt like saying :

" Could you not have so planned your plot as to have wreaked your venomous spirit upon me alone, without endangering or jeopardizing my precious cause also ? "

Thus all the pecuniary sacrifices I had made for this cause, by presenting each member of the Legislature with a copy of my book, amounting alone to over three hundred dollars, in addition to all the expenses attending a six months' campaign, added to my most indefatigable labors in Connecticut to bring about this most desirable change in the laws, that of removing some of the legal disabilities of married women, seemed, by this fell stroke, to be a dead failure, or in other words, "A Bull-run defeat!"

Another most formidable foe which I had to encounter in this field was "*clandestine letters*," sent to individual members, asking them to circulate them secretly, without letting me know of this fact or the infamous character of these letters.

Besides these members, I have been told that Dr. Bacon and Dr. Abbott and other clergymen in the city had copies of these same letters sent them, accompanied with most earnest appeals to use all their influence in trying to defeat my efforts in the Legislature!

From one who read these letters I was informed they were very derogatory to me and my character, even more scandalous if possible, than the published article.

Knowing nothing of this occult influence at work against me, I could not help feeling surprised and hurt, when meeting upon the street, the morning of the appearance of these scandalous articles, some members of my personal acquaintances, instead of giving me their usual polite salutation, accompanied by a tip of the beaver, evidently avoided me, by crossing over to the opposite side of the street, or passing by apparently unconscious of my presence. And it was in consequence of my speaking of this fact to one of my patrons, which led him to make me the above revelation, as an explanation of the cause of this neglect and coldness thus manifested. Said I:

"Why could not this ministerial influence Mr. Packard has thus rallied as an antagonism to defeat the reform I am trying to inaugurate, have met me in an open field of fair discussion instead of thus secretly attacking the moral character of its defender?"

"Because they could not afford to do this openly, as this movement has already received the popular voice in its favor, and this brutal assault upon the character of a woman, so utterly defenseless and so self-dependent also, might react upon themselves, and thus endanger their popularity."

" But, sir, it would not be so reprehensible an act in itself ? "

" No, Mrs. Packard, but it might bring an unenviable notoriety upon themselves, as deserving public censure, while this secret attack might defeat this reform, and at the same time, shield them from detection as opposers to humanitarian reforms."

" But ministers of Christ have no license to act unmanly any more than any other class."

" Certainly they have not, still their mistakes are often times allowed to pass unnoticed lest " the cause " suffer by their actions being subjected to criticism in common with others—in other words, their position shields them."

" But, sir, I think this is wrong, for the ministerial office does not insure men against the commission of sins of the darkest hue, for the ministry is composed of men, who are subject to like frailties and passions with other men. And ministers, like all other men, must stand just where their own actions place them, not where their position ought always to find them. They ought to be men whose characters should be unimpeachable. But they are not all so.

" Neither are all other men what they should be in their position.

" It is as much the duty of the minister to be true to himself—true to the instincts of his God-given nature, as it is of other men. And any deviation from the path of rectitude which would not be tolerated in any other man, ought not to be tolerated in a minister.

" In short, ministers must stand on a common level with the rest of the human race in judgment. That is, they, like others, must stand just where their own conduct and actions place them. If their conduct entitles them to respect, we should respect them.

" But if their conduct makes them unworthy of our respect and confidence, it is a sin to bestow it upon them, for this very respect which we give them under such circumstances, only countenances their sins and encourages them in iniquity, and thus puts their own souls in jeopardy, as well as reflects guilt on those who thus helped them to work out their own destruction, when they ought to have helped them work out their own repentance for evil doing."

But even in spite of this array of powerful influence against the petition, and their ostensible triumph for a time, I have reason to think the good seed did take root, and although thus buried, for a time, beneath the sod of ignorance and prejudice, yet, the sun-light of truth and righteousness can and will permeate these elements and not only cause the good seed to germinate, but also to mature it into perfected fruit, and thus ensure the blessings of spiritual freedom to mothers of future generations, as their rightful heritage.

CHAPTER XLII.

Tribute to Dr. Bushnell and Dr. Hawes, of Hartford, Connecticut.

It is with the most unfeigned and grateful pleasure that I am permitted here to chronicle the manly acts of two ministers in Connecticut, who I fondly believe represent the majority of Christian ministers in that as well as other States.

These two, who have embalmed the memory of their God-like deeds upon the tablets of my heart, are Rev. Horace Bushnell and Rev. Joel Hawes, of Hartford, both of whom were my efficient helpers and co-workers in prosecuting my business in that city, and their certificates I now have as proof of what I say, and were it not that such testimonials might be considered as immodestly abundant already in my book, I would here give them.

As it is, I will simply state a few facts respecting each, corroborating this statement.

I called upon Dr. Bushnell at his residence in Hartford, and after patiently listening to my statements, illustrating the reform that is needed by a recital of my own experiences, he seemed at once to comprehend the whole subject, and paying me for my book, he retired to his study leaving me with Mrs. Bushnell, and soon returned with his voluntary certificate, which he handed to me, saying :

" This may aid you in getting patrons in this city."

And it did give me a ready passport to the confidence of that community, and was the direct means of securing me many patrons.

He then said :

" Mrs. Packard, this outrage ought not to go unnoticed by

our courts. You ought to enter a prosecution against this Conspiracy in the name of the commonwealth, and were I a lawyer I would gladly take the case through myself. But as I am not, I will recommend you to Mr. Francis Fellowes, as your counsel in this matter—I will give you a letter of introduction to him, and wish you to state the case as you have to me, and I will meet him this evening at seven o'clock at the vestry of our church where we will confer together upon the subject, and report to you the result."

"Thank you, Dr. Bushnell, for your generous espousal of my cause. But permit me to say, I think there is no way to prosecute parties for doing legal acts."

"Legal act! It is not a legal act to imprison an American citizen for religious belief, and I believe it can be prosecuted, if conducted by one who understands the subject. And Mr. Fellowes does. I am willing to abide by his judgment in this matter."

I accordingly went to Mr. Fellowes; made my statement, and delivered his message, and the result was, Mr. Fellowes said : -

"I will take the subject under consideration, and examine the laws on this subject."

And he did so, and as the final result, he came to the conclusion there was no legal redress for me under the statute laws of Illinois, and so reported to Dr. Bushnell, where the matter was dropped. But the act showed where Dr. Bushnell stood on the subject of religious toleration, and also proved him to be a noble and firm advocate and defender of the American principle of free religious toleration.

And my interview with Dr. Hawes, although different in its character, yet was equally characteristic of the man, and the Christian.

His great sympathizing heart was actually moved to tears at the recital of my case, and after expressing his manly sympathy in words of true comfort and encouragement, I left him with the promise that I would accept his invitation to call again after he had read my book, which he bought most promptly and cheerfully.

I accordingly did so, and took tea with his happy family. As we conversed, I inquired:

" Doctor, how do you like my book ? "

" Before answering that question, I wish to ask you one question.   Do you believe in future punishments ? "

" Indeed I do !   There can be no true government without justice—but ɲ ɲishments under a just government must be reformatory n t vindictive."

" I am satis ied—I endorse your book—I believe you are taught by the spirit, and are living up to your highest convictions. - I think your books are going to do great good in the world.   Could your principles of reform be sustained by our laws, it would put an end to divorce in a great measure, and this would be a great blessing to society.   I am exceedingly well pleased with your book.   I would recommend it to my people as a book worthy the perusal of every family."

Again was his great heart moved at a recital of some events not given in the book, and while the tears of true sympathy were coursing down his cheek, he remarked:

" Well, Mrs. Packard, if you can live through all you have had to suffer and maintain a Christian spirit, you deserve heaven ! "

" What ! Dr. Hawes, ' *deserve* heaven ! ' "

" Yes, I say again, if you can maintain a Christian spirit through all your terrible experiences, I say you deserve heaven ! "

Thus I saw that in this instance both his theology and his intellect had been taken captive by his great sympathizing, Christ-like heart of pity for others' woes.

CHAPTER XLIII.

Passage of the Bill in Iowa Legislature, to Protect the Inmates of Insane Asylums by Law.

During the Session of the Iowa Legislature of 1872, I sent to Mr. J. Vanderventer, a member of the House, a "Bill to Protect the Insane," with a request that he see that it be presented, and report to me its progress; and if in his judgment any effort of mine could facilitate its passage, I stood ready to meet such an emergency.

On the 13th of March Mr. Vanderventer thus replied:

"The Bill sent to me was presented by Mr. Merrill on the 16th of February and referred to the Committee on Insane Asylums. No report has been made by the Committee, and I am informed the bill is not favorably regarded.

Without wishing to influence your action in any way, I deem it no more than right to say that I do not believe the bill would be considered favorably by the General Assembly, and the expense you could have to incur, while waiting action on the bill, would necessarily be large. Very truly yours,

J. VANDERVENTER."

"Rather dubious prospect!" thought I. "Nevertheless Mr. Vanderventer is only one, and possibly represents the minority in his private opinion; therefore I will write to the Chairman of the Committee to whom my bill is referred and test his opinion on this subject."

I accordingly did so, and received the following reply:

"Yours of the 17th is received and considered, and in answer I would say that the bill to which you refer is reported back to the House with the unanimous recommendation that it be indefinitely postponed!   Respectfully yours,

J. M. Hovey."

" Worse and worse!" thought I, " 'Tis even now past redemption, I fear, since the Legislature seldom acts contrary to the recommendation of their Committee."

" But shall the claims of this defenseless class be thus summarily ignored, with none to plead for them?"

" Nay, verily, I will do what I can to bring their claims to the notice of the Legislature, the only power that can help them."

I therefore sent to Mr. Hovey the following "brief" in defense of the bill, and asked him to show it to the other members of the Committee, viz.:

Defense of a bill to protect the rights of the Insane.

The main feature of this bill is to remove the censorship from the correspondence of the patients, as one means of protecting them in their right to be treated kindly and justly by their keepers.   My reasons are these:

1st.   A free and unrestricted correspondence will be a re-restraint upon the exercise of tyranny.

2d.   It will afford them an innocent gratification.

3d.   It will cultivate their affection for their relatives, which under the present censorship, is most cruelly shaken, if not destroyed.

4th.   It will mitigate their mental torture by allowing it a natural vent or expression.

5th.   As this censorship is regarded by them as an outrage upon their rights, its removal will help to reinstate in their minds the principle of justice.

6th.   It will give their friends a test of their mental condition.

7th. They now have no opportunity for self-defense, and this would afford them this reasonable right.

8th. It might prevent the culmination of evils developed by the Investigating Committee of Illinois State Asylum, by affording each case a chance for settlement when the charges were reported.

9th. If the complaints of abuse are delusive it could hurt no one—if true, they could be corrected without public exposure.

I followed this effort with editorials which I got written upon this subject, one of which I give my readers as a type of the others. This was written by the able editor and proprietor of the Davenport *Gazette* of Iowa. It was published March 19, 1872.

Rights of the Insane.

" Experience proves that the best instrumentalities are liable to abuse, and that institutions based upon philanthropy and having their sanction in the noblest promptings of the popular heart, are oftentimes turned into engines of oppression and cruelty.

Lunatic Asylums were founded in the interest of humanity, for the purpose of relieving the victims of mental delusion from the barbarities to which they had been formerly subjected by confinement in barns and sheds, jails and poor-houses, and bringing them under such restraint as should be necessary, while giving them the benefit of enlightened medical treatment.

Yet, exposures which have been made within a few years, have developed the fact that these palatial structures, built and supported at the public expense, have been converted into prison houses of persons not insane, especially married women, that oftentimes great cruelties and outrages were practiced within their walls, and that owing to the internal regulations adopted, concerning correspondence and intercourse with the outside world, these practices have been for a long time covered from the public eye.

In these cases the Superintendent, possessing powers well nigh autocratic, has been enabled to stifle the voice of complaint, and to defeat any investigation of the most glaring abuses. Judging from the testimony which we have seen and heard on this subject, we have no doubt that some have been made insane, and that the insanity of others has been aggravated by asylum treatment; and that in many institutions there is scarcely a pretence of scientific effort for the cure of the mental malady.

Within a few years several interesting works have been published by those familiar with the interior of asylum life, which have led, and are leading to important reforms in the management of these institutions.

In Jacksonville, Ill., a few years ago, there was a general jail delivery of married women from the Asylum in that place, who had been emancipated by the passage of a law requiring an inquiry into the reason of their detention ! The mental torture and anguish suffered by these innocent women, imprisoned on the pretence of insanity, the imagination can hardly conceive, and no pen can fully describe.

But while the forcible capture and detention of sane persons is not now as feasible as it has been, anywhere, and certainly is not legal, as it was in Illinois in the case of married women, yet it is quite clear that other reforms in asylum management are demanded.

One of these, and perhaps the most important, is the *removal of the censorship from the correspondence of the patients.*

A bill for this purpose is now before the Legislature of Iowa, and trust it will meet with favorable consideration and action.

At first blush it might seem a dangerous innovation upon the rules of a Lunatic Asylum to allow the inmates to write when and what they pleased to their families and friends. It might occasion some annoyance to keepers and superintendents to have their conduct freely criticised by the people in all stages of insanity. But experience shows that the enforced silence of the victims has been the bulwark of all the abuses that have crept into these institutions.

The inconvenience, therefore, which the officials might suffer from unfounded complaints would be trifling compared to the benefits that will flow from the abolition of the censorship. Unrestricted correspondence will tend to keep the management wholesome and economical. It will insure the inmates kind and considerate treatment, and restrain keepers and physicians from acts of tyranny and violence. It will tend to alleviate the mental malady by affording an innocent gratification ; by cultivating affection for relatives, and by giving the mind a rational theme for reflection. It will give their friends a test of the condition of their minds, and show the prospects of recovery or otherwise. In short it will operate wholly in the interests of the class for whom asylums are established, and of the public whose munificence supports them.

It is a reform that is needed, and we trust Iowa will not be slow in adopting it."

I accompanied these editorials with the inquiry, cannot the bill be rescued from the vortex into which you have cast it, and it be yet considered ?

In reply came this cheering intelligence :

" I must say that your perseverance and devotion to the cause you have espoused, challenges my admiration. And your appeal shall not pass unheeded, for my warmest sympathies are enlisted in behalf of the insane.

The bill you speak of has not passed beyond the control of the House, and I will have steps taken to have it re-referred to Committee so that you can be heard before them towards the last of this week.

You can notify myself or Newbold or Keables or Stewart at the State-House, and you will receive an early hearing. Yours respectfully,   J. M. HOVEY."

Elated with this prospect, I immediately left my home in Chicago and started for Des Moines. Upon arrival, I engaged board at the Pacific House, and early the next morning I went to the State-House in pursuit of some of the parties referred to.

Being an entire stranger in the city, and having no one on whom to rely for introduction to the members, alone I sought and found the Legislative Hall, when I was directed by the door-keeper to the side seats occupied by strangers and lobbyists.

Soon my correspondent, Mr. Hovey, came and introduced himself, and extended to me a cordial welcome, and so did several other members of this Committee to whom he introduced me.

After consultation, it was agreed I should have as early a hearing as possible in the Library-Room, before a committee of both houses.

During the three days which intervened, I formed the acquaintance of Governor Carpenter and the State Officers, and as many of the members and employees about the house as possible.

Governor Carpenter gave me his most hearty approval of the bill, and from his first acquaintance he became my private counselor in all matters relating to the fate of the bill. And of him it may truly be said no State ever had the honor of having a more worthy, humane and Christian governor than Iowa now has. In this noble man the unfortunate and oppressed will ever find a true friend and efficient helper, as his enforcement of the law will doubtless demonstrate.

The Committee allowed me two hearings in the Library-Room of about one-half hour each time. At the last meeting a large number of the legislative body were present besides the Committee on Public Institutions of both Houses.

My defense of the bill led the committee to look at the subject from an entirely different standpoint from what Dr. Ranney, Superintendent of Mount Pleasant Asylum, had presented. Previous to the committee's recommendation to indefinitely postpone the bill, Dr. Ranney had been notified of the character of the bill, and his request to be heard in reference to it had been cheerfully granted, by allowing him a patient hearing of one hour and a half. Upon which, the committee unanimously decided to give the subject no further attention.

From one who heard him, I was told that the chief point he made against the bill was, that if the inmates were allowed to write to their friends it would render the task of " subduing his patients " more difficult, and perhaps a hopeless one.

" Subduing his Patients ! " They were not placed under his care to be subdued, like criminals—but to be treated as unfortunates, with kindness and suitable medical treatment.

Thus I used the Doctor's argument against the bill as the most potent one in its defense—viz. :

If he does treat them as criminals, as he thus acknowledges, there is all the more need of some mode of self-defense on the part of his patients—and this bill affords just the kind of protection they need.

In short, my argument led the committee to reverse the decision Dr. Ranney's argument had led them to make, and now unanimously recommended that the bill be passed.

They advised me to lobby for the bill with the members until a vote of the House should be taken upon the subject.

The bill was ordered to be printed and laid upon the table of each member, and I commenced lobbying for it. Nearly three weeks of indefatigable labor I spent with the members at the legislative hall, and at their boarding places.

So very constant and unremitted were my efforts during this time—not allowing even a single day, however stormy, to pass, without filling my seat among the lobbyists at the State-House, that the remark was sometimes elicited from the members :

"Well, Mrs. Packard, you are faithful to your constituents!"

"Yes, gentlemen, I am like the importunate widow, who was determined she would not be put off with the denial of her request. Now, gentlemen, when you pass my bill you can get rid of me, but not before!"

My first effort in the lobbying department commenced on the evening of my arrival at the Pacific House, where I met about twenty members in the reception room, to whom the kind-hearted landlord introduced me at my request. For about one hour I held their attention to the object of my mission, hoping by this elucidation of the subject to secure their intelligent co-operation. And as they left one by one, remarking :

"Mrs. Packard, you may rely upon me as a helper,"

I felt that I had made a propitious beginning in the unique business of female lobbying.

At my first call at the Savery House as a lobbyist, I asked for an introduction to the "hardest case" they could produce, for me to convert into a defender of my bill. Hon. Mr. Claussen of the Senate, was then introduced to me in the public parlor, as "just the man," where we conversed for about one hour.

This Mr. Claussen was a most avowed *anti*-Woman's Right man, and it was mainly through his influence that the bill for woman's right to the ballot in Iowa had been "killed" in the Senate, the day after my arrival. So fearlessly and powerfully did he carry his magnetic force against the bill in a long speech he made in the Senate, that he was ever afterwards regarded as woman's greatest foe, by those who claim for her the right to the ballot.

Ignorant of these facts of his thus avowed committal against woman's cause, in my usual way, I dauntlessly defended her as the partner of her husband, who needed to be protected, as such. He patiently and silently listened until his manliness became so quickened into action as led him to exclaim :

" Well, Mrs. Packard, you have aroused a feeling of pity for woman. I do think you have been the victim of great injustice. What can I do to help prevent another such outrage against woman ? "

" To please defend the merits of this bill, in the manner your own good judgment dictates ; for you see we women are entirely dependent on your manliness for the enactment of laws for our protection."

" Yes, Mrs. Packard, I will gladly do so, for I never felt so much sympathy for woman's cause before. Have you any books on this subject ? "

" Yes, Mr. Claussen, here is a history of my persecution, written by myself."

And handing him my book he took it, and paid me for it, saying :

" I shall read this book with the greatest pleasure."

From this date, I found in Mr. Claussen not only a firm friend, but also an able and efficient co-worker and advocate of my cause. Through his influence other members called for my books, and thus their silent influence was at work in connection with my own personal efforts in defense of our cause.

But the most unpropitious prospect I had to encounter in this line of lobbying business was presented on the evening of the day I changed my boarding place for one nearer the State-House, where I found two Senators and two House members boarding. These members, like many others, I found had been " bored," as they termed it, by the female " Woman Rights " lobbyists, with their lectures on the subject of " Woman's Rights " so long and so persistently, that the subject had become a hackneyed one ; and now to have a new recruit arrive, just as they had supposed they had finished their woman campaign for that season, by the death of the Woman's Rights Bill the previous day, they could not but feel too great a degree of impatience and indignation at this prospect of another attack, to prevent its manifestation in a hasty and premature condemnation of my cause!

Therefore, upon a partial announcement of my mission, they interrupted me, and took the laboring oar entirely out of my hands, and did the talking themselves.

I concluded quietly and patiently to "bide my time," and let them have a fair opportunity to let off their superabundant steam so concentrated against the cause of woman. Now, when I had reason to think they had fired off all their own artillery, and thus exhausted their own ammunition, I asked for the floor, by saying:

"Gentlemen, I have listened to you without interrupting you, now will you please allow me to talk a little also?"

"Oh, yes, certainly, we will now allow you the floor!"

I then defined my mission as I had before attempted to do, and this time was not interrupted. Therefore, I had a fair opportunity to make myself understood.

This being done, these combatants began to apologize for their rudeness in ranking me with the "Woman's Rights" defenders, and for this reason mistreating me as they had, by saying:

"It is of no use for you to attempt anything with this body, for we have been button-holed already by the women longer than our patience can bear. There is no chance for you to succeed at all. It is a dead-lock for this session. Certainly no woman can introduce a reform so radical, with the least chance of succeeding!"

Among them, was one physician, who had been a Trustee of an Insane Asylum in Wisconsin, and he was especially down upon me, assuring me that Dr. Ranney would defeat such a bill summarily, and he would do so himself were he in his place. That no intelligent body would think of passing such a bill!

But now, after hearing my defense of the bill, he, together with the others, changed their tone of remark by saying:

"We see, you, Mrs. Packard, are not of this offensive class. You are reasonable and sensible on the subject of 'Woman's Rights.' Coming with such views as yours, there is more hope, at least, of your making it a success. Still, we think the opposition will be more than you can withstand, for the asylum influences will be concentrated against you."

Yes, they certainly were concentrated against me, and so also was the influence of these four members that evening secured as a concentrated force, with which to meet and repel it! Yes, this very physician became one of the ablest defenders I had, in the help he rendered me by suggesting some very important features in the bill to adapt it to meet the emergencies of the case.

And another learned Judge of this party, who, I noticed was moved to tears before I had finished my appeal, volunteered his very important assistance in helping me put my bill into a suitable legal form for action.

Thus these, at first, apparently antagonistic powers were thus impressed into most important service for the cause, the proof of which they that evening gave, by each laying upon the table before me the price of my book, which I gave them in exchange.

After about three weeks of this kind of lobbying in connection with that done at the State-House, before and after session hours, I felt fully confident that the popular current was in favor of the bill, when it was taken up, discussed, and the vote taken upon it. The House vote was seventy-eight in its favor and one against it.

But in the Senate it had a hard contested battle. Dr. Ranney had determined the bill should be defeated if possible,

14

and had therefore engaged his agents to work for him in the Senate.

They did strive most strenuously to "kill the bill," but it could not be done. The intrinsic merits of the bill secured for it a triumphant passage in defiance of this persistent opposition.

The vote in the Senate was thirty-two in its favor and sixteen against it—being two to one.

The congratulations I received at this important crisis of the bill from the state officers, members, and others of distinguished influence in the community almost compensated me for all the toil and expense I had incurred in working for this issue.

Meeting the Speaker of the House on the street on my return from the State-House, after hearing the result of this fierce battle in the Senate against it, he actually took off his hat, and while holding my hand in his, remarked:

"Permit me to congratulate you, Mrs. Packard, upon the triumph of your bill, for, that bill never would have been passed if you had not been here to work for it. It may truly be styled your bill."

Ex-Governor Merrill remarked:

"I congratulate you, Mrs. Packard, on the achievement of a great good, by the passage of your bill. It is a wonder no one has taken up this subject before. It has been an oversight in modern legislation which has excluded this class of American citizens from the protection of law for so long a time. While I was Governor, I often visited the institution at Mount Pleasant at irregular times for the express purpose of detecting evils if they did exist. But I found that this was no way to look into its secret workings. But your bill not only detects the evils but also applies the remedy of the laws to meet them. I wonder I never thought of this plan myself, for it is simply the dictates of common philanthropy to protect the inmates of

Insane Asylums by law. I do hope you will succeed in your avowed purpose of getting such a law through every Legislature in the United States. And I will buy your book not only because I would like to read it, but also to encourage you in your good work."

From several of the members I heard this remark:

"Mrs. Packard, I as much believe you are raised up by Providence for this special work as I believe Lincoln was raised up for his work of emancipating the slaves! for I do not think any other person could have got this bill through our legislature but yourself."

And I remember one compliment which flattered my vanity so much that I do not easily forget it, when I think with what misgivings I commenced lobbying with the members after that noted evening when female influence was acknowledged as being at so low an ebb in Iowa Legislature as that in which the "Woman's Rights" defenders left it. Said he:

"Mrs. Packard, your work has been prosecuted in our body in a very lady-like manner. You have neither 'bored' us, nor intruded upon our time or attention, and we hope you may be equally successful with other legislators."

"Thank you, gentlemen, for your good wish, for it is my intention to get this same law through every legislature in this Union before I die, if my life is spared a few years longer."

But the consideration which in my mind rose paramount to all others was the glorious thought that the reign of terror is now ended in asylums in Iowa, with the enforcement of this law, and the reign of justice commenced, which really caused my heart to thrill with joy.

But here as in Connecticut, the conspiracy followed me, when I supposed they had lost track of my programme, having remained quiet so long with my children in Chicago. But lo! the morning after the bill had passed the Senate, I heard the members at my boarding-house disputing at the breakfast table about who was the author of certain clandestine letters which were being circulated among the Senators, when I plainly saw the enemy was in the camp! but fortunately, had arrived one day too late to do the injury they had been commissioned to do. Speaking with one of these gentlemen upon this subject, he remarked, for my comfort, as he saw me affected to tears under the influence of this sudden and unexpected attack upon my character.

"Mrs. Packard, never mind! The bill is safe! They were a little too late this time to harm your cause!"

"Yes, Doctor, this is indeed my only consolation, for of what consequence is it now to me to be held in esteem by your honorable body, when my cause has been so valiantly sustained by them? I only desire to stand in their estimation just where my own actions will place me, instead of where these lying scandals may tempt them to put me."

Governor Carpenter signs the Bill to protect the Insane.

"Mrs. Packard, your Bill is all right!" See page 317.

"The Reign of Terror is ended!—The Reign of Justice is begun!" See page 317.

CHAPTER XLIV.

Opposition to the Enforcement of the Law.

Of course, the Governor's signature was promptly obtained, so also was my request for a certified copy of the bill most kindly granted by Mr. E. Wright, the worthy Secretary of State, who, like Secretary Tyndal, of Illinois, made me a present of it, not only as a token of respect from him, but as a testimonial of the success of my work in that State. When this elegant certified manuscript copy was handed me, with the great seal of the State of Iowa upon it, after thanking Secretary Wright, I hastened with it to the Governor's office, to show to him this elegant memento of my Iowa campaign, when he, after examining it carefully and seeing his own name suitably transcribed, handed it back, saying:

"Yes, Mrs. Packard, your bill is all right—and I rejoice with you in the success attending your effort in our State. I think it is a much needed law, and I shall do all in my power to have all its provisions enforced."

"Thank you, Governor Carpenter, I now feel that the highest honor I covet is that of posting the names of the Committee you appoint upon the Asylum walls, myself, for it would be virtually proclaiming to the imprisoned captives there confined: 'The Reign of Terror is ended!—The Reign of Justice is begun!'"

The Visiting Committee were appointed by the Governor, as the law required, and in compliance with his wishes I repaired to Mount Pleasant to meet this Committee at their first meeting, to instruct them into the importance of the law, said he:

"I wish you to present to them the same argument for the

enforcement of the law which you have used with me and the Legislature for its enactment."

But lo! Here, too, Dr. Ranney had superseded me and this appointment of the Governor! I saw at once that the opposition from the Legislature was but a small part of the opposition to be overcome.

When Dr. Ranney found the bill had actually passed into a law, thereby opening a direct communication between his patients and the outside world, he became alarmed lest the public know what is done behind the curtain in Mount Pleasant Asylum.

The Trustees were therefore instructed to regard this law as an innovation, which the good of the patients demanded should be most strenuously opposed!

A meeting of the Trustees was called at the time of the first meeting of the Visiting Committee to educate them into the folly of such an enactment, and to influence them to regard its provisions as worse than useless in their application to the interests of the patients!

And, I am very sorry to add, this artful policy of Dr. Ranney, manifested through the Trustees, prevailed in forcing upon this Committee the conviction, that the law had better be regarded as a dead letter until subsequent legislation should repeal it!

As evidence of this determination, the Committee avoided me at their first meeting, when they knew I was then in Mount Pleasant, waiting there at the Governor's request, for the express purpose of educating them into the importance and need of the law being enforced.

At their second appointment I met Mrs. Darwin alone, whose conduct and words more than confirmed the fact that the law was regarded by them as not only a useless enactment, but as one they did not hesitate to openly ridicule and deride.

To shield Dr. Ranney seemed their settled purpose and firm determination! But to shield his patients from his arbitrary power was no part of their programme up to this date. In Mrs. Darwin I failed entirely to awaken one feeling of sympathy in favor of the law, or that unfortunate class the law was designed to shield from harm.

At this crisis I wrote to Judge R. Lowe, of Keokuk, Ex Governor of Iowa, who was chairman of this Committee, the following letter:

MOUNT PLEASANT, June, 27, 1872.

JUDGE LOWE—Sir, I learn from Mrs. Darwin that your adjourned meeting of the 25th is deferred until July 2d. It was the Governor's wish that I meet this Committee in Mount Pleasant, and present for their consideration the same argument and appeal for the enforcement of the law, which I had used before him and the Legislature for its enactment, adding:

"I had never before realized its importance, and the committee may be equally ignorant on this subject."

To comply with his wishes, I accordingly suspended my business at a sacrifice of four hundred dollars already, and have been waiting here eight weeks to present the Governor's letter of introduction to this Committee.

I have offered to pay this Committee three thousand dollars of my own hard earnings, if necessary, to secure men who were capacitated for this important trust.

I have the names of four thousand men of the first standing in Iowa, who stand as my backers in enacting and enforcing this law, and this number is constantly increasing.

I have also a petition sent me from others, praying this Committee to enforce the law in every particular and begging me also to be their representative to defend their wishes to this Committee.

My object in writing to you, Sir, is to express my earnest desire to discharge these obligations, by meeting with you, July 2d, if agreeable on your part. I do not deem it my duty to intrude upon you an unwelcome elucidation of this subject. If, however, you desire light such as I can impart, I shall be happy to meet this appointment of the Governor and citizens of Iowa. It will take me one hour at least to do justice to this subject, and shall hold myself in readiness to meet this appointment at any hour after six o'clock, A. M., July 2d, at my son's house in Mount Pleasant, T. Packard, the third house north of Asbury Church in this city. Very respectfully yours, for the oppressed,

E. P. W. P.

Judge Lowe called upon me on July 2d, and allowed an interview of four hours and a half in all, and left, as I have reason to believe, a different man so far as his views of the need of the law were concerned. He now, like the Legislature, saw both sides, and therefore like them he changed from a derider of the law to its defender. Said he:

"This law shall be enforced! I have taken my oath to do it, and it shall be done!"

In coming to this determination he considered the following petition, from Iowa citizens, representing the wishes of the people, viz.:

Petition.

" *To the Visiting Committee appointed to carry out the provisions of the law to* " *Protect the Insane.*"

Approved, April 23, 1872.

" We, the undersigned, fully satisfied that the law to ' Protect the Insane ' is reasonable, just, humane, and much needed, do hereby petition you, the executors of the law, to thoroughly enforce it, in every particular, and thereby carry out the wishes of the people of Iowa to extend to this unfortunate class the protection of law while confined in their Insane Asylums."

He also considered an array of testimony of which the following is a type, showing Mount Pleasant Institution to be like others, in a corrupt condition, needing ventilation and reform, viz.:

A gentleman and lady living in this city, are willing to testify, under oath, that their daughter-in-law was taken from the asylum in a condition indicating both neglect and abuse. She had been there only two weeks, but her health and mental and physical condition were far more deplorable than when she was entered. From her shoulders down both her arms were completely covered with black and blue spots. One side of her head was badly swollen, indicating violent usage, which was confirmed by a physician extracting a stick of wood from her head, one or two inches in length.

The same party testify of one man who had an eye gouged out so that it hung upon his cheek, done by his attendant. Another man had his ribs broken from a kick given him by his attendant, when laying upon the floor. Another jumped upon his stomach, etc.

Another gentleman and lady of this city stand ready to testify that their son who was there three months, was taken out in an almost starved condition, and with many unmistakable marks of violence and torture inflicted upon him. He was so nearly starved to death, that a few days more of like treatment would have killed him. His entire body was covered with black and blue spots, and some wounds in a state of corruption. Ridges both upon his arms and legs showed he had had circulation so long impeded by confinement in the " crib " as to cause these marks to become indelible. He was suffering from chronic diarrhœa in its last stages, with no treatment to check it. His food was entirely inappropriate to his condition—so unfit for human beings as to have poisoned his system—so that all his finger and toe nails came off, having previously received their first serious injury from his rash attendants, by shutting them under the heavy crib, as they forced him into it, and shut it suddenly down upon him, while his fingers and toes were thus caught under it.

These parents assert that they believe there is no worse

place in the universe where human beings can be placed than our insane asylums under their present management, with no law to protect the patients.

A man in Des Moines, who has been a clerk in the Asylum for two years, asserts: There is no place in the world, in his opinion, where criminals are treated with greater cruelty than in Mt. Pleasant Asylum.   He testifies he saw a young man suspended in the air, with his hands tied to a rope, and then whipped until the blood flowed from his body.

Another, who had been for years an attendant there, says, the attendants treat the patients very roughly, but the Doctor knows but little about it.   He once saw an attendant knock a patient down with a chair.   He says what I say in my book of the treatment at Jacksonville is true of Mt. Pleasant Asylum.

I hear almost universal complaint of the increased unwillingness of the Doctor to allow the friends to see their relatives, while in the asylum, and also complaints of want of food and false imprisonments.

The above facts of cruel treatment I gave him in substance over the names of the witnesses, accompanied by the following letter:

MOUNT PLEASANT, July 4, 1872.

JUDGE LOWE—DEAR SIR—I send herewith the testimony I promised you.   These witnesses are competent and are ready and willing to be used in any manner you may desire for your great and arduous work.   Mr. Walters is a Quaker minister, and the peace principles under which his son was educated at home conflicted sadly with the discipline of the asylum, which is punishment for exhibitions of insanity!

Judge Lowe, 'tis a fact, patients in our insane asylums are treated as criminals, not as unfortunates.   But, sir, every obstacle which it is possible to interpose to prevent your knowing this fact will be thrown in your way.

The By-Laws of the institution will deny it.   But in their application to practice they are "By-Lies," designed to deceive and blind the inquisitive public.

The physicians and keepers will deny it in words, but own it in practice. These " honor God with their lips, but their hearts are far from him," as a God of truth.

It is to prevent this being known as the asylum treatment that the patients are not allowed to converse with visitors— that they have not been allowed to write to their friends— that friends are so reluctantly admitted to converse with their friends in the wards—that the employees are instructed not to tell outside of the asylum what passes within its walls.

Now, Judge Lowe, it stands to reason that if the patients were treated with reason, justice and humanity, they would not be so extremely anxious to conceal it. But it is because they are not treated reasonably that they are so afraid to have it known how they are treated.

Certainly these pad-locks ought to be removed from the lips of both patients and employees so that the public can know how the inmates are treated, and every attempt at concealment ought to be regarded as a suspicious omen, that there is something going on which ought not to be. Good deeds and good acts court the light. It is only the evil which seek darkness. And we may be almost always sure that deeds of darkness or concealment are evil deeds.

Legislators and trustees have hitherto let superintendents have things their own way almost entirely in the laws controlling them. Therefore this innovation of recognizing inmates of insane asylums as beings possessing human rights in common with other citizens, is a kind of new dispensation inaugurated, by restoring to them their long usurped Post-Office rights. And you, sir, are the man on whom the eyes of this republic are fastened to see that this single right is in no case ignored, and thereby the right of free communication be established between the patients and the outside world.

This law well enforced, must necessarily terminate the reign of terror and despotism and introduce the reign of justice and rectitude. I do hope before the next meeting of your Board a concert of action will be instituted, and the law be put into working order, thorough and efficient.

Respectfully yours, for the oppressed,

E. P. W. P.

After making a faithful report to the Governor of the disposition the Committee had shown to shirk the responsibilities of the law, and Judge Lowe's subsequent verbal committal in its favor, I received the following reply:

DES MOINES, July 23, 1872.

Mrs. E. P. W. PACKARD,

No. 1496, *Prairie Avenue, Chicago, Illinois.*

RESPECTED MADAME—The Governor was away from the capital and at Mt. Pleasant, when your letter of July 14th, with enclosures, was received. Upon his return it was laid before him. In reply he directs me to say that your statements will receive due and full consideration.

The Governor hopes however that your first impressions of the Visiting Committee, or at least one of its members, you will find to be incorrect, and that their official course will be such as to deserve and receive the highest approval.

Nevertheless, the Governor is determined to the extent of his power and information to secure an enforcement of the Legislative will, as expressed in the " Act to Protect the Insane."

Your articles have been handed to Mr. Clarkson for insertion in the *Register*, as requested by you.

Very respectfully,   WM. H. FLEMING,

Private Secretary.

While superintending the publication of my book in New York city, I wrote to Governor Carpenter for his picture, to form a part of one of my illustrations, and in reply received the following letter, the perusal of which affords me the cheering gratification of finding that the mode of conducting my campaign in Iowa Legislature receives the approval of this most highly-esteemed and worthy man and Governor.

STATE OF IOWA—EXECUTIVE DEPARTMENT, }
DES MOINES, November 9, 1872. }

Mrs. E. P. W. PACKARD,
>211 *Skillman Street, Brooklyn, N. Y.*

DEAR MADAME—I enclose you, in compliance with your request, a photograph of myself.

I think you give me entirely too much credit in reference to my connection with the passage of the " Act to Protect the Insane." The success of that measure was entirely due to your persistent advocacy, and the good judgment with which you presented its merits to the members of the General Assembly.

I regret not sending this photograph sooner, as your letter of October 7th would imply some haste, but absence from home, and the fact that I had no photograph at hand, is my apology. Very truly, yours,

C. C. CARPENTER.

CHAPTER XLV.

An Act to Protect the Insane by Law.

SECTION 1. *Be it enacted by the General Assembly of the State of Iowa:* That there shall be a Visiting Committee of three, appointed by the Governor, to visit the Insane Asylums of the State at their discretion, with power to send for persons and papers, and to examine witnesses on oath, to ascertain whether any of the inmates are improperly detained in the hospital, or unjustly placed there, and whether the inmates are humanely and kindly treated, with full power to correct any abuses found to exist; and any injury inflicted upon the insane shall be treated as an offense, misdemeanor, or crime, as the like offense would be regarded when inflicted upon any other citizen outside of the Insane Asylums. They shall have power to discharge any attendant or employee, who is found to have been guilty of misdemeanor, meriting such discharge; and in all their trials for misdemeanor, offense, or crime, the testimony of patients shall be taken and considered for what it is worth, and no employee at the Asylum shall be allowed to sit upon any jury before whom these cases are tried. Said committee shall make an annual report to the Governor of the State.

SEC. 2. The names of this Visiting Committee, and their post-office address shall be kept posted in every ward in the asylum, and every inmate in the asylum shall be allowed to write, when and what they please to this committee, and to any other person they may choose. *Provided,* The Superintendent may, if he thinks proper, send letters addressed to other parties, to the Visiting Committee for inspection, before forwarding to the individual addressed. And any member of the committee who shall neglect to heed the calls of the patient to him for protection, when proved to have been needed, shall be deemed unfit for his office and shall be discharged by the Governor.

SEC. 3.   Each and every person confined in any Insane Asylum within the State of Iowa, shall be furnished by the superintendent or party having charge of such person, at least once in each week while so confined, with suitable materials for writing, enclosing, sealing, and mailing letters. *Provided*, they request the same, unless otherwise ordered by the Visiting Committee, which order shall continue in force until countermanded by said committee.

SEC. 4.   It is hereby made the duty of the Superintendent, or party having charge of any person under confinement to receive, if requested to do so by the person so confined, at least one letter in each week, without opening or reading the same, and without delay to deposit it in the post-office, for transmittal by mails, with a proper postage stamp affixed thereto.

SEC. 5.   It is hereby made the duty of the Superintendent, or party having charge of any person confined on account of insanity, to deliver to said person any letter or writing to him or her directed, without opening or reading the same ; *Provided*, This letter has been forwarded by the Visiting Committee.

SEC. 6.   In the event of the sudden and mysterious death of any person so confined, a coroner's inquest shall be held as provided for by law in other cases.

SEC. 7. Any person neglecting to comply with, or willfully and knowingly violating any of the provisions of this act, shall, upon conviction thereof, be .punished for a term not exceeding three (3) years, or by a fine not exceeding one thousand (1,000) dollars, or by both fine and imprisonment, in the discretion of the court, and by ineligibility for this office in future, and upon trial had for such offense, the testimony of any person, whether insane or otherwise, shall be taken and considered for what it is worth.

SEC. 8. At least one member of said committee shall visit the asylum for the insane every month.

SEC. 9. That there shall be allowed as salary of such Visiting Committee the sum of five dollars per day for the time taken in visiting such insane asylums, and the same mileage as is now by law allowed members of the General Assembly. And the disbursing officer of such insane asylum shall pay the per diem and mileage allowed such Visiting Committee under the provisions of this act, and each member of such Visiting Committee shall certify under oath to such disbursing officer, the number of days he has served and the number of miles traveled.

SEC. 10. This act being deemed of immediate importance, shall take effect and be in force from and after two weeks publication in *Daily Iowa State Register* and *Leader*, newspapers published in Des Moines.

Approved, April 23d, 1872.

CHAPTER XLVI.

Educating the People.

The surest guarantee for the enforcement of any law is the voice of the people in its defense. Although confident the influence of the four thousand books which I had sold in Iowa, would be in the support of the new law, yet, since the territory thus canvassed was but a moiety of the entire State, I deemed it important to enlist the agency of the Press of the State in its behalf.

After the Committee had refused me a hearing at their first meeting, and while I was waiting at Mount Pleasant to make a second attempt to present the Governor's letter of introduction at their second meeting, the editors of Iowa held a mass-meeting of two days in that city, during which time they allowed me a hearing of ten minutes in defense of the law.

Thus I hoped to secure their aid in educating the masses into the importance of the new law.

Several, I am happy to say, volunteered me the use of their columns in helping on this reform.

The Mount Pleasant *Journal* had hitherto been committed to the interests of Dr. Ranney, regarding the law as an unnecessary act of legislation. I prepared an article in defense of the law, and sought the advice of some of the leading and most influential men in Mount Pleasant, who were my patrons, as to its publication.

They assured me it was of no use to try to get any article of that kind into the *Journal*, for said they:

"The *Journal* is governed by a ring, and therefore 'tis of no use to try; but the *Press* is governed by principle, and will therefore publish your article."

I accordingly went to the *Press* and read my article, and asked them if they would publish it.

They refused, saying:

" We have just refused an article from the Trustees condemning the law, and now it will not do to publish yours in favor of it. Perhaps at some future time we may open our columns to a discussion of both sides, but at present we must decline."

I told them they would disappoint some of their patrons to refuse, for they have told me:

" You were governed by principle, and would therefore publish it, while the *Journal* was governed by a ring and therefore they would not." Still they refused.

I then took the article to the *Journal* office and said:

" I have been told by leading men in this city that you were governed by a ring and therefore would not publish my article ; but that the *Press* was governed by principle and therefore would. I have asked them to publish it, but they cannot be prevailed upon to do so ; and now I wish to test these papers to see which is governed by a ring, and which by principle ! "

I then read them my article and said:

" Will you publish this article or not ? "

" Yes, we will publish it ! "

They did so, and also afterwards published " My Visit to Mount Pleasant Asylum," and several papers in Iowa reprinted these articles, as their editors had volunteered to do.

Thus the Mount Pleasant *Journal*, by daring to take the lead in this reform, has not only secured many additional subscribers, but has also by so doing paralyzed the efforts of its opponents to scandalize it. And the *Press* has lost some who would otherwise have become its subscribers, and has brought the suspicion upon it that it has too much policy, and too little principle to secure for it a sure passport to the confidence of the people.

The following is the article which the *Press* refused and the *Journal* published:

Self-Defense an Inalienable Right.

C. C. Carpenter, the present humane Governor of Iowa, in his defense of the Bill to Protect the Rights of the Insane, remarked:

" I want the right of self-defense myself, and I also want every citizen of Iowa to have this right; but under our present legislation every citizen of our State is constantly exposed to lose this right by an incarceration in an insane asylum, since these institutions must necessarily be based upon the principles of an autocracy, under which government the right of self-defense is annihilated.

" Now, simply for a misfortune to place any citizen outside the pale of justice, while inside an insane asylum is not only unjust but inhuman.

" There should, therefore, be a superior power inaugurated, by this Legislature, by which this autocratic power can be held amenable to the laws of our Republic, when abused."

And the Senate of Iowa argued in defense of this bill as follows:

" Since there now exists no link to connect the inmates of our Insane Asylums with the laws of our Republic—thus leaving them wholly at the mercy of an autocrat—there should be one, and the committee this bill creates forms just such a link; and we can well afford to pay our committee for fidelity to this important trust—that of extending to this unfortunate class the protection of the law, when needed."

It was argued that no absolute autocracy should be created and sustained by a Republic whose foundation principles require that every citizen shall be held amenable to the laws, and be able also to seek the protection of law, when needed, in defense of their inalienable rights.

Now the insane have the same inalienable right to be treated with reason, justice and humanity as the sane ; therefore the insane ought to have the same protection *of law* as the sane.

But under the present rule of Asylums they have none at all. No matter to what extent their right to justice is ignored, there is granted them no chance whatever of self-defense.

The single and only object of this committee is to ascertain if any individual, among all this unfortunate class, can be found who needs the protection of justice, and to administer it, when found without a question to be entitled to it.

This law gives to the committee a power superior to that of the superintendent, in that he himself is now held amenable to the laws, in his exercise of power over his patients, through this committee. For example, if this autocrat should be found to have been guilty of " assault and battery, manslaughter or murder," in his realm, he can now be held accountable to the laws like any other criminal found guilty of like offense outside of an Asylum, and this committee constitute the only link between him, as the superintendent and justice, as they do between his patients and justice.

It is a humane law. It is a much needed law. It is an honor to the State of Iowa to have passed such a law, for it places Iowa where she deserves to be placed, as the banner State in humanitarian reforms. She has thus immortalized herself as the pioneer State, in thus administering to her afflicted ones the right of self-defense while confined outside the pale of justice.

It is fondly hoped this bright example will speedily be followed by all the States in the Union, thus demonstrating the fact that this American Government is a Christian government, in that she can then claim, and be entitled to the honor of protecting by its laws, the right of self-defense, even to that most unfortunate of all classes of its citizens—the inmates of Insane Asylums.   THE PRISONER'S FRIEND.

Mt. Pleasant, June 20th, 1872.

CHAPTER XLVII.

My Visit to the Insane Asylum, Mount Pleasant, Iowa.

On the 25th of June, I accepted the invitation of Mrs. M. A. P. Darwin, of Burlington, one of the visiting committee, to meet her at the depot of Mount Pleasant, where I showed her my letter of introduction from Governor Carpenter, and we there engaged a 'bus to take us to the Insane Asylum.

Supposing her, of course, true to the cause she had come to defend—the enforcement of the law to protect the insane—to which the Governor's appointment required her oath of allegiance, I was both surprised and grieved to hear her not only criticise, but openly ridicule and deride the law in the presence of the depot and 'bus passengers.

Extremely cordial, bland and courteous was Dr. Ranney's welcome of Mrs. Darwin to the asylum, which he assured her was always ready and open for her inspection, as an official visitor. And Mrs. Darwin's introduction of me, as an intruder rather than an associate, evidently increased the obsequious attentions of Dr. Ranney to render himself agreeable to her by bestowing upon her his undivided attention. Their pleasure seemed reciprocal as they interchanged thoughts upon the character of " our noble institutions for the insane."

Dr. Ranney spoke of the Legislature as being so strangely infatuated as to reject light from those who are qualified to impart it, and to receive it from others. He accused them also of passing bills relative to asylums which *he* had not even recommended !

But neither of them showed the least disposition to elicit any opinions of my own, upon this, or any other subject they discussed. Indeed, the only word he addressed to me during the entire interview was a most indifferent:

" How do you do?" as Mrs. Darwin introduced me in these words:

" This is Mrs. Packard, whom I found at the depot, and she came along with me."

In a few moments after Dr. Ranney retired, Mrs. Ranney came in and took Mrs. Darwin directly into another room, leaving me entirely alone. In about fifteen or twenty minutes Dr. Ranney returned, and standing directly in front of me demanded, with the look and tone of a tyrant:

" Mrs. Packard, do you wish to see *me*?"

" No sir, I did not come for that purpose, I came to see the patients, and I should like to accompany Mrs. Darwin in her visits to the patients in their wards, as I have a letter of introduction from the Governor to this committee."

In the most peremptory manner, and authoritative tone, he replied:

" You can not accompany Mrs. Darwin to the wards! I forbid it! She has an official right to do so; you have no right at all, except that of a common visitor, and I shall grant you *only* that right. If you wish, my assistant will accompany you to such wards as are open on Tuesday and Friday from two to four o'clock, to visitors generally. But as to going into any others—*I forbid it!*"

I replied, " I will accept your offer to show me what you please."

The assistant soon came and took me into a female ward, where the first lady I saw ran up to me and grasped my hand with the utmost cordiality, and commenced talking, when I was informed by my guide:

" It is against the rules for a visitor to speak to a patient."

As I passed on many shook my hand and seemed evidently to desire to talk with their visitor.

I could not but mentally inquire, why are the social rights of society denied this class? Who has the right to deny these afflicted ones the right of free speech? Are they criminals? Why, then, should they be treated as such, in this particular? Can it be for the benefit of the patients that this right of free speech is annihilated in these wards?

In this silent manner I passed through the wards open to visitors, as I would through a menagerie, communicating no intelligence and receiving none. I saw nothing to criticise, but much to admire in the extreme neatness, quiet and order which everywhere prevailed.

I might have seen one hundred patients in all who looked comfortably and well cared for.

But how is it with the four hundred whom visitors cannot see? Are *they* as comfortable as is consistent with their condition?

This we are not allowed to know.

We must trust this portion of humanity to the unlimited power of one, who could be the tyrant to one of his parlor guests, and the polished sycophant to another!

Will we trust a valuable horse to the absolute power of one man without ever seeing or knowing how the animal is treated?

No, our property is too sacred to be thus exposed.

Shall we then trust our mother, father, wife, child or husband where we would not our property?

No! Iowa Legislature says emphatically, No! in its recent law " to protect the insane."

And one of the committee this law creates, was then in these wards visiting these inmates, *accompanied by Dr. Ranney*, in whose presence the inmates fear to complain, lest they receive their threatened punishment after she leaves!

Is this enforcing the law?

Nay, verily, it is merely making a wicked farce of it.

Let the people of Iowa watch this committee while they watch the internal machinery of their insane asylums. They are not sent to shield Doctor Ranney, but they are sent to shield his patients from his arbitrary power.

The people of Iowa are determined to look behind the curtain of their own institution; and if they cannot see these scenes through the eyes of their present committee, they will through some other agency.

The people of Iowa have a right to know how every inmate in this institution is treated.

And they have just the same right to place Doctor Ranney just where his own actions will place him that they have to apply this test to any of their other public servants. If he can stand upon this record of his own actions—Let him stand! If he cannot—Let him fall!

If Doctor Ranney is innocent, he will court investigation. If he is guilty, he will seek to avoid it.

E. P. W. PACKARD.

Mount Pleasant, July 10, 1872.

Additional Facts Respecting My Visit.

Since the above articles elicited no reply, I concluded Dr. Ranney was of the opinion expressed by Dr. McFarland under similar circumstances, viz.:

"The dignity of silence is the only safe course to pursue."

I therefore give my readers the few additional facts I had reserved for a future article, such as I had expected I should have an opportunity to give to the public in a rejoinder to his reply. But since he declines meeting my artillery in open combat, I preserve it in this form until called for.

After visiting the wards I returned to the reception-room, where Mrs. Ranney entertained me until called to their lunch.

She then politely inquired:

"Won't you, Mrs. Packard, take lunch with us?"

"Yes, Mrs. Ranney, I should be happy to do so."

At the same time commencing to take off my bonnet. Seeing this, she remarked:

"There is no neccessity for removing your bonnet, Mrs. Packard. Can't you eat with it on?"

"Yes, I can eat with it on without the least inconvenience, as I often do at hotels, as our present style of bonnets is little more than simply a head-dress."

When I had become seated by her side at the table, and caught one glimpse of the cold, forbidding frown of her husband, seated opposite her, I thought I could then account for this act, as well as the extreme nervous agitation which caused her hands to tremble so very perceptibly.

She knew she had incurred her husband's displeasure in even allowing me to come to the table at all. Still she could not wholly approve of her husband's course towards me, fearing it might be impolitic to treat me thus rudely.

The Doctor, however, firmly persisted in his uncourteous conduct—helping Mrs. Darwin, who sat at the other side of Mrs. Ranney, most politely and attentively to everything upon the table, but offered me nothing. He became so deeply absorbed in conversation with Mrs. Darwin that he seemed oblivious to everything, but to bestow upon her a "feast of reason and flow of soul," as well as a feast of table luxuries.

Mrs. Ranney carried out her programme also by passing everything to me which her husband offered to Mrs. Darwin, although still with a very trembling hand.

The Doctor, however, directed the eyes of four young gentlemen, who sat at the table and to whom Mrs. Ranney had given me an introduction, to me with a smile, as he finished one sentence in a very significant tone showing unmistakably for whom it was meant:

15

" The Legislature will reject these wise judicious bills, *and pass others!* "

The last three words were uttered in such a quick, cross, snappish tone that he for once forgot the gentleman and let his angry feelings boil over. I returned their smiles, as much as to say :

" I understand who that expression is meant for."

Doctor and Mrs. Ranney, Mrs. Darwin and myself all met in the rotunda as we left the table, where I, addressing Mrs. Darwin, said :

" How shall we get back to the village—the 'bus has gone back, and we cannot walk so far ? "

Dr. Ranney replied, " I will take *you* back, Mrs. Darwin, in the asylum carriage."

" But how shall *I* get back ? " I repeated, still looking at Mrs. Darwin, " I cannot walk so far this extremely hot day."

No response of any kind, from either of the trio, was made to this inquiry, and after a short silence Doctor Ranney walked off. I broke this silence by saying :

" Mrs. Ranney will you please excuse me while I take Mrs. Darwin into the reception-room for a private interview ?."

And we passed on. As we seated ourselves upon the lounge, Mrs. Darwin remarked, " I told the Doctor I should have a great many questions asked me."

" But the Doctor is a very bland and courteous gentleman, isn't he ? " said I.

" Yes, he is—I never saw him treat any one ungentlemanly and uncourteously until I saw him treat you so."

" In what condition did you find the patients ? "

" All very nice and comfortable ! "

" Did you go alone ? "

" No, Doctor Ranney insisted upon accompanying me ! "

" Don't you know, Mrs. Darwin, that this is no way to find out how the patients are treated ? "

" Yes, I know it is not, for one of the ladies said to me as Doctor Ranney stood by her, I can't tell you what I would like to, for the Doctor would have me punished when you leave, if I did ! "

Finding no way suggested, but for me to walk back in the burning noon-day sun of one of the hottest days of summer, I left her at the Asylum, promising to meet her at the depot in the evening, and started on my pedestrian tour. Following the winding road through the spacious Asylum grounds, with nothing to shade it from the scorching sun, before nearly reaching the gate I felt myself in danger of being sunstruck, and therefore sought the grateful shade of a large tree, under which reclined a number of male patients with their attendant, temporarily resting from their farm work. Accepting a chair offered me, and some of their cold water to drink from their tin pail, I commenced talking with them upon the mode the new law was enforced in their wards.

Their answers and remarks were evidently modified by the presence of their attendant, and as I arose to leave one of the intelligent ones, a sane man, started in the same direction, saying :

" I will fill my pipe."

We met at the gate, where the gate-house concealed us from the view of those we left under the tree, when he said :

" I wish to tell you, I have sent four letters to my wife, and I get no reply. I don't know as they are intercepted, but I think I should have had a reply if they were sent. And another thing," said he, in an undertone, " I want to tell you something more, may I ? "

" Certainly, tell me anything you like."

" I am almost afraid it is wrong, but I want to," and the big tears stood in his eyes.

" Oh, sir, you need not be afraid—tell me ! tell me all ! "

" I will then."

And just as he had uttered these words, his attendant called
out :

" Jim ! "

" Yes, I am here filling my pipe," at the same time crowd-
ing some tobacco into a hollow corn-cob with his fingers.

The attendant was now at his side, and taking hold of his
arm led him back to his companions under the tree.

This incident led me to recommend to the Committee the
Belgium mode of collecting the mail from inmates of insane
asylums, as seen in the following pages.

When once I had reached the public road I found no difficulty in hiring a passing team to carry me back to the village
depot, where I again met Mrs. Darwin, conveyed there in
the asylum carriage, accompanied by Mrs. Ranney. I then
presented her one of my books on condition she would read
it, which she promised to do, and without a " thank you,"
she turned from me and took a seat upon the opposite side of
the depot.

" How did you find the patients after I left ? "

" O, all nice and very comfortable. I like the appearance
of things at the asylum even better than I did at my former
visit ! "

" Did you see all the patients ? "

" Yes, all the female patients."

" Did Dr. Ranney accompany you this afternoon ? "

" Yes, he was with me all the time."

The public should know that Mrs. Darwin is the chosen
secretary of the Board of Visiting Committee. But unless
she changes her programme materially, the expense attending
getting up this Committee's report of the treatment of the
patients in Mount Pleasant Asylum will be a useless expendi-
ture, since this knowledge can be equally well obtained from
Dr. Ranney's own reports.

CHAPTER XLVIII.

The Belgium Mode of Collecting the Mail from Inmates of Insane Asylums.

A cotemporary has informed me through the New York Tribune that, "the Belgium government has recently ordered securely locked letter boxes, easily accessible to all the inmates to be placed in every Lunatic Asylum, public or private, in that country. No officer of the institution has any means of reaching the contents of these boxes, and the letters in them are collected weekly and are taken to the Procureur du Roi of the district for examination.

"If he thinks any complaint well founded, he at once institutes an inquiry into it, and takes steps to have the person released, if examination by impartial experts establishes his sanity.

"This certainly is a step in the right direction. All persons confined in Lunatic Asylums are thus placed in a direct communication with an officer of the law, who is sworn to see justice done them as far as possible. As we have said before, this letter-box system should be introduced by law into our own Asylums."

Another extract from the New York Tribune goes to confirm the statement that such a system is needed in our country. "It requires," says this writer, "a very plain statement of facts to arouse public attention to the conduct of our Lunatic Asylums. Such a plain statement is put forward to-day and supported by the affidavits of the principal parties concerned, a gentleman who has been confined for some time in Bloomingdale Asylum upon what he insists—and with apparent reason—

is a false charge of insanity, and two former employees of that Asylum.

" The statements of these three persons, amount to charges of the grossest cruelty, vindictiveness, and carelessness on the part of the officials of the prison, and these charges we are glad to see will be thoroughly sifted by able and determined men. The thought that we have at our doors a system of cruelty practiced upon those who can neither defend themselves, nor make their grievances known, is harrowing.

" Many of us are apt to think the powerful pictures of Charles Reade's " Hard Cash " overdrawn and exaggerated by the art of the novelist; but if the disclosures of Bloomingdale, coming close upon those of Vermont, should prove to be true, we may find the novel outdone in the strength of its coloring by history, and local history, too.

" An admirable suggestion has been adopted by the Belgium government which might be acted upon wisely by our own. The great fact of which the sane and insane of asylums complain, is, the utter want of means of communication with the outside world. It must be conceded that Lunatic Asylums are intended to be means of cure, and not alone places of safety, and that in many cases the means of communicating with friends would tend to the alleviation of mental and physical derangement.

" If the examination about to be made by the lawyers of J. T. Van Vleck, the gentleman who has been for a long time confined in Bloomingdale Asylum, upon what he asserts is a false charge, shall bring about so easy and still so important a reform as the letter-box system, it will have done one good thing by directing public attention to an important and ever increasing question."

Since this important feature of reform has now become already inaugurated in substance in Iowa, and regarding the Belgium mode of collecting the mail as superior to any plan our Committee had devised for this purpose, I cut out the above articles, and enclosed them in the following letter to the chairman of this Committee recommending its immediate adoption.

CHICAGO, August 12, 1872.

JUDGE LOWE—I am preparing a full and detailed account of my effort in Iowa Legislature and Mount Pleasant, to be published in my forthcoming book, and part of which is my last two letters I wrote to you, thus giving Judge Lowe, Ex-Governor of Iowa, and Chairman of the Visiting Committee, a very prominent place in this narrative.

Now, it is my desire to immortalize your name as the great pioneer of this now well inaugurated humanitarian reform. For this purpose I send you the enclosed practice of the Belgium government for you to adopt as the best devised mode of collecting the mail from the inmates of your insane asylums, and then report to me that it is done, or, how you do secure the enforcement of the legislative will of Iowa, so I can add this most commendable act as a new laurel to your crown of honor, in thus establishing a precedent worthy of imitation by every State in the United States.

Oh! how I should delight to say to other Legislators and Committees:

"Judge Lowe, of Iowa, the worthy chairman of the first Committee of the kind ever created in America, has established the best and most invulnerable system of communication with the outside world ever before adopted in America."

And this I could honestly say, by your adopting the Belgium practice of collecting the mail, free from any possibility of interference from interested parties. None but an authorized agent of the U. S. Mail should be allowed to hold the key to these mail-boxes.

Oh! Sir, do give to these unfortunates a sure guarantee, that their mail matter shall never again be interfered with by the asylum officials, and your passport to the gratitude of an appreciative Republic will be complete and unquestioned.

The good leaven is working in other States, since Iowa has taken her invincible stand to defend, by law, their unfortunate. I am now in correspondence with Governor Hoffman of New York on this subject, and he is looking to the operation of this humane law in Iowa for light to guide his actions.

Yes, Judge Lowe, "Your light is now set upon a hill where it cannot be hid." Oh, Let it shine! as the morning star heralding the millennial sun.

As ever, yours for the oppressed,

E. P. W. PACKARD.

In reply to the above, Judge Lowe wrote that, he saw no objection to adopting the Belgium mode of collecting the mail from the inmates of Insane Asylums in Iowa, and would recommend this course to the Committee at their next meeting, about the middle of September.

If the Committee do adopt this course, and secure the faithful enforcement of the law to "protect the Insane," Iowa can then make her boast of being the pioneer State in America in protecting the unfortunate inmates of Insane Asylums by the same laws by which other citizens of their State are protected.

CHAPTER XLIX.

Life in Bloomingdale Asylum, New York.

At a meeting of the Commissioners appointed by Governor Hoffman, convened Oct. 21st, 1872, at 118 East Thirtieth Street, New York, I listened to the following testimony, taken under oath before these commissioners, from a lady who had recently been confined three months at Bloomingdale Asylum, wherein she details the treatment there to be of the same barbarous character as the Committee of Illinois found it to be at their Asylum at Jacksonville.

She said she went of her own accord for treatment for epileptic fits, which she had been informed could be cured there. She was not insane, and did not go as an insane person, but as a boarder. She paid three hundred dollars upon entering, the sum required for three months, with a special contract that she should have all the medical care, treatment and attention her case required. The physician under whose care she had placed herself saw her only three times during the whole time. She took something four times a day, which she thinks was nothing but calomel, as she feels to this day such evil effects in her system as calomel produces.

The first night her attendant ordered her early to bed, without her supper.

She declined going so early, and without a light, and asked for her supper.

They refused her a mouthful of food and told her if she did not go immediately they should send her to the "Lodge."

She sent for the Doctor.

He came, and told her she must not have any supper, and must do as the attendants requested.

Still she told them she would not go until she pleased to do so.

Then they pushed her into her room and stripped off her clothing and tore it into ribbons before they left her.

They pinched and pounded her until her arms were covered with black and blue spots and also her entire body above her waist. They kept her in a straight-jacket part of the time and told her if she made any complaint they should send her down to the " lodge."

Her food was not only very scanty, but so poor that it was more suitable food for dogs and cats than human beings ; and if they refused to eat this it was forced down their throats with the fingers of the attendants.

She had seen a feeble patient, while in a straight-jacket, pulled from her bed by the hair of her head, and then dragged to the shower-bath and there held under it so long as they chose. And this was done to torture her, and not for hydropathic treatment. And such cases were not of rare occurrence but daily practiced there.

Her clothes were all taken from her and have never been returned.

She often tried to get away, and often begged of the Doctor to send her off, but he would not.

She showed her black and blue arms to the commissioners when they passed through, and one remarked as he beheld them :

" 'Tis shameful ! "

There was always extra scrubbing and cleaning about the house and premises, whenever the commissioners were expected. At other times neglect and disorder sometimes prevailed to a reprehensible degree.

The patients, the boarders of the house, were required to do all their own chamber-work, and most of the ward work, and the Irish servant girls would sit and sew while they compelled the patients to do the work for which they, as attendants, were paid for doing. Whether sick or well, she adds :

" We were required to make our own beds, empty our slops and clean our own rooms, and when I made complaint to the Doctor of this injustice, telling him I was not able to do this work, the only reply he made was :

" 'It is good exercise for you ! '

" We were sometimes allowed to walk out, but within very circumscribed limits, and never without the watch and scrutiny of these contemptible'and often very insolent attendants. In fact, I often refused to go at all, to avoid the petty persecutions and contemptible authority they loved to exercise over us.

" In all their treatment of the patients they endeavored to impress the feeling upon the mind of every boarder :

" ' You are merely our under-servants, subject wholly to our rule and dictation, as your keepers, while you are our prisoners.'

" In fact, the patients in Bloomingdale Asylum are treated more like brutes than human beings.

" I did not often make complaints to the Doctors of our attendants' ill-treatment of the patients, because I found the remark the Doctor once made to me, in reply to my report of mistreatment, to be too true, viz. :

" ' Mrs. —, we must take the statements of our attendants to be true rather than the counter-statements of the patients.'

" And it was the habitual practice of the attendants to deny the charges brought against them by the patients, no matter how abundant and consistent the testimony in support of these charges ; and besides, the attendants would threaten us with the straight-jacket and a consignment to the " lodge " if we did report them to the Doctor.

" Bad as it was, the treatment I received would have been much more cruel, had my friends failed to visit the asylum as often as they did.

" This manifested solicitude on their part was a great restraint upon them, for my friends would not be put off with their excuses, but would insist upon seeing me when they came.

" I wrote many letters which I gave to my attendants to mail for me, but not a single one of the whole number thus entrusted ever reached the friend to whom it was directed.

" I am very sure that had my imprisonment been continued two months longer, I should have become a raving maniac.

" But at the expiration of my term of three months, my friends insisted upon taking me out, and thus I was saved from this impending fate, which has already befallen many an inmate now confined in Bloomingdale Asylum."

At the request of the Commissioners and the witness herself, I withhold her name. She is a married woman and a resident of New York city, of good and respectable standing.

Testimony of a Gentleman's Experience of Life in Bloomingdale Asylum.

The following statement was given to the public, August 8, 1872, through the columns of the New York *Tribune:*

" One gentleman, for twenty years a prosperous merchant of this city, had an opportunity, not long ago, of giving a few months study to the internal workings of the Asylum at Bloomingdale.

" The question of his sanity had never been raised, to his knowledge, until in the course of conversation he betrayed a knowledge of some painful domestic matters in the family of a relative.

" On the following morning he was taken to a police station, and thence to a police court, where, on the testimony of two physicians who had never seen him until that day, he was committed to the Bloomingdale Asylum, his brother appearing as prime mover in the matter.

He remained a prisoner about three months, when, some friends having learned of his situation through letters which he was enabled to smuggle out of the asylum, a writ of habeas corpus was issued in his case, whereupon he was at once released by Dr. Brown. Although he did not intentionally take advantage of the release, it was adjudged that he had technically done so, having left the grounds and returned voluntarily; and his purpose of obtaining legal redress was thus thwarted.

In conversation with a New York *Tribune* reporter, this gentleman gave a minute account of the management of the asylum during the period when he was an inmate.

A prominent cause of complaint was that the establishment seemed to him to be run as a money-making institution, with little reference to the comfort or recovery of the patients. There was nothing to interest them—no books, papers, or magazines except a few old copies of some British reviews. There were no sources of amusement except a billiard-table, and the inmates could do nothing but sit in straight-backed wooden chairs and walk in the halls.

The attendants were rough and ignorant men, who could be hired on the most moderate terms. Foul and profane language was frequently addressed by them to the patients, and he had seen personal violence used at times.

A man by the name of Bissel was subject to epileptic fits, but was not insane; frequently he had been dragged by an arm or leg into his room, and there flung violently upon the floor. Bissel was placed at one time in the "lodge," a quarter reserved for the most violent lunatics.

Dr. Brown, in this gentleman's opinion, is an indolent man, who fails to oversee the institution personally, and his deputies and attendants take advantage of this fact to neglect their duties.

Thirty or forty patients were lodged in the rooms leading

into each hall, and the night watchmen were frequently absent from these halls until a late hour. The doors of the rooms were not locked, and the inmates were thus left for long periods at the mercy of the most violent of their number.

He had been locked into his room on several occasions at his own request as a precautionary measure.

The bath-rooms and water-closets were arranged without the slightest attempt at comfort or even decency. They were insufficient in number and filthy in the extreme.

The patients were treated rather as servants than as gentleman; he was expected to take care of his own room and to make his own bed.

In fact, in his opinion, the whole course of treatment to which the inmate of the Bloomingdale Asylum is subjected is of a nature to intensify rather than alleviate any symptoms of insanity which he may manifest, and to make a sane man mad.

During the short time that he was there he was able to find no occupation, and could amuse himself only by walking backward and forward in the hall—an exercise which his keepers regarded as a conclusive proof of his unsoundness of mind!"

The name of this informant is withheld for the present, as its publication might interfere with the legal proceedings which he proposes to begin.

Mr. Chambers' Testimony.

A very unique and sensible method of ventilating this asylum, has recently been adopted by the New York *Tribune* company, by sending one of their most reliable reporters to that institution under the guise of a patient, under which assumed character, he made investigations of the most important and reprehensible character, both in reference to the present mode of committal, and also the mode of treatment which the patients receive at Bloomingdale Asylum.

This energetic and capable young man, Mr. Chambers, the reporter, has immortalized himself in the hearts of the human_itarians, not only of his own but all future ages, by the good this effort has secured to this department of humanitarian reform.

His testimony with regard to his admission, and the treatment he received as a patient while there, are most graphically and fully reported by himself, and have already been given to the public through the columns of the New York *Tribune*, of August 30th and 31st, 1872, proving without a question that all the charges of the above witnesses are founded truth; that they are not either exaggerated or overdrawn pictures in any particular.

The summing up of this reporter's mission, I can give in no better language than is given in the editorial of the *Tribune*, containing his report, viz. :

" The narrative now published establishes, beyond any sort of doubt, that greater facilities are offered for getting a sane man into an insane asylum than out of it. The whole medical profession is at the beck and call of all who can pay to aid in the commitment. The same man, once committed, has only the medical skill of a single physician to call to his succor; and that physician was already prejudiced against him for divers reasons. It is his interest—to put the baser motive first and dismiss it soonest—to keep the paying boarder as long as his friends pay his keeping. Then the endorsement of his infirmity by two reputable professional brethren leads the asylum physicians to hesitate at reversing their sworn decision. It is not merely a thing that seems to lack professional courtesy, but a delicate one; if a mistake be made it is damaging to the reputation of himself or associates, and in any event is derogatory to a profession in which the members take unusual pride. Thus prejudiced, it is natural that there should be hesitation on part of the asylum physicians, and a disposition to torture a patient's protest of sanity and appeals for release into evidences of idiocy, confirmatory of the certificate of commitment.

No perfect or proper asylum or hospital for the treatment of special diseases, and particularly of insanity, can exist without strict adherence to a well considered system of classification.

The report which we publish to-day is conclusive proof that there is no such system pursued at Bloomingdale.

The proof is not in the assertions of the writer; it lies in the fact that he, feigning nothing, appearing a quiet person, without even eccentricities, daily visited by an "expert" physician, and constantly watched by "professional" keepers, was kept four days in the excited wards, surrounded by dangerous maniacs, without suggestion of removal. And during all this time the ward was never once visited by the Chief Physician or Superintendent, Dr. Brown.

The Bloomingdale Asylum is a private institution, owned and conducted by personal enterprise. It is evident, also, that it is a speculative institution, and is maintained at a profit at the expense and abuse of the unfortunate boarders. The lowest rate per week charged is twenty dollars.

Now it is evident from the plain, brief, and careful statements of the reporter, that the accommodations are not better than can be had in any second-class boarding-house in this city for seven dollars a week, room and meals included.

As for the other conditions, the food is not particularly nutritious, the supply of the costlier materials is small and grudgingly given, the food is not clean, nor is it well cooked, and the attendance at table is simply beastly.

The conversation of the keepers while serving at table is not fairly reported, but it is because their disgusting language cannot be expressed in print, and it is impossible to describe it. Uttered in a public bar-room, some of the words reported to us by the reporter as repeatedly spoken by the attendants while serving at table in the asylum, would have subjected the speaker to summary and violent ejection at the hands of the most besotted of proprietors.

The constant punishment of an imbecile youth by forcing him to perform the duties of a menial—the violent hurling of a harmless idiot half across a room for the offense of not knowing which way to turn—the brutal beating of an old and blind idiot for protesting against rude treatment—the toasting of a poor boy naked in the sun while confined in what is nothing other than an iron cage—these are among the instances of cruelty which the reporter cites as having been witnessed by himself.

Others are also named, but none are of such a painful nature as those enumerated above. We have vainly endeavored to imagine a plausible excuse for these acts of violence which we have not the heart to recite in detail. They appear to have been wanton acts done in moments of passion by the keepers, and were not necessary apparently to the maintenance of any system of discipline, for discipline and classification alike seem to have no part in the Bloomingdale management."

CHAPTER L

Testimony from Ward's Island, Taunton, Trenton, and Brattleboro Asylums.

Death and Burial of Louis C. Samuels, Victim of Ward's Island Asylum, New York.

In the New York *Sun*, of November 4th, 1872, appeared the following:

"On Saturday Coroner Herrman held an inquest over the remains of Louis C. Samuels, the lunatic alleged to have died at the city Insane Asylum at Ward's Island last Monday night, from the effects of mal-treatment at the hands of the keeper, James McDonald. The first witness examined was Dr. Joseph Cushman, who testified that the result of a *post-mortem* examination, made by him, was to show that Samuels was laboring under no acute complaint likely to have caused death, which, he thought, was brought about by exhaustion, the body being very much emaciated.

Dr. Gonzales Echeverria, resident physician of the asylum, testified that Samuels was admitted into the asylum last August. He was a person of some mental ability as far as he could judge. In September he was suffering from acute mania, but wholly inoffensive. He was also troubled with diarrhœa, from which he did not fully recover until about two weeks ago, when his mental condition also improved.

He frequently complained of being starved and mal-treated by the attendants in the ward, and especially by McDonald, who, he said, was greatly addicted to drinking. Witness was not at first disposed to place much credence in his statements, but a careful investigation satisfied him that the charge of inebriety at least was true.

On the morning of October 26th he found another patient, named Patrick Cassidy, in the ward with Samuels, with his face and shirt stained with blood, and on inquiry ascertained that McDonald had broken his nose. As this fact was admitted by the keeper, witness, considering him an unsafe man to have charge of insane patients, reported the fact to the Commissioners of Charities and Correction, and the following morning, on visiting the asylum, he was again appealed to by Samuels, who was evidently suffering severely, and who complained that McDonald had forced him to take a cold bath as a punishment.

He was at this time so emaciated that, according to witness, nothing but skin and bone were left. Seeing that he was suffering from lack of sufficient nourishment, the doctor ordered him some invigorating food. The next morning Samuels was in a still feebler condition, and complained that McDonald had again maltreated him, kicking him in the stomach with his knee on this occasion. He wished to write to his brother concerning his treatment, but witness assured him he would present the case to the proper authorities. He accordingly wrote a letter to the President of the Commissioners of Charities and Correction.

Witness here cited several instances of brutality which had occurred in the asylum within the past six weeks, one of which had resulted in the death of one Herman Eilers. On the night of Monday, October 28, Samuels died, and, in his opinion, his death was attributable solely to the cruelty of McDonald. After the examination of other witnesses the case was adjourned.

On Saturday the body of Samuels was taken to Bellevue Hospital, and yesterday the members of Olympic Lodge assembled at 193 Bowery to pay the last tribute of respect to their deceased brother.

Despite the inclemency of the weather nearly every lodge in the city was represented. Brother Lipenan delivered an eloquent address, and resolutions were adopted concerning the inhuman treatment to which Brother Samuels had been subjected. A long procession marched to Washington Cemetery in Brooklyn."

Death of James Parks, Victim of Taunton Asylum, Massachusetts.

" A coroner's jury has this week investigated the last days and death of James Parks, who died at the Taunton Lunatic Asylum on March 3d.

He was a truckman in Cambridge, and during Thursday, February 26th, was observed to act strangely about his work. In the evening he went to an Irish wake in Charlestown and acted on his return homeward with a boisterous turbulence, apparently resulting from intoxication, sometimes on horseback and sometimes off.

Two policeman, after a severe struggle in which they several times struck him with a billy on the head, arrested him and took him to a station house.

In the morning he was adjudged insane, and after several days of detention in the station house, was sent to the Taunton hospital. Here he became very violent, and one of the attendants, in defending himself against Park's maniacal fury, threw him down and kneeled on his chest in order to keep him under. Thereafter Parks lost his vigorous strength, and the next day died.

Post-mortem examination showed some heavy scalp wounds, bruises in various parts of his body, and fourteen broken ribs, a fracture of the breast bone, and the right lung perforated in several places. The doctors of the asylum endeavored to lay the blame of death upon the previous struggle, and for that purpose tried to prove that maniacal excitement could mask severe physical injuries.

The weight of testimony was inexorable against their hypothesis, and the verdict attributed his death to the fierce fight in the hospital.

No blame was cast upon the men who thus became his unintentional murderers! But it is evident that constant familiarity with such cases leads to a criminally reckless handling of human life; and it is unlikely that three stalwart men should have been unable in any other way to master this one man without recourse to crushing breath and blood from his body."

Mr. Bischoffsberger, Victim of Trenton Asylum, New Jersey.

"In Newark, a Mrs. Bischoffsberger, wife of a well-to-do grocer, and her brother-in-law, Simon Stentz, were taken into custody upon a charge of unlawfully depriving Mr. Bischoffsberger of his liberty and attempting to defraud him of his property.

Mr. Bischoffsberger's friends claim that his wife, in order to get possession of the property, induced a physician to give a certificate that he was insane. In this project, as alleged, the wife was assisted by Stentz. Upon the above mentioned certificate, it is further alleged, Mr. Bischoffsberger was hurried to the Lunatic Asylum at Trenton, where no careful examination of his case was made. Mr. Bischoffsberger protested that he was perfectly sane, and that his incarceration was the result of a base conspiracy.

The wife paid six months board in advance for the "patient." Once rid of the old man, the wife commenced measures to get possession of the property, which is valued at forty thousand dollars. In the meantime some of Mr. Bischoffsberger's friends became suspicious of the stories that had been given out relative to his whereabouts and instituted a search.   They were aided by the Doctor above alluded to, who had fallen out with Mrs. Bischoffsberger, because she would not pay him his promised fee.

Having discovered the old man's whereabouts, steps were at once taken to secure his release.

The Superintendent of the asylum suddenly discovered that Mr. Bischoffsberger was not insane, and wrote to his wife informing her of the fact, and ordering her to come and take her husband away.   Mrs. Bischoffsberger, who had not yet succeeded in her schemes of getting possession of the property, refused to do this, and sent money to the asylum authorities for three months' more board.   Mr. Bischoffsberger's friends still persevered, and at length succeeded in securing his liberation.

The " patient " is now in Newark, apparently as sane as any one.

Mrs. Bischoffsberger and Stentz, as above stated, have been arrested and committed to the City Prison, in default of bail, to await trial.   There is a sensation ahead for Newark."

Brattleboro Asylum Horrors.

This terrible Asylum, so long notorious for its cruelties to the inmates, is now undergoing a thorough ventilation, and when the forty witnesses who are now summoned to meet at Montpelier, come forward before the public with their testimony, it will doubtless more than confirm the present reputation it has acquired of being one of the most cruel of all these American bastiles.

It will doubtlessly show that the remark of a victim who suffered one years' torture there to be no exaggeration of the truth.   Said he :

" If ever my friends decide to return me again, as a patient, into that institution, there is one request I have to make, which I beg of them with all sincerity to comply with, which is, that before they put me there, to begin at my toes and with pinchers pick off all the flesh from my entire body, and it will be a mercy to me to have them thus do, before they send me to Brattleboro asylum again!'"

Another case is that of a lady, whom the Doctor decided to subdue by the starvation " treatment," which process was so long continued that the smell of food even drove her almost frantic, so that she would risk almost any exposure to get it. To prevent this they jacketed her, so that with her arms thus pinioned they could better restrain her efforts to help herself when in the dining-room.

One day as she entered the dining-hall in this straight-jacket, the sight and smell of food so stimulated her appetite in her now emaciated and nearly deathly condition from so long a deprivation of food sufficient for nature's demands, that in her agony she bent her head towards the table and, was just in the act of clutching a mouthful of food between her teeth, when her attendant saw her and seized her to drag her away, when she, instead of securing the food she aimed at, caught the table-cloth between her teeth in its place, and by the violent and sudden act of her attendant in dragging her off, she dragged off with her patient the table-cloth, and with it the dishes upon it, so that a general break-up was the result.

Now the starved patient was taken off to receive her condign punishment for breaking the asylum crockery, which she was as certain of getting as she had been of getting the counterpart of her "treatment"—starvation—from the decree of the same despot.

She was stripped, pinioned, and whipped until the blood flowed from her body so profusely as to stand in puddles about her feet!

And this is the " treatment " our Christian Government has legalized as the cure for insanity !

Knowing, as I do, that this is true, and liable to occur in every asylum in our country, whether public or private, shall I be innocent in God's sight if I fail to lift up my voice, cry aloud and spare not, until every inmate within the pale of these despotic institutions has access to the strong arm of law to protect them from such violence and injustice ?

Nay, if I were silent under these circumstances, well might I expect, under the government of a just God, to receive myself, sooner or later, these same punishments inflicted upon myself, which I had not tried to ward off from my unfortunate brothers and sisters in God's great family.

Indeed, I verily believe, that if the truth were known, there would be found in every asylum on this continent cases of just as false imprisonment in each of them, as mine was in Jacksonville.

It is therefore my settled and determined purpose to rest not from my labors until they are all thoroughly ventilated.

CHAPTER LI.

Is Man the Lord of Creation?

The response I received to the congratulation I gave Doctor McFarland, one day, on his return from his Chicago trip, pained me a little. His wife standing by, I said:

"We welcome your return; still, we congratulate you on being able to leave the superintendence of the house in so good hands as your wife's, in your absence. We feel that kindness rules her actions towards the patients."

"Your words are always so sweet and honied!"

"No more so than my feelings. They are correct reporters of my heart."

"Would that some of these sweet and honied words could be bestowed upon the husband you promised to love and honor!"

"He has had them in more abundance than any other man, but he shall never have another, until he repents.

"Oh, how determined you men are to break down the conscience of woman, and thus annihilate her identity. Only let her be your *echo* or parasite and she is all right!

"Doctor, there should be no individual sovereignty in opposition to God's government. Therefore, no husband should require the subjection of his wife's conscience to his will, when it opposes what *she regards* as God's will. God grant, that the time may never wear away in me this spirit of resistance to such oppression."

"But Mrs. Packard, these principles would be subversive of all family government; for, the government of the family is vested entirely in the husband, the wife has no right to her identity; she must live, move and have her being in him alone."

16

" I admit that the recognition of her identity will endanger the overthrow of a family despotism, because the marital power will then be so limited as to compel a respectful regard to the inalienable rights of the wife; for, on this principle, the husband must have the power to ignore all her rights, or he cannot be ' lord over all ' in his family !

" I claim that every family established on such a basis ought to be overthrown, as well as all other despotisms ; and it is this principle which is at the present day sending devastation throughout the whole social fabric of society.

" Despotism cannot live on freedom's soil.

" Divorce and disunion are demonstrating this fact, and they will continue to demonstrate and remonstrate too, against family-despotism, until this government will extend the right of life, liberty and the pursuit of happiness, to the wives of the government as well as the husbands.

"Married woman has as good a right to her moral accountability as a married man ; and God is her sovereign as well as he is man's sovereign.   Man has no more right to interfere with her allegiance to Christ's government, than she has to interfere with his.   Both must be judged independently before this highest tribunal, therefore each should be morally free to live up to their highest convictions of right."

" Mrs. Packard, what is meant by ' Wives, obey your husbands ? ' "

" It means to obey them in what is right, and not in what is wrong."

" What is meant by the husband being the ' head of the wife ? ' "

" It means that he is the head, or the senior partner of the firm, and the wife the junior partner, or companion.   He has this headship assigned to him instead of the wife, because he is the best fitted in nature to defend and protect the wife and children.   He is the head, to protect, but not to subject the rights of the other members of the household. This headship gives him no more right to become the despot, than the junior position of the wife allows her to become his slave. Being associated as partners, does not confer on either the right of usurpation."

" But what shall be done, when, on a point of common interest, they cannot agree ? "

" The junior must yield her views to the senior's."

" But supposing the wife feels that the husband's plans will bring disaster upon the family interests ? "

"It is her duty to yield, notwithstanding, after she has urged all her strong reasons against it, for unless she does, she trespasses on his right as a ' head' of the firm. The risk must be assumed by some one, and as the ' head' is compelled to bear this responsibility, he ought to be allowed to act in accordance with his own judgment, after the opinions of his junior partner have been candidly weighed. Then, if disaster follows, she has no right to complain, for this is one of the indispensable liabilities of a co-partnership relation. Understanding this principle when she entered the firm, she would be domineering over an inalienable right of her partner to do otherwise. Unless this principle of justice can be peaceably conceded, there is no alternative but a peaceable dissolution, or a civil war."

It is with a kind of patriotic pride that I can at this age chronicle one State as having already engrafted this just principle of legislation into their laws, and also add, that its application is pacific in its influence upon the social fabric.

Finding that Iowa was in advance of all the other States in this Union in removing the legal disabilities of common law in relation to married woman, and that she lacked only one more provision to render all the rights and responsibilities of the husband and wife equal before the law, I therefore, during my nine months labors in Iowa, in 1871-2, made a specialty of this defect, by obtaining thirty-six hundred names of patrons who consented to have their names used with their Legislature as those who wished to have this defect remedied. Therefore, in the winter of 1872, I sent to the Legislature the following Bill, together with these thirty-six hundred names as patrons in its support, viz.:

" Where the parents of children live separate and apart from each other, without fault of the wife, whether divorced or not, the Circuit-Court sitting as a court of Chancery shall have jurisdiction to regulate the custody and maintenance of the children, and determine with which of the parents the child or children shall remain, and who shall be entitled to the earnings, and liable for the support of the same—and the rights of the parents, in the absence of misconduct, shall be equal."

In reply came the intelligence that there had been a committee appointed to revise the statutes of Iowa and that they had reported that they would recommend to the Legislature to adopt this principle into their laws, for this reason, that as in all other respects the rights of the husband and wife were equal, they saw no reason why in relation to parentage they should not be equal also.

While at work, however, for my ' Bill to Protect the Insane,' in the Legislature of 1872, I also lobbied for this bill, and had every reason to think the recommendation of this Revising Committee would be adopted by the Legislature without opposition. But the sudden and rather premature adjournment of the Legislature left this part of their business unfinished, to be acted upon at their next Session.

When this bill is actually passed into a law, Iowa can then be justly entitled to the honor of not only being the pioneer State in protecting the inmates of insane asylums, but also in extending the same protection of law to the married women of their State which they do to the married men.

CHAPTER LII.

Getting my Children—A Re-united Family.

Finding as I had, that my property rights—my rights of conscience and opinion and my personal liberty were all at the mercy of my legal usurper, I inquired of my counsel with the most intense anxiety:

" How is it with my children ?. Can I not have children protected to me while I am a married woman ? "

" No, the children are all the husband's after the tender age. You can have no legal right to your own children, unless you get a divorce, and then the Judge will give you your children and alimony."

" Then your laws do protect children to the single woman, while they do not protect them to the married woman ? "

" Yes, the laws do respect the right of maternity in the single woman, but in the married woman this right, like all her other rights, is ignored by this suspension of rights during coverture."

" Now, we married women claim that the time has fully come to have our maternal rights established and protected by law, equally at least to those of the single woman, for by such laws a premium is offered on infidelity and encourages divorce ; whereas, the best interests of society demand that the sacred institution of marriage be based on the principle of right and justice to both parties so that neither party can ignore or usurp the inalienable rights of the other.

" Until this is done, the children of this Republic have only half their rights, in law. They can claim a legal right to a father's training, but none to a mother's care."

The obstacles in the way of getting my children seemed at first view almost insurmountable. The battle I was called upon to fight seemed to require more courage, fortitude and perseverance, than I could command, when I looked simply upon the obstacles.

But when my loving heart looked upon the end to be attained—the care of my own dear children—doubt, despon-dency and fear fled apace before the determined will and purpose to succeed, in spite of the mighty barriers to be overcome.

The laws of two States must first be changed, and my poverty be supplanted by plenty, before I could reasonably hope to succeed in getting the custody of my three minor children.

Fully-determined, however, to face these foes and conquer them all before giving the field to the enemy, I commenced writing and selling my own books, as heretofore delineated, and persevered in this business until I had sold enough to purchase a nice little cottage and lot in Chicago, free from all encumbrance.

But as the laws of Illinois then were, all my earnings which had paid for this home in full, were entirely subject to my husband's control, and thereby liable any day to be taken from me by my husband. The imperative necessity of self-protection drove me to seek a change in the laws of Illinois, to secure to me a safe title to the ownership of this property.

As a preparatory step, as soon as the legislature for 1869 was chosen, I mailed to each member of that body a copy of my book, the postage alone of which cost me forty dollars.

I considered this as throwing light across their path, in season for them to consider the subject impartially and calmly before being called upon to act, trusting that all that was needed was simply to inform them of the necessity of such legislation as would render impossible another such outrage.

In addition to this I suspended all other business, and paid my board in Springfield another entire session, trying to so bring the subject before the members, that its claims might not be forgotten or disregarded. I wrote anonymous articles for the *Chicago Tribune* and the Springfield State *Journal* upon the subject of my bill, which I had the honor to hear credited to Mrs. Livermore of Chicago. But this compliment, flattering as it was, did not supersede the need of direct personal effort for the success of the cause.

The bill which I had prepared had for its object—" To equalize the rights and responsibilities of the husband and wife."

It covered the whole ground of married woman's legal disabilities, the passage of which would not only entitle her to the rights of an individual property owner, the same as her husband, but also to the right of co-partnership with her husband in the use and control of the property acquired during coverture, and also the right of co-partnership with her husband in the guardianship, custody and control of the children, and also an equal right with her husband, as surviving partner, to the administration of the estate and guardianship of the children.

The two following are a specimen of the kind of articles to which I called the attention of the legislature through the columns of the public press.

The Rights of Children.

Every child has a right to a mother as well as a father. Neither should these rights be ignored by the laws of a Christian Government.

But as the law now is, the mother's legal right to the custody and control of the children, after " the tender age," is annihilated by the common law basis of marriage.

After " the tender age," this right of the mother is entirely subject to the will or wishes of the father. He may allow the mother the privilege of rearing her own children, or he may take from her this privilege and bestow it upon whom he pleases, regardless of her entreaties or protests to the contrary, and she is helpless in legal self-defense of this right of the child.

True, a court of chancery may award this right to the mother, if her claim to competency can be sustained; still the common law secures to the father the right to usurp this sacred right which God has given the mother to be the natural guardian of the child.

Supposing the reverse was true, and men had to be subject to such laws as these, which women had made for them.

Would they not cry out against the inhumanity of these laws of their woman government, so long as it allowed the father's right thus to be trampled into the dust by such unjust legislation?

But supposing the woman government should claim, in defense of these one-sided laws, that—

" It will not do to allow the father to have equal rights with the mother, lest our own rights be imperiled thereby.

" No, we must retain the full power to usurp the rights of the defenseless father, for there is no way under the laws of our woman government to protect the rights of the weak against the usurpations of the strong, except to grant the full power of usurpation and protection to the strong party alone!

" Yes, we will not only retain the law-making power as our own exclusive right, but we will also compel you to be subject to these laws of our one-sided legislation. This is our way of protecting the rights of men, for all our rights are forever gone just as soon as our right to usurp the rights of men is limited!"

" Oh! man's inhumanity to woman in such kind of legislation "makes countless millions mourn!"

Yes, under our man government it is the *un*married woman

alone who has any legal right to rear her own offspring, while the father is required to provide for it.

Illegitimate children are allowed a legal right to a mother's training and guardianship, while the legitimate offspring of the married woman have no legal right to the care and training of their own mothers!

Now we claim that the law should protect the rights of the married woman's children to a mother's care, equally at least with those of the single woman.

But it does not do so.

Therefore this Christian government thus offers a premium on infidelity, and encourages divorce or separation, as this is now the only way a married woman can get the legal custody of her own children. Woman must either have her children in a single state, or be divorced from the marriage relation in order to be possessed of the legal right to the custody or control of her children!

We do not want that the father's right to the control and custody of the children should be extirpated; we only want the mother's right to be established on the same basis.

The child has a right to a father, and therefore it is eminently proper that the law should establish and protect this right. And so also has the child a right to a mother, and, therefore, we claim that it is equally proper that this right also should be established and protected by law.

It is earnestly hoped that the Twenty-six General Assembly of Illinois will be magnanimous enough to boldly face these disgraceful facts, and dare 'to be the pioneer State in this Union in establishing and protecting the right of the children of this republic to the guardianship and training of the married mother, as well as the father, by passing the " bill for an act to equalize the rights and responsibilities of the husband and wife." In behalf of the children of Illinois,

Chicago, February 2d. 1869 A MOTHER.

The Mother's Legal Rights.

There is a bill before the Illinois Legislature calling for the legal recognition of the maternal rights of married women.

The provisions of the bill grant to the mother the same legal protection in law, which the enlightened public sentiment of the present age grants her in her social position in society.

We would most cheerfully admit that married woman's social position under the American flag is the best in the world, and if her legal position could but be made to correspond with it, ours would be the model government for woman.

By this bill the mother becomes legally a joint partner with the father, as the guardian of her children, and is equally entitled with him to the custody, control and earnings of the children, as long as they shall continue to be husband and wife. But in case of separation the children must be disposed of as the present statute law directs, in case of divorce, at the discretion of the judges before whom each party makes their claim.

As the law now is, all the natural rights of married women are annihilated by that principle of the non-existence of the wife, thus leaving all her rights wholly subject to the will of her husband. As the right of the mother to rear her own children is one of married woman's natural rights, which the common law of marriage entirely ignores, the manliness of the legislators of the present age should, by statute law so modify this unjust principle, as to recognize in married woman a legal right to be the guardian of her own offspring.

Another provision of the bill is, that as the mother has a right to rear her own offspring, she has therefore a right to a home to rear them in; and, as she assumes equal responsibilities with the father in the training of the children, she must therefore become a joint owner with him in their common property, thus allowing the mother means for discharging her responsibilities equal to those of the father

But some object that woman is not prepared to assume these important trusts and responsibilities.

But how is she to become prepared?

By perpetuating her dependence, or by lifting her up on this plane of responsibility, and thus educating her for her high duties?

It was once argued that the negro slave must first be fitted for freedom before he could be trusted with it; but the more enlightened claimed that the very best way to fit him for freedom was to elevate him to the position of a free man.

Responsibility does elevate, and therefore the most sure and effectual method of capacitating married woman for these trusts is to lift her out of her dependent condition, and entrust her with those high and noble duties and responsibilities which cluster around the mother's heaven-assigned sphere.

Only once let our legislators try the experiment and test us by endowing married woman with her natural rights as a woman, they need not be surprised if her clamor for the rights of men should cease.

But so long as the law-makers will stifle her cry to them for the protection of this, the first right of woman's nature, they must still expect to hear that most unwelcome cry for " the right to be their own protectors ! "

Mothers of Illinois! let us suspend our condemnation of our man legislation until we see what action they take upon this bill, wherein we make our appeal to them for the protection of our maternal rights, trusting that they may yet be induced to give to married woman as sure a guarantee of her rights as a mother, as they provide for themselves as fathers.

In behalf of the mothers of Illinois,

Chicago, January 29th, 1869.　　　A Female Parent.

To secure the passage of this bill, I met the Judiciary Committee of the House to whom the bill had been referred, at the

Leland House, by appointment, and there presented my defense of the bill to a crowded audience in the committee's room.

But I am sorry to add, it did not seem to be appreciated or favorably regarded.

The chairman told me they would like to see many of the provisions of the bill introduced into the statute laws of Illinois, but did not consider it expedient to recommend a bill including so many radical changes at once—but would report it back without their recommendation, and leave it to the action of the House to accept or reject it independent of their opinion, if it was my wish for them so to do. He told me it was his candid opinion the House would reject it by a large majority, if presented as it was, for there were too many changes, although good in themselves, to introduce at one time.

I therefore concluded not to urge the bill any farther in its present comprehensive character, but wrote at once to Judge Bradwell, of Chicago, to know if his business would render it possible for him to visit Springfield, and allow me his advice and assistance in this matter.

He came, and I met him with Mrs. Bradwell at the Leland House, where, after thoroughly canvassing the subject, he advised that, instead of mutilating my bill, which in his judgment was admirable, to lay it by for this session, and present one which simply included a married woman's right to hold and use her own earnings, independent of the interference of her husband.

To this I consented and also accepted his kind offer to draft the bill, which he promptly did, and reads thus on the statute book of Illinois, viz:

"A married woman shall be entitled to receive, use, and possess her own earnings, and sue for the same in her own name, free from the interference of her husband or his creditors."

The bill was presented, referred to the Judiciary, recommended, and passed without opposition ; and thereby, I, in common with other married women in Illinois, am now protected by law in my right to my home, bought with my own earnings.

I sent on the " Bill to equalize the rights and responsibilities of husband and wife," to the next legislature of 1871, and it was presented by Senator Dore of Chicago, and freely discussed on the floor of the Senate, and through the columns of the papers, and before the Session closed, I received a letter from Senator Dore, stating that the main features of the Bill had passed into a law, so that now a married woman is equally with the husband entitled to the custody, control and earnings of the children, and can administer upon the estate, and is equally with the husband the natural and legal guardian of the children on the death of her partner, and her right to her own property is protected equally with that of her husband.

Thus I felt that the good seed so prayerfully sown in tears was at length quickened into life, and had arisen to be a power and a blessing to the mothers of all future time in Illinois.

And here a mother's pride prompts me to pay a passing tribute to my son, Samuel, now a lawyer of good standing in Chicago, for to this, now filial son, am I indebted more than to any other one person for the assistance I received in the drafting of this Bill.

This dear child worked with a hearty good will in this noble cause, since his developed manhood has led him to see and feel the need of legal protection to his oppressed mother, in suffering the highest love in her nature—the maternal—to be thus ruthlessly strangled and crucified, not only to her anguish, but also the detriment of the children. This son, in common with almost every other member of the bar with whom I have conversed upon this subject, has often expressed his surprise at finding the statutes so defective on this subject. He once said :

" Mother, I do not think there is one lawyer in ten who knows how absolutely helpless married woman is under the common law, nor how defective our statutes have been in regard to the legal protection of married women. I never fully realized it until my attention was called to it by your experiences. I will gladly do anything in my power to aid you in bringing about this most needed change. If you wish I will go to Springfield myself to help you in this matter, if necessary, to get this important bill through.''

Thus I found that this dear son, who once in his childish ignorance sustained his father in his wicked course, had now become his mother's real and efficient defender and protector, and no restitution he can now make is regarded by him as too great, such as his more developed and now enlightened manhood prompts him to make, as a free-will offering upon the altar of filial love for his esteemed and honored mother.

My next step was to get possession of my children, then in Massachusetts. But as the laws were, when Mr. Packard fled with them to that State, he was solely entitled to the custody, control and earnings of the children, while the mother had no rights at all.

But in the meantime I had sent a bill to Hon. S. E. Sewall, of Boston, requesting him to present it to the Massachusetts Legislature and defend it before the Committee, if necessary, in order to secure its passage.

In response to this came the most welcome intelligence, in the Spring of 1869, that the laws of Massachusetts had been so changed that a mother had now an equal right before the law to the custody and control of the children, with that of the father, and that in case of separation, the Court must determine, by the merits of each individual case, with which of the parents the children should remain.

I therefore decided to go directly to Boston to petition the Court for the custody of my children.

To prepare myself for this campaign I obtained some certificates from my friends in Chicago relative to my capacities to assume the responsibilities of the training and support of my children. And also certificates from real estate agents in relation to the value and amount of the property which I held in my own right. And in addition to these I took the voluntary certificates of my two oldest sons, then doing business in Chicago, with me to Boston to use, if necessary, instead of their going themselves with me to the Court, as witnesses, which, however, they both volunteered to do if I needed them to help me in any manner, to secure the custody of their sister and two younger brothers.

Some of these certificates I will here give to my readers for two reasons—one of which is, that they may see in what estimation I was held in the community where I had made my home since my sanity had been vindicated by the court at Kankakee.

And the other is to show the evidence that these dear sons ever stood the noble defenders of their mother's sanity and her rights; for among other false charges brought against me, by this Conspiracy, is, that most cruel charge, that these dear sons have been disloyal to their mother!

Therefore it is a plain duty I owe these devoted sons, as their mother, to defend their characters against this most unjust charge, by allowing them to speak for themselves, in their own words as found in their own certificates, viz.:

CHICAGO, ILL., April 20, 1869.

To Whom it may Concern:

This is to certify, that I, Theophilus Packard, am the oldest son of Theophilus and Elizabeth P. W. Packard; that I am twenty-seven years of age; that the first sixteen years of my life I spent under my mother's care and supervision, and nearly fitted for college under her teachings.

That from my own judgment and knowledge, without extraneous influence, I solemnly believe that my mother is the only proper person who has both the will and ability to take charge of and maintain her infant children.

That she is *my mother* in every sense of the term, and her councils I may rely upon ; that her loving care and disregard of self to minister to our best interests, merits our most filial regard.

I do not consider her as ever having been insane.

By her indefatigable efforts she has bought and paid for a nice little house and lot in Chicago, to which she has a good title, free from all incumbrance.

It is my earnest and sincere desire that she may obtain possession and control of the minor children, in which case I intend to live in her family.

THEOPHILUS PACKARD, JR.

CHICAGO, ILL., April 12, 1869.

To Whom it may Concern :

This is to certify, that I am the second son of Mrs. E. P. W. Packard and Rev. Theophilus Packard. That 1 am twenty-four years of age. I can say that my mother is every way able and competent to take charge of my younger brothers, who are now under age, educate and bring them up.

From my early youth until I was sixteen, I have been reared under her influence. She has always been a kind and affectionate mother, and all of her children always respected and loved her so long as she was permitted to live with them.

She was separated from them contrary to her wishes.

I consider the charge of insanity against her wholly unfounded.

She is a most excellent mother, her judgment good, and her moral character without a stain. The tribulations and sufferings she has undergone in the past, I feel can be but partially atoned for, by unremitting filial love and the care and custody of her minor children.

She has a house and lot in this city worth thirty-five hundred dollars, unincumbered.

It is my wish and desire that she may take charge of my two brothers, George H. and Arthur D. Packard, for it is my opinion they would be better brought up under her care than under the care of any one else.

Should this desire of her heart be realized, I intend to make my home in her family.

I. W. PACKARD.

———

CHICAGO, ILL., April 12, 1869.

To all whom it may concern:

I hereby certify, that I have been acquainted with Mrs. E. P. W. Packard since 1861. That I have often met and conversed with her upon various general subjects, as well as relative to business matters. That she has at all times exhibited a high order of mind upon all subjects touched upon.

That her character for morality and sterling integrity is, and during the whole period of my acquaintance with her has been, wholly beyond reproach. That she has ever exhibited the most kindly feelings, and when speaking of her children, great affection for them.

I have no hesitancy in saying that she is in every way eminently qualified to have the care, custody, control, and education of all her minor children.

J. H. KNOWLTON,
Counsellor at Law, and ex-Judge.

CHICAGO, ILL., April 12, 1869.

To all whom it may concern:

This is to certify, that I have known Mrs. Elizabeth P. W. Packard for many years. That she is a lady of wonderful business capacity. Is comfortable in her circumstances, the owner of real and personal estate to quite an amount. Is an able and ready writer, an energetic, capable, and worthy woman and mother.

As a mother she is not only able and capable of bringing up her minor children in a proper manner, but I would add, that I know of few, if any ladies, that would excel her in taking care of and educating children.

She is a very superior lady, and in my opinion should have the aid of all good citizens in getting the care of her own children.

JAMES B. BRADWELL,
Judge of the Court of Cook County.

———

CHICAGO, ILL., April 12, 1869.

To whom it may concern:

This is to certify that I have known Mrs. E. P. W. Packard personally for above five years. That I have transacted business with her as publisher and printer—printing several thousand copies of her work—and have invariably found her prompt to meet business engagements, and accurate in the details of business affairs.

W. H. RAND,
Of Chicago Tribune Co.

The above are a mere specimen of the character of the certificates I took from my acquaintances, found among the most respectable and renowned citizens of Chicago, which, with

The Re-united Family. Mrs. Packard and all her Children. See page 379.

their silent influence, aided my Boston lawyers so to present my case to the Court as to secure my object, without the need of either child or any other witness going with me before the Court in my defense.

Hon. S. E. Sewall and T. Currier, lawyers of Boston, acting as my attorneys, the case was formally presented, and met with all the favor from the Court we could desire.

Mr. Packard seeing there was no chance of his retaining the children, by opposition, took the advice of his attorney Mr. Griswold, of Greenfield Mass., then a member of the Mass. Legislature, and superseded the Court's decision, by giving up the children to me, as his own voluntary act—voluntary—in the sense that he chose to give them up in this manner, rather than have me come into possession of them by the Court's decision, which seemed to be inevitably certain, if he did not.

I objected to taking them in this manner, lest I might by thus getting them leave it optional with Mr. Packard whether I retain them or not.

But my counsel said, it was of no material advantage to me to get them by a decree of the court of Massachusetts, since her laws were not binding upon Illinois citizens, and therefore counselled me to take them from his hands, rather than insist upon taking them by the Court's decree.

I accordingly yielded my judgment to theirs and took them with me, without opposition, to Chicago, Illinois, in June, 1869, where I have since lived with them in my own house at 1496 Prairie Avenue.

My three oldest boys in their majority, doing business in Chicago, boarded with me and my three minor children, thus obtained, constituting "The Re-united Family" of seven, living in peace and harmony.

Thus the mother's battle was fought, and the victory won!

It has been a nine years' battle with despotism—three of which were spent within the gloomy walls of the most terrible prison which could be found on this continent, and six in most excessive toil and labor to provide a home for my dear children.

As the sum of these six years toil, I wrote seven different books and published them myself, without either begging or borrowing money to aid me in so doing; and also sold twenty-eight thousand of these books myself, by single sales, besides doing the arduous and expensive work of lobbying for my four bills, during four different legislative sessions.

The only capital I had to commence with was health, education, and energy, and this capital is still entire and complete as when first invested. There have been no perceptible drafts upon the principal, but, on the contrary, have been adding annual interest to the principal continually!

From this experience I am prepared to infer, that vigorous, active, energetic, persevering exercise of both body and mind is a healthy, and, as I think, a natural condition, favorable to both intellectual and spiritual growth.

And that maternal love is the most potent element in the universe to lighten toil and render wearisome exertion a pleasure instead of a burden.

And here, too, the law of compensation and retribution is too evident to be passed unnoticed.

Six years previous to this triumph Mr. Parkard turned me out upon the cold world homeless, penniless and childless. He had the home, property and the children.

Now he is homeless, penniless, and childless; while I have a home of my own, property, and the children.

Yes, God has been at work through the immutable laws he has established in his government in rewarding honest toil with a competency; while idleness has brought poverty and shame and a tendency to mental imbecility as its natural result. Since 1866 he has had no ministerial charge, and been dependent for support upon the charity of others.

Since in the author's opinion maternal duties are paramount to all others, I have most cheerfully laid aside all public duties, except the sale of books sufficient to support my family comfortably, which took me from them about three months in a year.

The remaining nine months I have devoted almost exclusively to my family, refusing all the calls of social life and its varied responsibilities, that I might devote all my energies in moulding and shaping the characters of my long neglected children.

To my mind the claims of the public are secondary at least to those of maternity. Never primary when her children's training is at stake. Could I have prevented it **my children** would never have been separated from their mother.

CHAPTER LIII.

The Family Disperse.

In the order God has established the period in which an entire family live an unbroken unit, is usually a limited one. Ours was no exception to this law of our earthly existence.

Indeed, the memorable 3d of July, 1869, was the first day our family had ever met, an entire unit. The oldest and the youngest, then eleven years, had never before met in the same family circle. My oldest son was attending school at Mount Pleasant, Iowa, when our youngest was born, and before he returned home his mother was kidnapped! and this was the first day the father, mother, and all the children ever met under the same roof.

And the first and the only time we all ever worshiped God in his sanctuary together, was this memorable Sabbath evening when we all went in one solemn company to a Methodist church service in the vicinity of my home.

When I took the children from Mr. Packard in Massachusetts and brought them to Chicago, Illinois, he followed us, and has since lived in Manteno, Kankakee county, Illinois, in the family of his brother-in-law, Deacon Dole. While in Chicago, on his way to his final destination, he called upon his children to see them cozily living in their mother's home. My filial son, Theophilus, now standing as the guardian and protector of my family, told his father as he met him at the door:

"Father, you know this is mother's home. You have no right here. Our mother shall never be molested in her own home."

"Yes, I know it is—I acknowledge I have no right here—I shall not trouble your mother."

Acting upon the principle of doing unto others as we would wish to be done by, I have never denied Mr. Packard the privilege of seeing his children at my house whenever he chose, or their writing to him when and what they pleased, and also allowed them to visit him occasionally.

But from me he has never received anything but the respectful treatment of a stranger gentleman in my family. For I never have had the least occasion for believing he has ever repented in the slightest degree of the course he has pursued towards me.

Therefore, as I claim to be a follower of Christ, I am not allowed to extend to him forgiveness, except upon the gospel terms of repentance. And since he does not repent he will not allow me to forgive him.

For nine years subsequent to my incarceration I withdrew all fellowship from him, not even so much as to speak or write to him: but when he restored the children to my guardianship and care, although it was a mere act of compulsion on his part, since he saw it was certain the court would give them to me if he did not, yet, as I told him:

"I am happy I can regard this act in the light of an act of restitution on your part so far, as to allow me to treat you henceforth as a gentleman."

From that time I have felt justified in simply speaking to him as I would to any stranger gentleman.

Within three years from this date my two oldest sons both married, and removed to Iowa where they still live.

My third son, Samuel, has been obliged to sojourn for a time, in a Southern climate to recuperate his health.

And my fourth son, George, thought it best to suspend, for a time at least, his educational course at the High School at Chicago, where he stood in the highest rank, both in deportment and scholarship, and accept an offer from his uncle in New York city to go into business with him as his bookkeeper.

I consented to this arrangement and he is now in New York city with his uncle.

My dear daughter, Elizabeth, is teaching school.

Arthur, my youngest son, is at work on a farm in the country. This disposition of Arthur was secured by his father, in opposition to my will and wishes. It was my intention to give him and George both a superior education, and I made them each this offer, and in George's case this offer is still a standing one. But in Arthur's case, since his father has taken him from my guardianship, care and custody, without my consent, I consider myself as henceforth exonerated from all my previous offers for his support and education.

Although so far as Arthur's welfare is concerned, I regret this arrangement. Yet, for myself, I feel greatly relieved of a heavy responsibility ; for by the great fire in Chicago my business capital was all burned up, so that from that date I have had no income to depend upon for my own or my children's support, except the rent of part of my house. And until I can earn a new capital to start business again with, it would have been quite a burden upon me to furnish means for their support and education.

Looking therefore upon these circumstances as only parts of the wise plan of an unerring Providence, I cannot but feel that God has thus emancipated me from all family cares and responsibilities, so that I can now devote my undivided energies to the great work, I seem peculiarly capacitated by my experiences, to perform. Indeed, I cannot but regard myself as one of God's agents to do the especial work He has assigned me to do.

He has kindly gratified the great desire of my maternal heart—the care and custody of my own children, for a time —and now He seems to say to me :

" Will you trust your children with me, and go work in my vineyard ? "

My heart responds, " I will."

CHAPTER LIV.

An Appeal to the Government to Equalize the Rights and Responsibilities of the Husband and Wife.

As my case now stands delineated by the foregoing narrative, all the States on this Continent can see just where the common law places all married women. And no one can help saying, that any law that can be used in support of such a Persecution, is a disgrace to any government—Christian or Heathen. It is not only a disgrace—a blot on such a government—but it is a crime against God and humanity, to let confiding, trusting woman, be so unprotected in law, from such outrageous abuses.

Mr. Packard has never impeached my conduct in a single instance, that I know of; neither has he ever charged me guilty of one insane act—except that of teaching my children doctrines which I believed, and he did not!

This is all he ever alleges against me.

He himself confirms the testimony of all my friends, that I always did discharge my household duties in a very orderly, systematic, kind, and faithful manner. In short, they maintain that I, during all my married life, have been a very self-sacrificing wife and mother, as well as an active and exemplary co-worker with him in his ministerial duties.

Now I have mentioned these facts, not for self-glorification, but for this reason, that it may be seen that good conduct, even the best and most praiseworthy, does not protect a married woman from the most flagrant wrongs, and wrongs, too, for which she has no redress in the present laws.

If a man had suffered a tithe of the wrongs which I have suffered, the laws stand ready to give him redress, and thus

17

shield him from a repetition of them. But not so with me. I must suffer not only this tithe, with no chance of redress, but ten times this amount, and no redress then.

I even now stand exposed to a life-long imprisonment in States where committals on certificates are legal, so long as my husband lives, while I not only have never committed any crime, but on the contrary, have ever lived a life of self-sacrificing benevolence, ever toiling for the best interests of humanity.

Think again! After this life of faithful service for others, I am thrown adrift, at fifty years of age, upon the cold world, with no place on earth I can call home, and not a penny to supply my wants with, except what my own exertion secures to me. Why is this?

Because he who should have been my protector, has been my robber, and has stolen all my life-long earnings.

And yet the law does not call this stealing, because the husband is legally authorized to steal from the wife without leave or license from her!

Now, I say it is a poor rule that don't work both ways. Why can't the wife steal all the husband has? I am sure she can't support herself as well as he can, and the right of justice seems to be on our side, in our view. But this is not what we want; we don't wish to rob our husbands, we only want they should be stopped from robbing us.

We just ask for the reasonable right to use our own property as if it were our own, that is, just as we please, just according to the dictates of our own judgment. And when we insist upon this right, we don't want our husbands to have power to imprison us for so doing, as my husband did me. It was simply that I insisted upon my right to my property, when this fatal issue resulted therefrom as seen in the foregoing narrative.

Now, I ask any developed man, who holds property which is rightfully his own, and no one's else, how he would like to exchange places with me, and be treated just as I have been treated ? Now, I say it is only fair that the law makers should be subject to their own laws. That is, they should not make laws for others, that they would not be willing to submit to themselves in exchange of circumstances.

Just put the case to yourselves, and ask how would you like to be imprisoned without any sort of trial, or any chance for self-defense, and then be robbed of all your life earnings, by a law which women made for your good (!) as your God-appointed protectors ?

Oh, my Government—the men of these United States—do bear with me long enough to just make our case your own for one moment, and then let me kindly ask you this question :

Won't you please stop this robbery of our inalienable right to our own property, by some law, dictated by some of your noble, manly hearts ? Do let us have a right to our own home —a right to our own earnings—a right to our own patrimony. A right, I mean, as partners in the family firm.

We do not ask for a separate interest. We want an identification of interests, and then be allowed a legal right to this common fund as the junior partners of this company interest. We most cheerfully allow you the rights of a senior partner ; but we do not want you to be senior, junior, and all, leaving us no rights at all, in a common interest.

Again, we true, natural women, want our own children too —we can't live without them. We had rather die than have them torn from us as your laws allow them to be.

Only consider for one moment, what your laws are, in relation to our own flesh and blood. The husband has all the children of the married woman secured to himself, to do with them just as he pleases, regardless of her protests, or wishes, or entreaties to the contrary ; while the children of the single women are all given to her as her right by nature !

Here the maternal nature of the single woman is respected

and protected, as it should be; while the nature of the married woman is ignored and set at naught, and the holiest instinct of woman is trampled in the dust of an utter despotism.

In other words, the legitimate offspring of the wife are not protected to her, but given to the husband, while the illegitimate offspring of the unmarried women are protected to her. So that the only way to be sure of having our maternity respected, and our offspring legally protected to us, is to have our children in the single instead of the married state!

With shame I ask the question, does not our Government here offer a premium on infidelity?

And yet this is a Christian Government!

Why can't the inalienable rights of the lawful wife be as much respected as those of the open prostitute? I ask, why?

Is it because a woman has no individuality, after she is joined to a man? Are her conscience, and her reason, and her thoughts, all lost in him?

So my case demonstrates the law to be, when practically tested.

And does not this legalized despotism put our souls in jeopardy, as well as our bodies, and our children?

It verily does!

It was to secure the interests of my immortal soul, that I have suffered all I have in testing these despotic laws. I would have succumbed long ago, and said I believe what I did not believe, had it not been that I cared more for the safety of my own soul, than I did the temporal welfare of my own dear offspring.

I could not be true to God, and also true to the mandates of a will in opposition to God. And whose will was to be my guide, my husband's will, or God's will? I deliberately chose to obey God rather than man, and in that choice I made shipwreck of all my earthly good things.

And one good thing I sorely disliked to lose, was my fair,

untarnished reputation and influence. This has been submerged under the insane elements of this cruel persecution.

But my character is not lost, thank God! nor is it tarnished by this persecution. For my character stands above the reach of slander to harm.

Nothing can harm this treasure but my own actions, and these I intend in future shall all be guided and controlled by Him, for whose cause I have suffered so much.

Yes, to God's grace alone, I can say it, that from the first to the last of all my persecutions, I have had the comforting consciousness of duty performed, and an humble confidence in the approval of Heaven. Strong only in the justice of my cause, and in faith in God, I have stood alone, and defied the powers of darkness to cast me down to any destruction which extended beyond this life.

And this desperate treason against manliness which has sought to overwhelm me, may yet be the occasion of the speedier triumph of my spiritual freedom, and that also of my sisters in like bondage with myself.

The laws of our Government most significantly require us " to work out our own salvation with much fear and trembling," lest the iron will which would hold us in subjection, should take from us all our earthly enjoyments, if we dare to be true to the God-principle within us. So bitter has been my cup of spiritual suffering, while passing through this crucible of married servitude, that it seems like a miracle almost, that I have not been driven by it into insanity, or at least into misanthropy. But a happy elasticity of temperament, combined with an inward consciousness of rectitude, and disinterestedness, has enabled me to withstand these fiery darts of the adversary, as few women could.

And I cherish such a reverence for my nature, as God has made it, that I cannot be transformed into a " man-hater." I thank God, I was made, and still continue to be a " man-lover."

Indeed, my native respect for the manhood almost approaches to the feeling of reverence, when I consider that man is God's representative to me—that he is endowed with the very same attributes and feelings towards woman that God has—a protector of the weak, not a subjector of them.

It is the exceptions, not the masses of the men, who have perverted or depraved their God-like natures into the subjectors of the dependent. The characteristic mark of this depraved class is a "woman-hater," instead of a "woman-lover," as God by nature made him. This depraved class of men find their counterpart in those women, who have perverted their natures from "men-lovers," into "men-haters."

And man, with a man-hating wife, may need laws to protect his rights, as much as a woman, with a woman-hater for her husband. Laws should take cognizance of improper actions, regardless of sex or position.

All we ask of our Government is, to let us stand just where our actions would place us, without giving us either the right or power to harm any one, not even our own husbands. At least, give us the power to defend ourselves, legally, against our husband's abuses, since you have licensed him with almost almighty power to abuse us.

And it will be taking from these women-haters no right to take from them the right to abuse us. It may, on the contrary, do them good, to be compelled to treat us with justice, just as you claim that it will do the slave-holder good to compel him to treat his slave with justice.

It is oppression and abuse alone we ask you to protect us against, and this we are confident you will do, as soon as you are convinced that there is a need or necessity for so doing.

In summing up this argument, based on this dark chapter of a married woman's bitter experience of the evils growing out of the law of married servitude, I would close with a petition to the legislatures of all the States of this Union, that they would so revolutionize their statute laws, as to expunge them entirely from that most cruel and degrading kind of despotism, which identifies high, noble woman as its victim. Let the magnanimity of your holy, God-like natures, be reflected from your statute books, in the women protective laws which emanate from them.

And may God grant that in each and all of these codes may soon be found such laws as guarantee to married woman a right to her own home, and a right to be mistress of her own household, and a right to the guardianship of her own minor children. Let the interests of the maternity be as much respected, at least, as those of the paternity; and thus surround the hallowed place of the wife's and mother's sphere of action, with a fortress so strong and invincible that the single will of a perverted man cannot overthrow it.

For home is woman's proper sphere or orbit, where, in my opinion, God designed she should be the sovereign and supreme; and also designed that man should see that this sphere of woman's sovereignty should be unmolested and shielded from any invasions, either foreign or internal. In other words, the husband is the God-appointed agent to guard and protect woman in her God-appointed orbit. Just as the moon is sovereign and supreme in her minor orbit, being guarded and protected there by the sovereign power of the sun, revolving in his mighty orbit.

The appropriate sphere of woman being the home sphere, she should have a legal right here, secured to her by statute laws, so that in case the man who swore to protect his wife's rights here, perjures himself by an usurpation of her inalienable rights, she can have redress, and thus secure that protection in the law which is denied her by her husband.

In short, woman needs legal protection *as a married woman.* She has a right to be a married woman, therefore she has a right to be protected as a married woman. If she cannot have protection as a married woman, it is not safe for her to marry, for my case demonstrates the fact, that the good conduct of the wife is no guarantee of protection to her; neither are the most promising developments of manhood, proof against depravity of nature, approximating very near to the point of "total depravity," and then woe to that wife and mother who has no protection except that of a totally depraved man!

But, some may argue, that woman is already recognized in several of the states as an individual property owner, and as one who can do business on a capital of her own, independent of her husband.

Yes, we do most gratefully acknowledge this as the day-star of hope to us, that the tide has even now set in the right direction. But allow me to say, this does not reach the main point we are aiming to establish, which is, that the woman should be a legal partner in the family firm, not a mere appendage to it. We want an equality of rights, so far as co-partners are concerned.

Then, and only till then, is she his companion on an equality, in legal standing, with her husband, and sharing with him the protection of that Government which she has done so much to sustain; which Government is based on the great fundamental principle of God's Government, namely, an equality of rights to all accountable moral agents. Our Government can never echo this heavenly principle, until it defends "equal rights," independent of sex or color.

APPENDIX.

My Plea for Married Woman's Emancipation made before Connecticut Legislature in New Haven State House, June, 1866.

Gentlemen of the Judiciary Committee:

In compliance with the kind invitation your gallantry has prompted you to extend to me, to meet you here in session, to consider the merits of the " Petition for the Protection of the Rights of Married Women," which the General Assembly has respectfully referred for your consideration, I have come to plead in its defense.

And here, gentlemen of the Judiciary Committee, allow me first to extend to you my thanks, for allowing me the high honor and privilege of defending so noble a cause as woman —and to defend it, too, in the presence of intelligent, manly gentlemen, whose God-like natures predispose and capacitate you to view this subject from this most favorable stand-point.

Indeed, gentlemen, just consider for one moment the noble position you now occupy. Here are the names of two hundred and fifty *men*, citizens of the first character and standing in this city, who have sent up a petition in behalf of the rights of married women and ask you, the law-makers of this Republic, to consider, and, if possible, to so ameliorate married woman's legal position, as to remove some of her many legal disabilities.

Really is not this fact of itself, a speaking proof of the principle, that man is woman's protector? And does he not ever esteem it his highest honor thus to identify himself with this most God-like principle? And have not we, women, everything to hope for, from this instinctive uprising of the manly element in our defense ?

We do not desire, nor ask, for the privilege of defending ourselves.

No, neither do our petitioners give us any occasion for so doing; for they have anticipated us, in thus proposing to ameliorate our legal position, without even waiting for us to ask them to do so.

Again, men are not only our petitioners, but they have asked the men, not us, to devise how this can be done. They do not ask us to frame their laws for our protection, but have even volunteered to do it for us.

All that they have thus left us to do, is, to fulfill woman's appointed mission—to bless and sanctify home, by her refined influence, and leave it wholly to the men to protect us, in this our hallowed sphere.

Is it not an honor, much to be coveted, in us natural women, to live in Connecticut, where the manliness of our protectors not only allows us the high privilege of fulfilling the duties of our heaven-appointed sphere, but also proposes to protect us in this sphere, so long as our good conduct deserves such protection ?

Yes, for one, I rejoice that man is the law maker of this Republic, fully satisfied as I am that woman's cause could not be in better or safer hands, were she allowed to be her own protector. Nature and the Bible, both harmonize with this most manly feature of Connecticut's espousal of woman's cause, and thus being in the track of Nature, we are sanguine of ultimate success.

Yes, sanguine, that Connecticut is to secure to herself the high honor of being the van of this great American Republic, by being the pioneer State in woman's Emancipation.

Woman's Emancipation! What! Is woman a slave in Connecticut ? Have we not emancipated all our slaves long ago ?

Yes, thank heaven! Connecticut was one of the pioneer states in negro emancipation, and she now intends to secure to herself the highest kind of honor, as a State, in being the honored pioneer in emancipating woman from the chains of married servitude!

"Chains of married servitude! Are our women, in Connecticut, in chains?

"Away with such an idea! Our wives are our companions, our partners, the best part of ourselves, how then is it, Mrs. Packard, that you can call them our slaves?"

Bear with me, my gallant brothers, and I will tell you, for your ignorance is a sure passport to your gallantry, in that you have never used your power, as a master, over your slave. They are, socially, as you say, your companions, your partners, your better halves; but legally, they are your slaves, and it is to break their fetters, to legally emancipate woman, that your petitioners have sent up this petition.

Let us test this question. What is a slave?

A slave is a dependent, one mancipated to a master, one in the power of another, one who has lost the power of resistance; and married woman, being legally a "nonentity," on the principle of "common law," throughout the United States, is therefore an American slave, while she is a married woman, in that she loses all power of resistance when she becomes, legally, a wife; for henceforth, she is wholly at the mercy and will of one man, with no sort of legal power to resist this will, than the slave has to resist the will of his master. He has the same legal power to subject his wife, that the master has to subject his slave.

And now, since America has emancipated the negro slave from bondage to a one man power, we married slaves fondly hope that our emancipation draws near—yea, may quickly follow in the wake of negro emancipation!

But, gentlemen, in securing our emancipation you will have

to encounter the same pro-slavery arguments and spirit, as their emancipators did, viz. :

That the slaves are better off as they now are—that they are taken better care of by their masters than they could take of themselves—that the interest of the master demands the good treatment of his slave—that public sentiment is a sufficient law of protection to the slave's interest—that the subjection of the wife is the Bible law of marriage—and besides, there is not one married woman in a thousand who even knows that she is a slave.

Blissful ignorance! Would that there were no exceptions! But alas! the exceptions are fast becoming the rule, looking from the stand-point of applications for a divorce.

Indeed, gentlemen, there is a cause for this terrible upheaving of the social element. Our divorce laws are destroying the very structures of civilized society. Yes, the monogamic principle of Christianity and civilization is being rapidly supplanted by the polygamic principles of barbarism.

And you know, gentlemen, that it is an infallible principle of ethics, that all effects have a cause, somewhere. And now I wish to present this one great question to you—the law-makers of this Republic—for your candid, calm consideration, viz. :

Does not the radical cause for these divorces lie in the non-entity principle of the wife? that is—in your holding her legally, as a slave, with no power of resistance to this " one man power," and no protection from its abuse, except the law of divorce?

And, besides, since the principle of slavery is wrong, and the principle of freedom is right, is it not right in itself, that woman should be legally emancipated?

The only right I came here to claim for woman is her right to be protected by our man government. Not protected as a slave, wholly dependent upon the will of one man : but protected as a woman, as a companion of her husband, as one who has rights, as a woman equally dear and sacred to her, as man has rights, as a man equally dear and sacred to himself. Our rights are not man's rights, neither are man's rights woman's rights. Both are different, yet both are inalienable, and both equally sacred.

Man has rights as the head of the family which the wife has not. Even nature and the Bible both teach, that man is the head of the marriage firm.

As I view the subject, the different spheres of man and woman are definitely defined in the Bible. It seems to me to be the appointment of God, that man should bear the toil, and woman bear the children.

Now, if man is made the responsible head of the family so far as providing for its pecuniary interests are concerned, it seems to me he should be the head of finance, in the family realm, and every woman should consider it beneath the dignity of her nature to dictate to her husband in this department, in any such sense as to trammel his own reason and judgment in this matter. The man's reason should dictate his business, not his wife, and the manhood of that man's God-like nature, is yet in an undeveloped state, where he will consent to be dictated to, by his wife, in defiance of his own reason and judgment.

I say dictated—not influenced by his wife—for, I say further, that a man is less than a man who will not be influenced by his wife through his affection and reason, if her reasons are sound and logical, and her affections pure and chaste.

A being, in the form of a man, who will despise a sound argument—a truth—merely because a woman was its medium to him, is a being fit only to be despised; and deserves to be ranked among the woman haters of society.

But, thank God! this perverted class of human kind, are the exceptions, not the rule—for, in most cases, the manliness of his nature will prompt him to consult his wife's feelings and wishes as his better half—his junior partner even, in his family interests ; but, the ultimate decision in this department must, and should be left with the husband—the senior partner of the firm, as the responsible head of the financial department.

And it should be the first and paramount duty of this responsible senior, to provide a suitable home for his dependent family, and so secure it to them, that any financial failure on his part, would not endanger the family home. Then the wife could safely trust her fortune, where she could herself, knowing that her department of the finance—her home—is safe, and beyond the reach of his financial misfortunes to alienate.

And here, in this family home, made secure to her by the Government, she should be the legally constituted mistress, in this, her heaven-appointed sphere. And here too, she should be the legally appointed head of her own special department— viz—rearing the children. Here the Government should protect the mother as the natural guardian of her own children.

And the paternal power should be enforced as the natural protective power which the mother seeks as her own right by nature. And should any degree of depravity tempt him to betray this most manly of all trusts, the protection of the maternity to his own wife, let the Government enforce it, as an obligation.

Again, no man should be allowed to lord it over and dictate to his wife in this, her God-assigned sphere, any more than the wife should be allowed to dictate to her husband, in his God-appointed sphere. But the true woman, like the true man, will naturally consult the wishes and feelings of her husband, in this matter, as he does hers, in his department. But the ultimate decision in this department, must be left to the wife.

In other words the wife should be the legally constituted Queen at home, in the same sense in which the husband is the King abroad.

Again, the husband is the "head of the wife;" for God says,

"he shall rule over." Now this husband's rule over the wife is, as I view it, the rule of protection and love—not the rule of subjection and hate. For the practice of subjection in this conjugal sphere, is as inseparably connected with the feeling of hate, toward the one he has subjected, as the feeling of love is identified with the practice of protection towards the wife.

Our feelings grow out of our actions. If we act wrong, we shall feel wrong—if we act right, we shall feel right. And there is no other way to develop the feeling but by action.

For example, the only possible way for one to have a liar's feelings is to tell a lie, and then he will be sure of feeling like a liar—let him steal, and he can't help feeling like a thief. So also to know what it is to have a good, kind, generous, benevolent feeling, let him perform some good, kind, generous, benevolent deeds; these correspondent feelings are the inevitable result of his good actions.

So if this rule of the husband over the wife is confined to the rule of protection, his feelings will be confined to the love sphere. But if he can, and does subject his wife, his feelings pass directly on the opposite sphere of hate, and no power can prevent it; for God's laws are immutable.

So the only possible way to insure love and harmony in the marriage union, is to secure the natural order God has established, as its only inflexible, enduring basis.

The Government then, whose chief intent and purpose is, to protect the weak against the usurpation of the strong, should not allow the husband to rule over the wife in any other sense than that of protection.

This protection of her interests should be like that exercised by the sun, in his protecting his moon in her orbit. He should not be allowed to so exercise his compripetal power, as to draw the moon entirely out of her God-appointed orbit, and so completely absorb her into himself, as to leave her no orbit at all.

No, he should be satisfied to be the King of the day, and let her remain the Queen of the night, ruling with her soft and gentle influences, the mighty train of brilliant stars which God has assigned her, as her own most fitting companions and associates.

In short, all that we ask for woman is, that her natural rights, as a woman, such as a right to herself, a right to her children, a right to be the mistress of her own house, be as well protected, by law, after she is married, as they are when she is single, with this difference, only, viz: that after she is married, this protection come to her through her husband, the natural protector of his wife, instead of directly from the Government, as before marriage. And in case the husband fails in his obligations to his wife as her protector, let the Government hold him responsible for the discharge of these obligations, as his duty.

Then let two equally protected identities form one union, which neither can have cause for dissolving, without an illegal trespass upon each others' rights.

As the case now stands, the husband, being the only legally protected partner in the union, can legally usurp all the rights of the wife, leaving her no chance for self-defense, except that of leaving the union, by secession or divorce.

What we want is, protection in the union, not a separation or a divorce from it. Or in other words, we want protection from the cause of divorce.

No lady wants to be a divorced woman, but she wants to be a married woman, and protected as a married woman. So long as her good conduct deserves it, she wants protection for herself, and her children, in the home their joint interests have provided for them. She don't want to be driven into a divorced state in order to secure the protection of her natural rights, against the usurping power of her husband.

Now, gentlemen, I am sorry to own it, this seems to be the tendency of the legislation of the present day, in respect to the

marriage union. And it seems to me to be very unjust legislation. For, as woman's case now stands, good conduct, even
the best, is no sort of guarantee of protection for her, while
in the marriage union; since you have licensed her husband
with almost almighty power to oppress her, without giving
her the least chance for self-defense from this power, while
in the union.

Gentlemen—representatives of our manly Government—we
would not upbraid you for placing us in this legal position.
Indeed, it is not you who have done it, it is the antiquarians of
by-gone days, who subjected woman as the mere slave of her
husband, who have assigned us our present legal position.

And since the law of love protects the wife in most instances,
our Government may have felt that no modification of the nonentity principle of the wife, was needed, as a self-defensive
measure. They have doubtless considered the husband as the
only protection which the married woman needed, since the
God-like principle of manliness would prompt a true man to
protect his wife, even sooner than he would himself.

And so it is, and we most cheerfully admit, that it is only
for the exceptional cases, that the legal identity of the wife is
needed, as a means of self-defense.

But as you do in other cases, make laws for the exceptional
cases ; laws for criminals for example, do not imply that all
need such a restraint, but some cases do need them, therefore
they are made for the exceptional cases.

So in the exercise of this marital power, the cases where it
is abused demand some restraint to protect the oppressed
wife. And it certainly is very manly in our Government, to
protect confiding woman against this form of oppression, as
well as any other form of abuse.

Again, it is anti-Christian legislation. As we view it, there
is but one law of divorce permitted by the Great Founder of
the Christian dispensation ; and so, in cases where this cause

does not exist, there seems to be no Bible license for a divorce. Thus the conscientious, Christian wife is compelled to do violence to her conscience, in consenting to be divorced, contrary to the principles of the divine law. And where human and divine laws conflict, what can she do?

Is she not compelled, either to do violence to her enlightened conscience, by getting a divorce; or continue to suffer that oppression and abuse which is, to her, a lingering, living death?

Gentlemen, the legal protectors of my sex, will you not furnish these worthy, confiding dependants upon your magnanimity, with some safe refuge, which can save both their consciences and themselves from violence?

To illustrate and enforce my argument, gentlemen, may I not be allowed to cite my own case, egotistical as it may seem to be? Gentlemen, I have exercised the dauntless courage of true woman, in daring to assert my right to my individuality, in defiance of the nonentity principle of this American legislation. I have simply claimed the right to my own thoughts. And what has been the result?

Gentlemen, I have had to make shipwreck of all the most sacred, dearest rights of womanhood. A right to my husband—a right to my children—a right to my person—a right to my furniture—a right to my money—a right to my wardrobe—a right to my home—a right to my liberty. And, as an equivalent for all this mighty sacrifice, I retain only the legal right of being imprisoned for life, as a State pauper in a State Lunatic Asylum!

Yes, 'tis true, this is the only right my legally appointed guardian allows me. And no man, woman, or child, has any right to say it shall not be so. I am legally helpless in the absolute power of this one man tyrant.

My God-like brothers, can you deliver me? Can you befriend me?

If so, you can deliver, you can befriend all the dear sisterhood whom I represent.

Brothers, I need your protection! I need emancipation!

All my life-earnings, yea! myself, is in the absolute power of this unjust and cruel man. I have naught that I once possessed, save my stainless character, my education, and my health. On this capital alone have I staked my liberty, my emancipation. With this battery I am battling for my freedom, for justice, for right.

And, Oh, my God! sustain Thou me in this terrible conflict.

And, if it is possible, spare, Oh! spare! my earthly father, till the victory is achieved! for he is the only protector of whom my persecutor stands in any fear.

Oh, my Connecticut brothers, let him fear your laws—let him fear your legislation—and then your sisters will be delivered from liabilities like my own.

And will you not do it?

Can you consent to pass off the stage of action, and leave your darling daughter, your beloved sister, yea, even your better-half, legally exposed and liable to suffer all I have suffered, from this abuse of marital power? Will you not, for their sakes, cast your vote into the scales of woman's emancipation, and thus enter your God-like protest against married servitude?

Gentlemen, my case, although an extreme one, may not be so rare an exception as you may strive to fondly imagine it to be.

No, God only knows how many a sainted wife and mother has been ground down and trampled into the very dust, crushed by the arbitrary power of perverted manhood.

My brothers, 'tis true, many a nobly endowed woman has been crushed, subjected to a tyrant's control, and has been led to desire death, rather than such a life of cruel bondage.

Yea, God only knows how long is that train of living martyrs who have gone up to God's throne and God's tribunal to get their wrongs avenged on earth, because they had no protection, no claims for justice at their country's tribunal. Have they appealed to this higher court in vain?

No. The Judge of all the earth will do right. And will not the claims of this host of martyred married slaves be exacted from that government which would not protect their identity from the usurpation of perverted manhood?

Yes, 'tis true, this Government has a long account to settle for protecting, by its laws, that most guilty of all oppressors, an oppressive husband.

Gentlemen of the Judiciary Committee, on you now rests the responsibility of continuing to shelter these oppressors, under such laws, as obliterate the personal identity of the largest and best part of our American citizens.

Henceforth, may we not fondly hope that married woman's inalienable rights will be protected by the laws of Connecticut, so that on this great American continent there may be found one State where the married slave can find as safe a refuge from her oppressor as the negro slave once found in Canada?

Let the brave sons of Connecticut send forth their proclamation of freedom to woman! Then shall Connecticut's envied territory henceforth be the home of the free, as well as the brave.

Again, I am still in danger of another kidnapping, and thereby our noble cause is jeopardized.

Yes, the same wicked spirit which has been, and still is, my persecutor, is now following this dear cause of woman's emancipation, and is seeking its overthrow.

Gentlemen, have you not seen what a mighty avalanche of scandalous insinuations, and bare-faced lies, has just now been palmed off upon this credulous public, for the sole purpose of undermining my character as a sane person, knowing that just as soon as this public confidence in my sanity is destroyed, **I** shall be altogether helpless again, in the absolute power **of** my persecutor ; and then he can kidnap me again and **hide** me for life in some lunatic asylum. And since no laws defend me, this may yet be done.

Should public sentiment—the only law of self-defense **I** have—endorse the statements of this terrible conspiracy, against the personal liberty and stainless character of an innocent woman, I may be yet again entombed to die a martyr for the Christian principle of the identity of a married woman.

Three long years of false imprisonment does not satisfy this lust for power to oppress the helpless !

No—nothing but a life-long entombment can satisfy the selfhood of my only legal protector !

Brothers, should the credulous public suffer me thus to die a martyr for woman's cause, don't let this precious cause be entombed with me. Oh ! leave not this dear cause to the fickle decision of public sentiment, if you can afford me no other protection.

Public sentiment ! What protection does that ensure to me ?

Do you not see in our very midst, how very unstable is the verdict it renders me ? Does it not one day cry, Hosannah ! and the next, Crucify !

Oh ! I do want laws to defend me ; and as an American citizen, I not only ask, but I demand as my right, that my personal liberty shall depend upon the decision of a jury— not upon the verdict of public sentiment, or forged certificates either.

And here, I beg leave to enter my most solemn protest against the injustice of that legislation which suspends the personal liberty of any American citizen upon the certificate of any person, class, or oligarchy.

Again I say, my gallant brothers, be true to my cause, **if** false to me. Be true to woman! defend her, as your weak confiding sister, and heaven shall reward you.

This untimely bursting in upon our almost triumphant cause, of the spirit of this cruel conspiracy is designed by the woman-hating spirit which prompted it, to defeat the first progressive step of this new rallying army, in defense of woman's emancipation.

But, my brothers—my dauntless brothers! be not afraid of this wicked host which is encamped against us. Be valiant for woman! God is on her side, and " he always wins who sides with God."

Gentlemen of Connecticut Legislature, go forward! Emancipate woman! and put to flight this wicked host who have encamped against us. Fear not! Fear nothing so much as the sin of simply not doing your duty. Maintain your death grapple in defense of the heaven-born principles of liberty and justice to all human kind—especially to woman.

For above this cross hangs suspended a crown, of which, even our martyred Lincoln's crown of negro emancipation is but a mere type and shadow, in brilliancy. And God grant! that this immortal crown of unfading honor may be the rightful heritage, the well earned reward, of Connecticut's manly sons, as embodied in their Legislature of 1866, by the passage of the following bill, viz. :

" Any woman entering the marriage relation, shall retain the same legal existence which she possessed before marriage, and shall receive the same legal protection of her rights as a woman, which her husband does as a man. Should the husband's power over the wife become an oppressive power, by any unjust usurpation of her natural rights, she shall have the same right to appeal to the Government for redress and protection that the husband has."

End of Vol. II.

www.ingramcontent.com/pod-product-compliance
Lightning Source LLC
Chambersburg PA
CBHW032311280326
41932CB00009B/771